S0-FCS-564

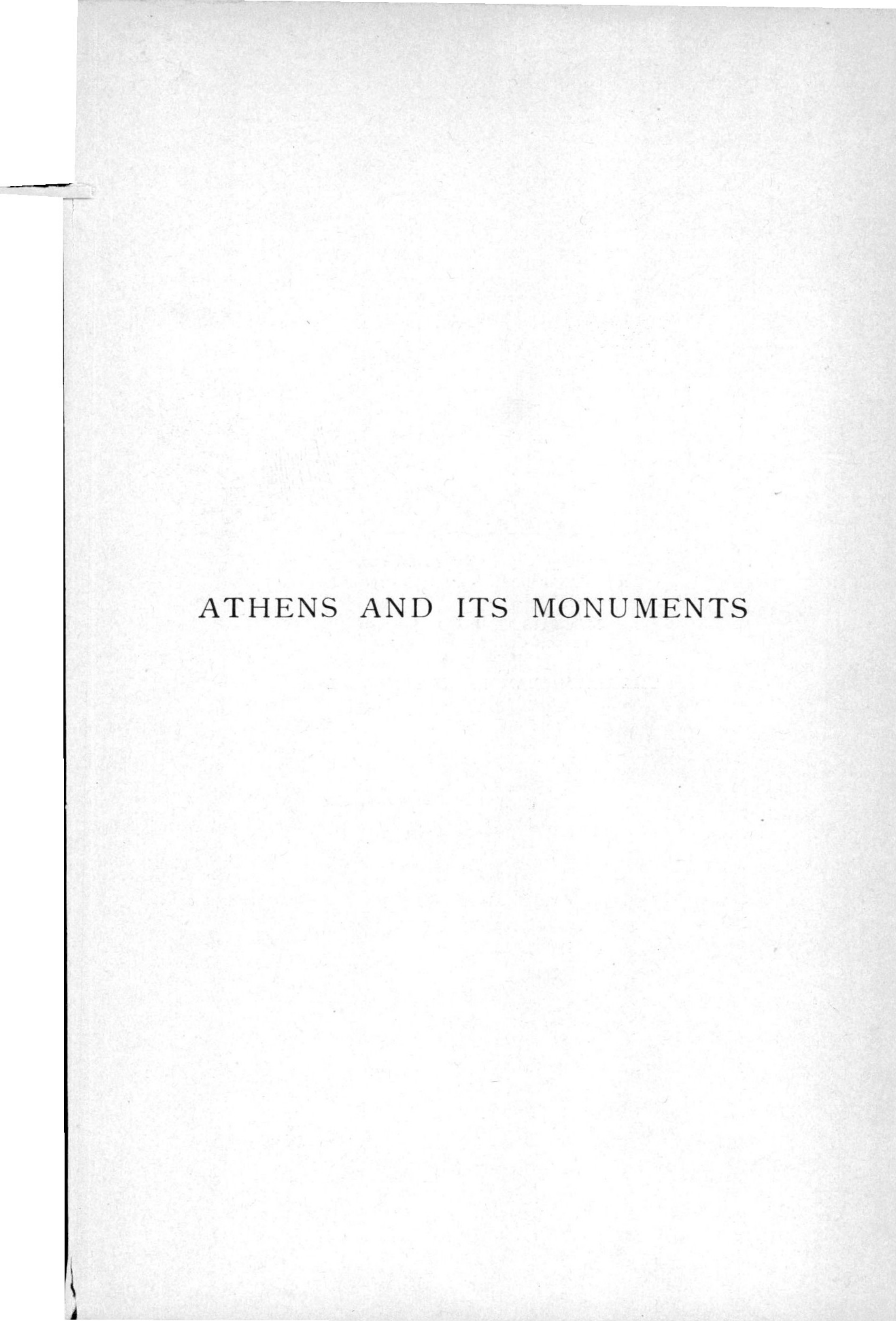

# ATHENS AND ITS MONUMENTS

THE MACMILLAN COMPANY
NEW YORK · BOSTON · CHICAGO · DALLAS
ATLANTA · SAN FRANCISCO

MACMILLAN & CO., LIMITED
LONDON · BOMBAY · CALCUTTA
MELBOURNE

THE MACMILLAN CO. OF CANADA, LTD.
TORONTO

FIG. 1. — Southeast Athens, from the east end of the Acropolis.

To the right are the Olympieum and the Arch of Hadrian, in the middle the Stadium, and in the background Mt. Hymettus.

# ATHENS
# AND ITS MONUMENTS

BY

CHARLES HEALD WELLER
THE UNIVERSITY OF IOWA

ἐμοὶ γένοιτο . . . Ἀθήνησι καὶ ζῆσαι καὶ τὸν βίον ἀπολιπεῖν
(*May it be my lot . . . in Athens to live and there my life to end*)
— ALCIPHRON, iii, 51, 4.





New York
THE MACMILLAN COMPANY
1913

Set up and electrotyped. Published November, 1913.

Norwood Press
J. S. Cushing Co. — Berwick & Smith Co.
Norwood, Mass., U.S.A.

τῇ ἐμῇ γυναικί

# PREFACE

THIS book is designed to provide a brief and untechnical account of the topography and monuments of ancient Athens for the general reader and the traveler, as well as an introduction to the subject for the student of archaeology and history; a few ideas that are new and worthy may perhaps be found by the specialist. In view of the wealth of material available, the maintenance of a proper balance and perspective is not easy; particularly strong is the temptation to allow recent discoveries to usurp more than their just share of attention. A straight course between doubt and dogmatism is also difficult to keep. Notwithstanding the effort to avoid confusion of fact and theory, and to present, so far as possible, the grounds for opinions expressed, the form of statement may now and then seem more positive than is justifiable. If, on the other hand, the use of "probably" and "perhaps" appears frequent, the point may be urged that many problems are still far from a solution; when evidence is scanty, doubt is more reasonable than dogmatism.

The topographical treatment adopted by Pausanias is so convenient and logical that it has seemed preferable to the historical order. Pausanias and other sources are quoted freely; the references, save in the case of direct quotations, could not be given without encumbering the pages. If the exigencies of space have also made imperative the omission of the names of modern scholars, appreciation of the obligation imposed by their labors is no less keen. My constant indebtedness to the works mentioned in the bibliography at the end of the book, particularly to

Dr. Judeich's *Topographie von Athen*, will be manifest to all who are acquainted with the literature of the subject. The general plan of the book was suggested by Miss Harrison's *Mythology and Monuments of Ancient Athens;* had she decided to revise her volume, this book would probably never have been written. In these days one can hardly write about Athens without an expression of gratitude to Dr. Wilhelm Dörpfeld, long the secretary of the German Institute there, whose genius has illumined many a dark corner of the ancient city, and whose personality has been an inspiration.

The list of those who gave me aid and encouragement in completing this task is long. I am under special obligation to the American editor of this series of Handbooks for reading the manuscript and offering suggestions; to Professor David M. Robinson, of Johns Hopkins University, for reading both manuscript and proof; to Professor Frank B. Tarbell, of the University of Chicago, and Mr. Lacey D. Caskey, of the Museum of Fine Arts in Boston, for reading a large part of the manuscript and for giving valuable suggestions. Deeply appreciating the kindly assistance of these scholars, I absolve them from responsibility for such errors and infelicities as still remain. The sources of the illustrations used in the book are indicated in the list at the beginning of the volume. I can here only express in general terms my thanks to those who have furnished photographs, especially to Mr. Ashton Sanborn and Mr. Carl W. Blegen for securing and sending photographs from Athens. Finally, I desire to express my thanks to my colleague, Mr. Robert B. Dale, who made many of the drawings.

CHARLES HEALD WELLER.

IOWA CITY,
June 1, 1913.

# CONTENTS

# ILLUSTRATIONS

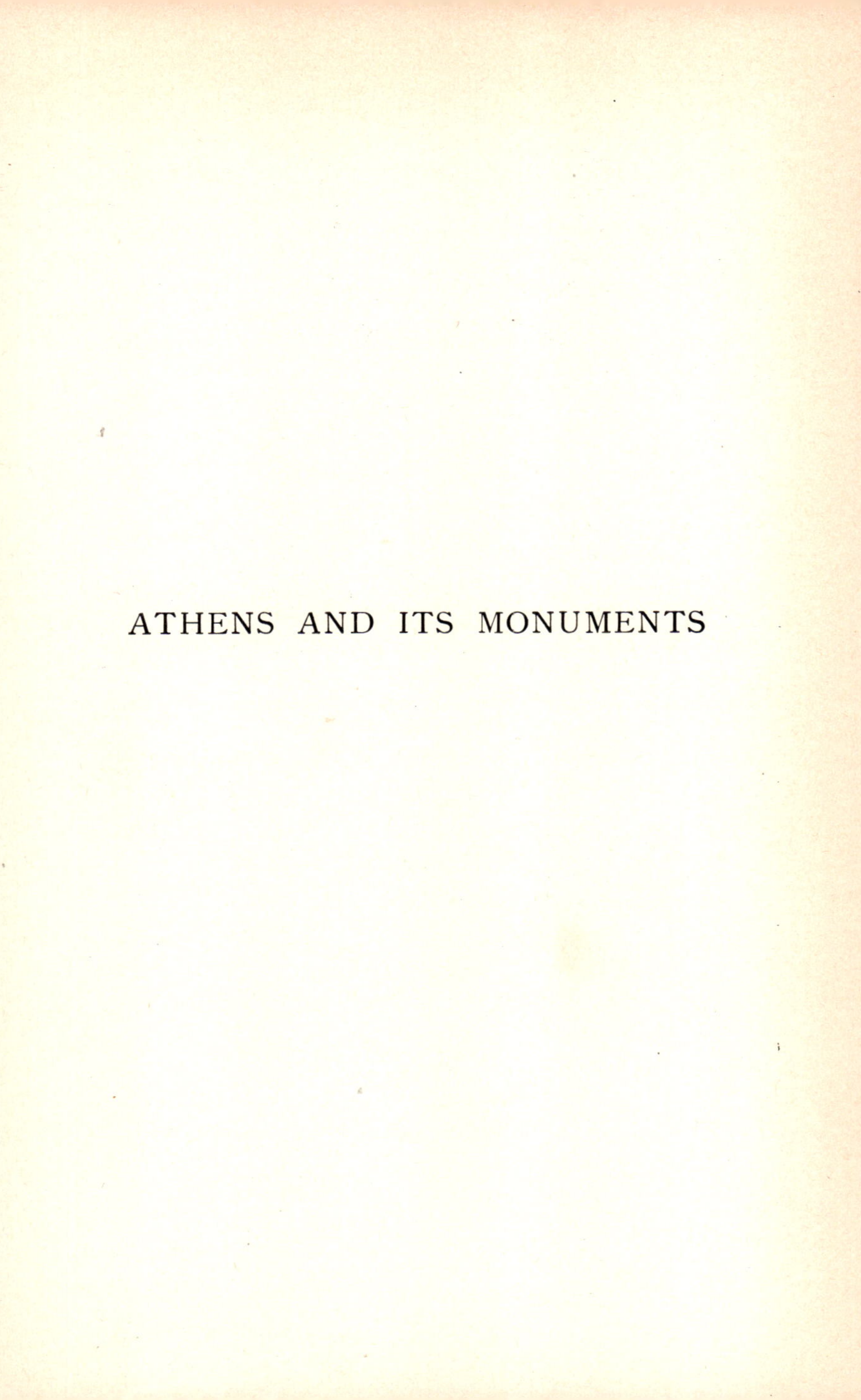

# ATHENS AND ITS MONUMENTS

# ATHENS AND ITS MONUMENTS

## INTRODUCTION

### Sources of Information

The most important sources for our knowledge of the topography and antiquities of ancient Athens are, of course, the monuments themselves; and under monuments we include not only buildings and sculpture, but also such remains as coins and inscriptions, though the latter may also be classed as a part of our most valuable literary evidence. Happily the monumental remains are abundant, and additions are constantly being made by means of excavation and various investigations.

Time, however, has dealt so harshly with most of the ruins, defacing some, destroying others, that we should be quite helpless in our effort to visualize the ancient city without the aid of the literary sources. Casual references in the writers of tragedy and comedy, in the historians, the orators, the philosophers, and many other authors, and their commentators, are of inestimable value. But we are still more indebted to special accounts of the city itself. Unfortunately the majority of these have come down to us in a very fragmentary condition. The most regrettable loss is that of the work of Polemo of Ilium (second century B.C.), who in antiquity was highly esteemed. His four books *On the Votive Offerings on the Acropolis*, his book *On the Sacred Way*, and his *Record of the Namesake*

*Heroes* (*Eponymi*) *of the Tribes and Demes*, would be invaluable to us, but we have of them only scanty fragments. The few pages of a book *On the Cities of Greece*, which has survived under the name of Dicaearchus (published by Heracleides the Critic about 205 B.C.), contain some notes on Athens. Only disconnected excerpts have been preserved, mostly by Byzantine lexicographers, of similar works by Diodorus the Periegete (fourth century B.C.), Heliodorus of Athens (second century B.C.), and several others.

But the greatest treasure of the student of Athenian topography is the extant treatise of Pausanias, in ten books. This author was a native of Asia Minor, his home probably being at or near Lydian Magnesia, in the vicinity of Mt. Sipylus; the journey on which his description seems to have been based was probably made in the period of the Antonines (138–180 A.D.). The first thirty chapters of his first book deal with the city of Athens and the demes of Phalerum and Peiraeus. Since in this book he describes the Stadium as it stood after it was completed by Herodes Atticus, in 143 A.D., and later remarks that the Odeum built by the same man in honor of his wife, who died about 161 A.D., was not built when the book was written, it must have been published between the dates mentioned, or very near the middle of the second century after Christ. Not only in respect to Athens, but also for Olympia, Delphi, and other places, the reliability of Pausanias has repeatedly been tested and not found wanting. His purpose seems to have been to compose an interesting narrative for distant readers and to provide a handbook for the traveler. Coming from Phalerum and Peiraeus and entering the city by the principal gate, he guides the reader systematically about the sites which seem to him "worth seeing." Of course we should not assume, as some have done, that Pausanias necessarily followed the same route himself, any more than this would be assumed for a modern guide-book.

Second only in importance to the ancient literature are records made by late mediaeval and early modern visitors to Athens. These comprise so numerous a group that only a few can be mentioned in our survey. For about twelve centuries after the period of Pausanias the study of the antiquities of the city received slight attention. In 1395 Niccolò da Martoni tarried a day there upon his return from a crusade to the Holy Land, and left in his journal a brief account of what he saw. A generation later, in 1436 and in 1447, Cyriac of Ancona spent some time in Athens, but of his commentaries and drawings only portions have survived. Much valuable material is given in the extant records of three anonymous visitors, two Greeks and an Italian, who were in the city just after the middle of the fifteenth century. The work of Martin Kraus, a professor of Tübingen, is also valuable.

References to Athens in the literature of the next two hundred years are few and unsatisfactory. About the middle of the seventeenth century, M. Giraud, consul of France and later of England, furnished material which was soon afterwards published by the scholar Guillet in his *Athènes ancienne et nouvelle* (1675), the first systematic account of the city to appear in modern times. To the seventeenth century belong also several plans of Athens, and especially of the Acropolis, the best being that made for the French Capuchins about 1660. The long letter from Athens of the Jesuit Babin to the Abbé Pécoil of Lyons is interesting, but not altogether trustworthy. Of greater moment are the descriptions and drawings made for the Marquis de Nointel, French ambassador to the Sublime Porte, who, with his retinue, spent some weeks in Athens in 1674. The most valuable part of the material consists of sketches, made by a Flemish painter in the company (probably not, as formerly supposed, by Jacques Carrey, the French artist) of various antiquities, notably the pedimental sculptures of the Parthenon (p. 284). Many of the originals were destined to perish a few years later; these sketches therefore are of prime importance. In the very year of De Nointel's visit, George Transfeldt, a runaway slave of a Turkish merchant, was in the city and has left a brief description. Two years later the French artist Jacob Spon and the Englishman Sir George Wheler visited Athens together, and the results of their observations form the first scientific publication of the ruins.

With the end of the seventeenth century came disasters; the capture of the city by the Venetians, in 1687, was accompanied by the explosion of powder stored in the Parthenon, and followed by the demolition or removal of works of art (p. 304); yet the attention of the western world was attracted to Athens and its monuments as never before. To the Venetian expedition were due several plans and descriptions; a panorama was also made, based on the Capuchin plans.

As the investigations of the seventeenth century had been mainly French, so those of the eighteenth were preëminently English. Of greatest importance is the work of the painter James Stuart and the architect Nicolas Revett. Supported by wealthy patrons, these men spent three years in Athens (1751–1754), making careful plans and measurements of the ruins and preparing sketches of ruins and of scenes in and about the city. The four sumptuous volumes of their *Antiquities of Athens* are epochal, and form an indispensable addition to the literature. Chandler, who was sent out by the Society of Dilettanti, Pococke, Dalton, Wilkins, and Dodwell also visited the city and made useful contributions. Finally Colonel William M. Leake, at the moment when the Greek revolution broke out (1821), closed the period with his illuminating study of the topography of Athens, a part of his larger study of Greece.

After the Revolution came the establishment of the kingdom of Greece, and an era of tranquillity. The appointment of a German prince, Otho of Bavaria, as king intensified the awakened interest of German scholars in the art and history of the country, and their efforts have been ably seconded by scholars of other lands. In Athens at the present time are the headquarters of a well-supported Greek National Archaeological Society, and foreign scholarship is represented by French, German, English, Austrian, and Italian, as well as American Schools.[1] The twentieth century has opened with a cordial coöperation among these various agencies established for the advancement of research in the field of Greek archaeology and antiquities.

## Building Materials and Methods of Construction

Architecture in any land is conditioned largely upon the building materials available; in this respect Athens was particularly favored. Not only limestones of excellent quality, but true marbles also, are quarried in unlimited quantities not far from the city. The earlier inhabitants

[1] The *National Archaeological Society* of Greece was organized in 1837. In 1846 the *École Française d'Athènes* was founded; in 1874 the Athenian section of the *Käiserlich Deutsches Archäologisches Institut*, with headquarters in Berlin; the *American School of Classical Studies* was established in 1881, the *British School at Athens* in 1883. The most recent accessions are the Athenian branch of the *Oesterreichisches Archäologisches Institut* and the *R. Scuola Archeologica Italiana*, founded, respectively, in 1908 and 1909; though Austrian and Italian archaelogical stations were maintained some years previously.

naturally turned to the material nearest at hand, the hard, dark-gray limestone of the Acropolis and the neighboring hills. Of this stone, with its crystalline veins and nodules, the old wall of the Acropolis was built, as well as the foundations and even the superstructures of early buildings. During a part of the sixth and fifth centuries B.C., considerable use was made of Karâ limestone. This was of dense texture, lighter in color than the rock of the Acropolis, and of a reddish gray tint. It was quarried near the modern village of Karâ, on the side of Mt. Hymettus, about three miles southeast of Athens. But the favorite building stone from the sixth century, or earlier, down into Roman times was a softer yellowish gray limestone from Peiraeus, the Peiraic limestone or poros. This is easily worked and was much used for walls and even for sculptures. During the Periclean age it was chiefly utilized for foundations, but in all periods after its introduction it was used for entire buildings. Visible surfaces of poros were often covered with stucco and painted, or, in Roman times, veneered with slabs of marble. A hard, coarse breccia was also employed, particularly from the fourth century B.C., but only for foundations and concealed backing or supporting walls.

But the Athenians were not slow to appreciate the advantages of marble. After the time of the Peisistratids, marble came more and more into use for the better buildings. The coarse-grained Parian and other island marbles seem to have been used at first in both architecture and sculpture, but they were soon left for the sculptor alone. From the end of the sixth century B.C., the fine-grained, milk-white marble from quarries still visible on the side of Mt. Pentelicus, was most employed for architecture and often for sculpture; especially noteworthy is its use in the splendid structures of the age of Pericles. The oxidization of the iron which Pentelic marble contains has produced a golden-brown patina, the rich tints of which add to the charm of Athenian ruins to-day. In later times the bluish and usually streaked marble of Mt. Hymettus[1] was greatly admired. From the fourth century B.C., and particularly in Hellenistic buildings, Hymettian marble was even preferred to Pentelic. Mention must also be made of a dark-gray Eleusinian stone, which is used as a decorative material in the Propylaea and the Erechtheum, but otherwise very rarely.

Kiln-dried bricks did not come into use at Athens until Roman times, and then only to a limited extent; better materials were too abundant. Sun-dried bricks, on the other hand, were numerous in all periods. Of them were built the walls of private houses and even the superstructure of the Themistoclean walls of the city and of Peiraeus. Roof tiles and ornaments, and water conduits, were usually made of terra cotta, but the public buildings of the best periods were constructed mostly of marble. In Roman days opus incertum, and other forms of concrete construction were introduced as elsewhere in the Roman world.

The earliest walls of Athens, such as the old wall of the Acropolis and the first house walls, were Cyclopean, that is, were built of stones of irregular shape and often of huge dimensions, slightly hewn, or quite unhewn; the interstices were filled with smaller stones and clay (Fig. 2). As the stones began to be more carefully cut and fitted, this style developed into the polygonal wall (Figs. 3 and 119). Polygonal masonry was most common in the sixth and fifth centuries B.C., but it is found also both earlier and later, so that its presence is not always a safe criterion of age.

The later and more regular polygonal wall, with its

[1] Some of the quarries of Pentelicus yield the same kind of marble.

FIG. 2. — Cyclopean wall belonging to the Pelargicum, at the east end of the Acropolis.

joints approximately horizontal and vertical, perhaps developed into ashlar masonry. The latter appeared at Athens as early as the seventh century B.C., and is the ordi-

FIG. 3. — Polygonal wall in the west ascent to the Acropolis.

nary style found in Athenian buildings. In the architecture of the best period the blocks were cut and joined with the utmost precision, so that the insertion even of the blade of a penknife between the stones is impossible. The heavier walls were ordinarily constructed of headers and stretchers, the former at right angles, the latter parallel, to the course of the wall. The surfaces of finished walls were carefully smoothed, but the blocks in many unfinished walls, as those of the Propylaea (p. 236), retain the depressed border to which the remainder of the surface was to be dressed, and often the "bosses" to which the lifting ropes had been attached; with reference to the process of moving the stones, however, we should add that most blocks were lifted with derricks by means of grappling hooks and lewises, as they are to-day. In later times the raised surface left within the border (the rustica, Figs. 4 and 82) was

FIG. 4.—Olympium and south wall of its precinct.

The upper portion of the wall is a modern restoration.

purposely kept as an ornament. In walls of the majority of buildings the course (orthostatae) above that which (euthynteria) lay on the foundation or floor was usually of double the height of the other courses of the wall.

Mortar made with lime was not used in walls until Roman times. The Greeks tied blocks of stone or marble together with various sorts of dowels and cramps, usually of bronze, fastened in their sockets with lead. The drums of columns, at least of the principal Athenian buildings, are held in place by round dowels of wood set in squared wooden blocks which fill the sockets in the stone (Fig. 5). Courses in a wall are kept from shifting by metal dowels; the blocks in the same course are held together by cramps. The forms of the cramps varied with the different periods, and furnish a convenient criterion for the determination of approximate dates. Z-shaped cramps (⌙⌐) seem to have been used mostly before the end of the sixth century B.C. Double-T-shaped cramps (⊢⊣) are characteristic of the best period, the sixth to the fourth centuries B.C. U-shaped cramps (┌─┐), with the extremities sinking vertically into the stones, are used from the fourth century B.C. Swallow-tailed cramps (⋈) are found in walls of various epochs (Fig. 6), and other kinds are occasionally used.

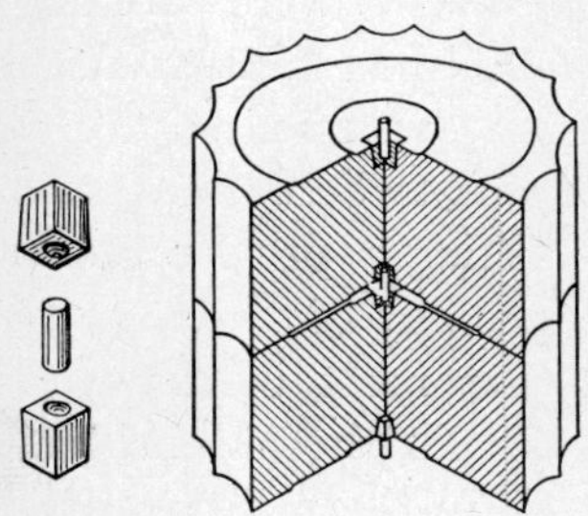

FIG. 5.—Method of joining the drums of a column.

Cramps are of different sizes. The double-T cramps of the Parthenon are about 12 inches long. The largest cramp known, in the Propylaea, is 31.5 inches long.

The three "orders" of architecture (Fig. 7), Doric, Ionic, and Corinthian, will be familiar to most readers. Their use in Athenian buildings, and the architectural forms most often employed, will be indicated in connection with the buildings studied in the following pages.

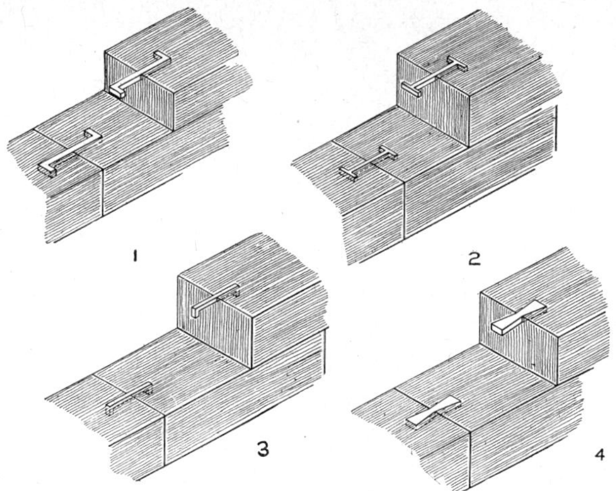


Fig. 6. — Various styles of cramps used in uniting the blocks of a wall.

Number 1 is the Z-shaped cramp, 2 the double-T-shaped, 3 the U-shaped, with extremities descending vertically into the stones, and 4 the swallow-tailed cramp.

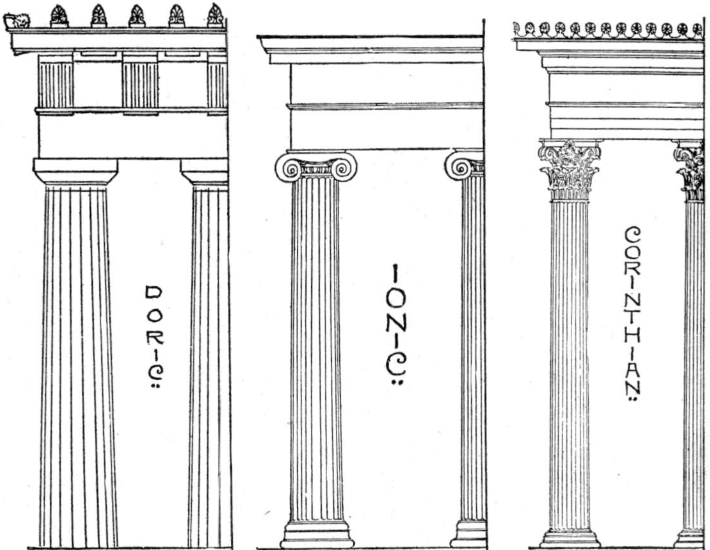


Fig. 7. — The "orders" of Greek architecture.

Fig. 8. — Panoramic view of Athens, from the Hill of the Nymphs.

At the right is the Acropolis with the Areopagus in front of it; at the left is Market Hill and the "Theseum;" in the background, at the left, are Anchesmus with Lycabettus at its end, the summit of Pentelicus, and, at the right, Hymettus.

# CHAPTER I

## Situation and Natural Environment

The city (Fig. 8) of Athens[1] lies in the midst of an irregular and undulating plain (Fig. 9), which extends from the northeast southwestwards to the Saronic Gulf and is, roughly speaking, about fifteen miles long by ten miles wide. On three sides the plain is hemmed in by mountains, whose foothills extend far out into the central area. The range of Parnes is the highest (4631 feet) and longest, extending westward into Mt. Cithaeron and eastward nearly to Mt. Pentelicus. High up in Parnes is the fort of Phyle, where Thrasybulus assembled the little band that was to terminate the Thirty's tyranny. The naked ridge of Harma was clearly visible to the Pythian priests at Athens, watching for the lightnings over its summit to tell them of the time to send sacrifices to Delphi (p. 61). Farther east is Decelea, whence at the end of the Peloponnesian War the Spartans spied upon the city; the king's summer palace is now in the vicinity, at Tatoï.

Northeast of Athens is the pyramidal peak (3637 feet) of Mt. Pentelicus (Fig. 10), or Brilessus; white scars in its side mark the site of the modern marble quarries, which are not far from the ancient. The summit of the mountain is about eleven and a half miles, in a direct line, from the

[1] The city lies in 37° 58′ north latitude and 23° 42′ east longitude (from Greenwich). The latitude is nearly the same as that of Palermo, Cordova, and San Francisco.

Acropolis. Hymettus (3369 feet) is the elongated mountain on the eastern borders of the plain. Its sides are

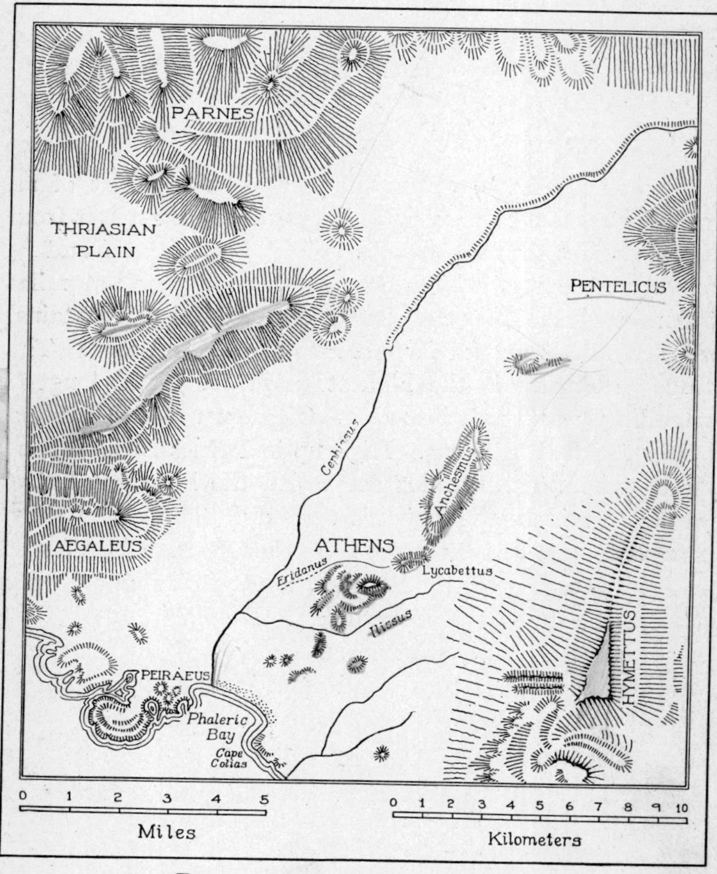


FIG. 9. — Map of the Athenian plain.

scored with deep and rugged ravines; the southern and lower third, cut off by a high pass, is the Anhydros or Waterless Hymettus. Even more than for its marble was the mountain famous for its bees, which gathered honey, as they do to-day, from the wild thyme and savory and other fragrant herbs growing on its rugged slopes. But its most wonderful feature is the glow cast over it by the setting sun; *purpureos colles florentis Hymetti* the poet Ovid called the deep-tinted heights. Marking the western

FIG. 10. — Mt. Pentelicus in winter, as seen from the American School.

border of the plain are the lower summits (1535 feet) of Mt. Aegaleus, or Corydallus, which divides the Athenian from the Eleusinian plain. Aegaleus is really a spur of Parnes and is joined to it by the low ridge (564 feet), over which the railroad to the Peloponnesus now passes. In Aegaleus, almost directly west of Athens, is a low pass (416 feet) where now is the mediaeval monastery of Daphní; here in antiquity ran the Sacred Way which led to the mystic close at Eleusis. In the middle of the plain is another low range, the ancient Anchesmus, which terminates abruptly at the south end in the conical hill of Lycabettus (912 feet, Fig. 11), at the northern edge of modern as of ancient Athens; it is now crowned by the little chapel of St. George.

In shape Athens formed an irregular ellipse (Fig. 22), about a mile and a half long from east to west and a mile wide from north to south. The northern half is fairly level, the southern, hilly. Near the middle of the ellipse is the lofty rock of the Acropolis, whose west slopes blend with those of the Areopagus and the Pnyx.

FIG. 11. — Mt. Lycabettus, from the Acropolis.

The palace lies at the right of Lycabettus; in the background is Mt. Pentelicus.

The hills of Athens were once connected geologically with Mt. Lycabettus, and so the ancients surmised, as we see from a passage in Plato's *Critias* (p. 112A). The Acropolis, by nature the most important hill, was the seat of earliest settlement. It is an abrupt and rocky plateau, nearly 1000 feet long by 445 feet wide; it reaches its greatest elevation (512 feet) northeast of the Parthenon. The west end descends gradually and provides the only natural approach; the other sides are precipitous, though the fall on the south side was less pronounced before the height was increased by filling, on the inside of the wall. Northwest of the Acropolis is the Areopagus (pp. 357 ff.), a triangular rock, precipitous about its east end, where it is highest (377 feet), and sloping away gently toward the west. Bounding the city on the southwest is the Pnyx Hill, which is divided by depressions into three parts. Of these the southernmost, the Museum Hill (Fig. 144), is the highest (485 feet); on its summit stands the conspicuous monument of Philopappus (Fig. 12), which has now lent its name to the hill. The central elevation, the Pnyx proper, held the ancient meeting place of the ecclesia (pp. 110 ff.). The northernmost hill is now called the Hill of the Nymphs, from an inscription hewn in its side; the ancient name is unknown. Here the national observatory now stands; behind it is the pit known as the Barathrum, into which were thrown the bodies of executed criminals. A low, flat ridge running north from between the Hill of the Nymphs and the Areopagus is the ancient Colonus Agoraeus (p. 88), the western boundary of the Agora, or market-place. Some hills of minor importance will be mentioned later in special connections.

Fig. 12. — Monument of Philopappus, on the summit of the Hill of the Muses.

The geological formation of the hills is shown in the accompanying diagram (Fig. 13).

The Athenian plain has always been scantily watered. The largest river, the Cephissus, has its sources in Parnes and Pentelicus, and flows through the middle of the plain, passing about two miles from the city; it empties into the Phaleric Bay. Except in time of freshets, however, its

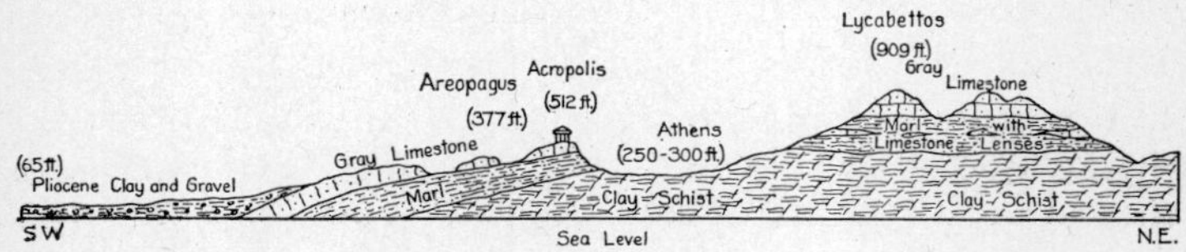


FIG. 13. — Geological formation of the hills of Athens.

water is either exhausted by irrigating ditches or sinks into the gravelly soil before its mouth is reached. Its moisture is not all wasted, for on either side of the stream are miles of luxuriant olive groves. The Ilissus River rises in Hymettus and flows westward past the southern borders of the city toward the Cephissus. Its bed (Fig. 56) is usually dry, save for a slender thread or an occasional pool, but a heavy rain sometimes turns the rivulet into a rushing torrent. A third river, the Eridanus, had its rise in springs on the side of Lycabettus, and flowed westward through the city, issuing at the Sacred Gate; but it has gradually been filled or arched over, and its very course until recently was lost. Even in antiquity it was turbid except near its sources. Of two other streams, the Sciron and the Cycloborus, we know little more than the names and the fact that they were north of the city.

The city contained a few natural springs; we have information concerning Callirrhoë, south of the Areopagus (pp. 108 ff.), the Clepsydra (pp. 351 f.), and the spring of the Asclepieum (p. 209), on the slopes of the Acropolis. Another Callirrhoë, in the bed of the Ilissus, is apparently supplied by subterranean streams of the river. Of cisterns the number was legion. Peisistratus, in the sixth century B.C., was probably the first to bring water into the city by a conduit to supplement Callirrhoë; near the other end of the city's life Hadrian began to build an aqueduct from Pentelicus, which Antoninus Pius completed. This aqueduct and its terminal reservoir on the side of Lycabettus have been restored and are in use to-day to supply the modern city.

The arid, calcareous soil of the Athenian plain produces little vegetation save olive and fig trees, though by irrigation considerable tracts are being redeemed for vineyards and gardens. Thucydides and other ancient writers mention the thinness of the soil, which, except along the Cephissus, in many places barely hides the rock beneath. The upper slopes of the mountains support the holm oak and a variety of shrubs, but the lower declivities and the strip of plain adjoining have forests, which are subject to destructive fires. Athens itself contains few trees, except those planted in the parks; apparently in antiquity it was not much better off in this respect, though we read of planes and other trees in the Agora and the parks and along the Ilissus.

Accurate meteorological observations have been taken at the national observatory for more than half a century, and comparisons have been made between the recent records and all available evidence regarding ancient conditions. Continued denudation of both mountains and plain has no doubt increased the aridity of the region, but the records show that forest fires and the destruction of timber by human agencies, such as charcoal burners, were familiar in antiquity; on the whole the climatic conditions seem not to have undergone material change.

The bright and clear Athenian air has ever been a subject of comment. Euripides remarked upon it, and the photographer of to-day can test it empirically. Only a ninth of the days in the year are sunless, and on not more than a dozen days is the sky completely overcast. Rain falls on not more than a hundred days, mostly during the months from October to January. The precipitation in summer is scanty or altogether lacking, as is also the dew, and the total yearly rainfall is only about sixteen inches.[1] Morning fogs are frequent, especially in summer, when the distant mountains are often shrouded in a light haze even throughout the day. Showers are sometimes accompanied by terrific lightnings, the thunderbolts of Zeus, and heat lightning is often incessant. During the night of August 30, 1862, some 56,000 flashes were counted inside of four hours. Snowfall in the city is rare and light, but the mountains are often snow-capped throughout the winter.

The average temperature of January, usually the coldest month, is about 46° F.; of July, the hottest month, about 81° F. The mean annual temperature is about 68° F., but the heat of July and August is often intense. The highest recorded temperature for the period of observation is 105.26° F., the lowest, 19.58° F. The heat of the soil has once been known to rise as high as 160° F. Dryness of the air is very marked, the percentage of saturation in July and August averaging only 47, from November to January about 75.

The winds keep the air of Athens in almost constant motion and frequently carry with them clouds of dust, which whiten the vegetation, and penetrate the houses; these, and the lack of water, are the bane of the city. Boreas, the stormy north wind from Thrace, which, says

[1] The average annual rainfall of Washington, D.C. is about 43 inches.

Alciphron's poor man (3, 42, 2), "goes through my sides like an arrow," is really not so frequent (average, 53.6 days in the year) as Caesias, the northeast wind (92.6 days), or Lips, the southwest wind (65 days), or Notus, the south wind (58.7 days). Zephyrus, the west wind (15 days), and Apeliotes, the east wind (10.5 days), are comparatively infrequent.[1]

### GENERAL ASPECT OF THE CITY

The extent and appearance of Athens naturally varied greatly with the different epochs of its history. The time, however, which we should choose, in order to see the city at the zenith of its glory, is the period of the Antonines, ending about 180 A.D., after all its public buildings had been completed and before the era of ruin and decay had set in. Fortunately this is just the period that we best know, thanks to the description of Pausanias.

How large a population Athens had cannot be accurately determined. It was never large. Modern estimates vary greatly, but we may well believe that the entire population, including Peiraeus, at no time exceeded 200,000.

Some years after the Persian Wars, Peiraeus was laid out by the Milesian architect Hippodamus in rectangular blocks, but Athens itself, like most ancient and, indeed, most modern cities until recent times, grew up after no comprehensive plan.



A few wide avenues led from the principal gates in the city wall. The broadest was the street leading from the Dipylum to the Agora (p. 79), which was lined with colonnades on both sides. At the eastern end of the Acropolis was the impressive street of the Tripods (p. 180), a favorite

[1] For the personifications of the winds in the reliefs of the Horologium, see pages 143 f.

promenade. South of the Areopagus a considerable stretch of the famous road along which the Panathenaic procession passed, has been uncovered, but this is found to be only thirteen to eighteen feet wide, and shut in closely on either side by blank walls of precincts and dwellings. The streets debouching on these main arteries were narrow, in great part like alleys. Few of the streets were paved, and side-walks were unknown.

We have little information about the private houses of the city and must depend chiefly for our knowledge upon

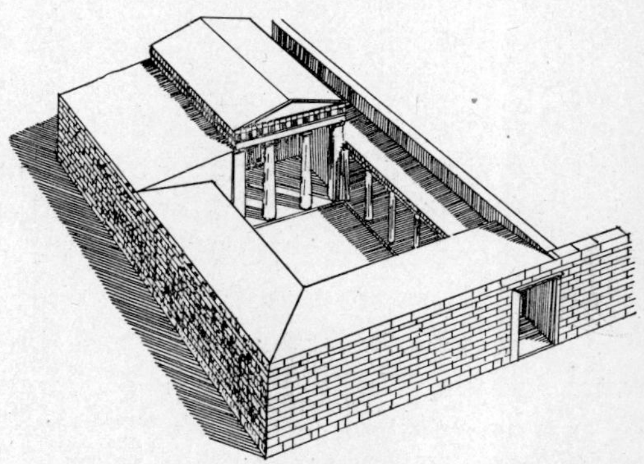

FIG. 14. — Reconstruction of a house at Priene, in Asia Minor.

those excavated at such places as Priene and Delos (Fig. 14). The houses were built about central courts, which afforded light and air, and most of them were but one story in height. The front wall, built on the edge of the street, was pierced only by an occasional window and by the door, the latter sometimes set back in a vestibule. A traveler of the Hellenistic period remarks (Ps.-Dicaearchus 1, 1): "The majority of the houses are cheap, but there are a few good ones; strangers who come upon them unexpectedly could hardly be made to believe that this is the celebrated city of the Athenians." This statement, however, has a bearing only upon the general appearance of the exterior, for the interiors of many houses must have been fairly ornate. Alcibiades is said to have had his walls decorated by a painter, and after his time some houses must have been still more sumptuous. In the fourth century B.C. we find Demosthenes complaining (3, 29) that "some have built private houses more magnificent than the public buildings."

Along the more frequented streets the lower front rooms seem often to have been used as shops, either by owners or tenants, as at Pompeii. The erection, in a niche or a vestibule before the house, of a pillar altar of Apollo of the Streets, or a herm, or a hecateum, or all three, was a general custom. Herms were also set up at street crossings. The location of a house was rarely or never designated by streets, the names of which, in fact, were usually without marked significance, but by some well-known building or site near which it stood.

The traces of dwellings in Coele, between the extremities of the Long Walls on the western slopes of the Pnyx hills, deserve mention. The exposed rock of this district is scarred by hundreds of cuttings where once stood the simple habitations of a considerable population. At one point, possibly an open meeting place, seven rude seats are hewn in the native rock (Fig. 15). Another deep cutting, with three adjacent rock-hewn chambers (now closed by iron gratings), has long been called the Prison of Socrates (Fig. 16), with whom it has nothing to do;

FIG. 15. — Seats hewn in the rock, on the side of the Hill of the Muses.

it was doubtless the site of an unusually pretentious dwelling.

The patriotic Athenian spent most of his time in the open, and the glory of his city was the public buildings. The center of Athenian life was the Agora, situated on the lower ground north of the Areopagus. It was entered

FIG. 16. — The so-called Prison of Socrates, a part of an ancient dwelling.

from the northwest by the brilliant avenue leading from the Dipylum gate, and was flanked on all sides by works of architecture, sculpture, and painting. To mention only the objects of chiefest note, the entering visitor, if he turned to the right, saw the Royal Stoa, or Colonnade, the Stoa of Zeus Savior, and the temple of Paternal Apollo. The ridge behind these bore the temple of Hephaestus and the shrine of the hero Eurysaces. Against the slope of the Areopagus stood the sanctuary of the Mother of the Gods, where were the public archives; in her precinct, too, were the senate house and the circular Tholus. Not far away were the Orchestra, with the revered images of the Tyrannicides, the temple of Ares, and the statues of the Namesake Heroes of the tribes. On the left stood the Painted Porch and the Theseum (pp. 152 ff.). Back of these rose the imposing Stoa of Attalus, and near it the Ptolemaeum. Still farther on stood the spacious Stoa of Hadrian and the great Market of Caesar and Augustus; in the rear of these the octagonal Tower of the Winds. Then, among and within all the buildings and precincts we must imagine almost countless images of gods and heroes and distinguished men; while everywhere graceful and brightly appareled men and women, not a few of whom are known and dear to us, round out the brilliant picture with warmth and life.

Following the road from the Prytaneum about the east end of the Acropolis, our traveler came upon another famous quarter in southeast Athens. Here the huge temple of Olympian Zeus and, across the river, the Stadium, stood out conspicuously; while not far away were the famous Gardens and the shaded parks of the Lyceum and Cynosarges. Or, following the street of Tripods at the east foot of the Acropolis, he passed the Music Hall of Pericles to the great theater of Dionysus and the two temples hard by; then continuing westward he came to the shrine of Asclepius and Health, or walked through the long colonnade of Eumenes to the lofty Music Hall of Herodes, with its spreading roof of cedar.

To crown all, the visitor ascended the Acropolis, past the delicate temple of Wingless Victory, between the exquisite columns and through the open doors of the Propylaea, into the middle of the sacred area. All about him were scores of statues, masterpieces in marble and bronze; on every side great works of architecture; the whole a marvelous harmony of brightness and color. Foremost among the buildings, the graceful Erechtheum and the stately Parthenon; and in the Parthenon, towering on its pedestal the awe-compelling statue, in gold and ivory, of Athena, the city's guardian.

### THE DEMES

Certain districts of Athens came to be known by special names. Limnae, the Marshes, was the region south of the Areopagus, in which lay the oldest precinct of Dionysus; this area has been laid bare by excavation (p. 83). Agrae, or Agra, sacred to Artemis Agrotera (Huntress), who had a temple there, embraced the district about the Stadium. Hiera Syke, or Sacred Fig Tree, lay just outside the city on the way to Eleusis. Near by was Sciron, a region not altogether reputable. Colonus included the hill west of the Agora. Hunger Plain (Limoupedion) was behind the Prytaneum, probably on the north slope of the Acropolis. The situation of the precinct Eretria is unknown. The eastern extension of the city founded by Hadrian was called New Athens, or the Athens of Hadrian.

More important than these districts were the divisions of the city into demes (Fig. 262), corresponding in a measure with American wards. The problems involved in determining the limits of the demes are complicated and do not demand attention here. Coele, as we have seen (p. 23), was the Hollow in the rear of the Pnyx hills. North of Coele was Melite, which embraced the hilly region west of the Agora. Besides numerous public buildings, Melite contained the residences of many prominent citizens, among them Themistocles, Phocion, Epicurus, and Callias. Cerameicus, the Potters' Quarter, included the Agora and the territory northwest, even beyond the city wall, which accordingly divided the deme into two parts, Outer and Inner Cerameicus. A shaft of Hymettian marble set up against the wall outside of the Dipylum (Fig. 17) bears the inscription in letters of the second century B.C., "boundary of Cerameicus," the only such terminal known. Outer Cerameicus is mentioned by Thucydides (2, 34, 5) as "the most beautiful suburb of the city." In both sections of the deme, public and private buildings were numerous. Since the Agora was included in the deme, the terms "Cerameicus" and "Agora" were used by late writers without distinction of meaning (p. 82).

FIG. 17. — Boundary stone of the deme of Cerameicus, near the Dipylum.

The stone bears the inscription: ὅρος Κεραμεικου.

Beyond those which have been mentioned, there is little certainty in the location of the demes. Collytus was one of the favorite quarters of the city; it bordered on Melite and probably extended south of the Areopagus and the Acropolis. Aeschines and Diogeiton are said to have lived in Collytus, and the street of the same name that ran through the deme is reported to have been a veritable bazaar. Tertullian (*De anima* 20) gravely asserts that boys learned to talk a month earlier in Collytus than elsewhere, but the statement doubtless came from the witticism of some comic poet, who, as has been suggested, may have attributed such precocity to the deme because of the proximity of the orators' bema on the Pnyx. If Collytus was south, then Cydathenaeum perhaps extended north of the Acropolis to the Eridanus, on whose bank may have been the tannery of Cleon, a Cydathenaean. Scambonidae may have been north of the Eridanus.

Of the demes outside the wall, Laciadae was at the northwest along the Sacred Way, and contained a precinct of the Hero Lacius. Ceiriadae lay to the west of Melite and included the Barathrum (p. 17). Diomeia was probably southeast of the city (p. 65), and embraced the Cynosarges. Ancyle included the district of Agrae and the Stadium. Agryle lay to the east of the city. Peiraeus and Phalerum were south; they will be discussed at greater length later on (pp. 383 ff.). Only one other deme need be mentioned, that of Colonus, which included the famous hill of Colonus Hippius (pp. 379 ff.), a mile north of the city, and probably the Academy. Whether or not the Colonus in the city was a separate deme, is a moot point.

The various demes in the city, like those scattered as villages throughout Attica, were political subdivisions of the ten tribes as organized by Cleisthenes.

## CHAPTER II

### HISTORICAL SKETCH

ALONG with the proud claim that they were autochthonous, the Athenians preserved a distinct tradition of an original race of Pelasgians driven out by later Ionians. The excavations of the last generation have shown that this tradition contains more than a kernel of truth. The Pelasgians are perhaps to be identified with the Mycenaean race, which, as we now know, reached a high stage of civilization in Greece, as well as the islands and coasts of the eastern Mediterranean, and was displaced before the beginning of the first millennium before Christ by an Achaean people, coming we know not whence. From the Achaeans the Athenians of history were sprung. A considerable admixture of Oriental influence may indicate that the tradition of an Egyptian Cecrops as the city's founder is something besides a myth.

Of the early Mycenaean settlement we have material evidence in the ruins of the strong wall, the Pelasgicum, or Pelargicum, that encompassed the Acropolis (pp. 48 ff.), and the numerous remains of houses of Cyclopean masonry that once crowned the hill. We can even locate the palace of the old Mycenaean lord — be he Cecrops or Pandion or Erechtheus — near the middle of the north side of the Acropolis (p. 312); his retainers had their houses at its foot.

The history of this early period was soon veiled in myth, and the facts were forgotten by the Athenians of the classical age. Writing centuries later, when Athens is at the zenith of her power, Thucydides (2, 15) tries on archaeological grounds to determine the outlines of the city which succeeded the first settlement, or, as he calls it, "The city before Theseus." "Before his time," says the historian, "the city consisted of what is now the Acropolis and the land which lies at its foot and faces, in a general way, toward the south. The evidence is as follows: The sanctuaries in the Acropolis belong also to other gods," — that is, besides Athena, the presiding deity of the Acropolis, — "and those outside are situated more towards this part of the city, as, the sanctuary of Olympian Zeus, the Pythium, the sanctuary of Earth, and that of Dionysus in the Marshes, in whose honor the older Dionysia are celebrated on the twelfth of the month Anthesterion, as the Ionians descended from the Athenians still keep up the custom; and other sanctuaries are also situated here. And the fountain which now, since the tyrants so reconstructed it, is called Nine-spouts (Enneacrunus), but long ago, when the natural springs were visible, was named Fair-flowing (Callirrhoë), this, because it was near at hand, they used for the most important purposes, and even to-day the custom is kept up of using its water before weddings and for other holy rites. On account of the old settlement there, the Athenians up to the present time call the Acropolis Polis," or City.

This passage has been much discussed, and the situation of every one of the sanctuaries that Thucydides mentions has been brought into question. But assuming, as seems warranted, that our author has in mind the sanctuaries best known, we observe that he names them in their proper order from east to west (Fig. 18), — Olympieum, Pythium, sanctuary of Earth, Dionysium, and Nine-spouts (pp. 161 ff. and 108 ff.). The hoary antiquity of each of these is beyond a doubt. Not one of them, strictly speaking, is south of the Acropolis, nor does Thucydides claim that they are; but the argument suffices to show that the pre-Thesean city lay in this general direction.

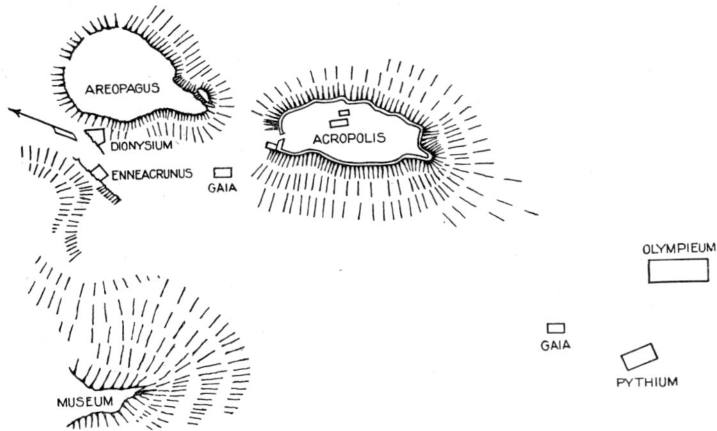


FIG. 18.—The situation of ancient sanctuaries, according to Thucydides.

Cecrops is said to have divided Attica into twelve independent states; Theseus, to have united it into one kingdom, with Athens as its capital. This "synoecism" of Theseus, or whoever accomplished it, may be put somewhere near a thousand years before Christ — tradition gives 1259 B.C. as the date — and marks the beginning of Athens's greatness. We need not linger further in the misty period of the kings, or trace the gradual evolution of the democracy; our present purpose is to sketch the material growth of the city rather than to review her constitutional development. The building of new shrines for the new divinities introduced from the newly allied demes is the most that we can definitely ascribe to those remote times; of this the antiquity of their worship is sufficient evidence. But the construction of other buildings must have gone on apace, and to an early epoch must be attributed the Ancient Agora, which was near the entrance to the Acropolis, and surrounded by public and private edifices.

The city rapidly outgrew the narrow district south of the Acropolis and the Areopagus, and the newer shrines were built on their northern slopes. Soon the center of the city's life was transferred to the valley north of the Areopagus, and here the public buildings began to be constructed.

The old Pelargicum about the Acropolis no longer sufficed to protect the city, and a new wall was built (pp. 52 ff.), following on the west the summits of the hills and extending on the south and north to the Ilissus and Eridanus rivers. Precisely when this wall was built we do not know, but it seems to have existed before the unsuccessful attempt of Cylon, about 630 B.C., to express the popular dislike of Draco's laws and make himself tyrant of the city.

What contributions the lawgiver Solon may have made to the material development of the city, we cannot tell. The successors of Solon, however, the tyrant Peisistratus and his family, set their stamp on Athenian architecture. To Peisistratus is to be credited the beginning of the great temple of Olympian Zeus (pp. 162 f.), which was destined to wait seven centuries for its completion. He, too, was probably responsible for the system of aqueducts that brought water from Hymettus to the ancient spring of Callirrhoë and transformed it into the elaborate fountain of Enneacrunus (pp. 108 ff.). His son Hippias began the fortification of the hill Munychia at Peiraeus; his other son Hipparchus founded the gymnasium in the Academy (p. 367); and his grandson Peisistratus dedicated an altar of the Twelve Gods at the new center of the city, where all roads met (p. 99), as well as an altar of Pythian Apollo (p. 168) near the Olympieum.

The Acropolis the Peisistratids especially adorned. They strengthened and added to its old wall, and built an ornamental Propylum (p. 226) at the western entrance. The old "hundred-foot" temple they surrounded with a peristyle and adorned with new sculpture (p. 314); the origin of various other buildings and sculptures of the sacred hill was due to them or to their inspiration.

The artists whom the fame, or the largesses, of the Peisistratids drew to the city beautified it with statues and other works of art, as the poets and philosophers whom they attracted glorified it intellectually and spiritually. The final blow which made Peisistratus master of the state was struck in 540 B.C.; Hippias was banished in 510 B.C., his brother having been assassinated four years earlier. The half-century of the rule of the "tyrants" was the first of the brilliant periods in the history of Athens.

The legislation of Cleisthenes followed close on the banishment of Hippias, and the arrested democracy began to develop anew. The tyrannicides, Harmodius and Aristogeiton, who had killed Hipparchus, were honored with statues, by the sculptor Antenor (p. 105); and Leaena (Lioness), the mistress of Aristogeiton, who under torture had refused to betray the other conspirators, was commemorated in a statue of a tongueless lioness (p. 253). The enthusiastic Demus obliterated the inscription on the altar of the Twelve Gods, and stopped work on the Olympieum, but the upbuilding of the city by no means ceased. Statues of the Namesake Heroes of the ten new tribes were set up (p. 98); a bronze chariot was dedicated on the Acropolis in honor of a victory over the Boeotians and Chalcidians in 506 B.C. (p. 229); the Tholus, or Rotunda, was built for the prytanists of the senate (p. 98); and probably a beginning was made of the first temple on the site of the Parthenon (p. 272). The accidental collapse of the wooden bleachers during a dramatic contest (about 500 B.C., p. 192) led to the construction of the first stone seats in the theater. During his archonship (493/2 B.C.) the astute Themistocles began the fortification of Peiraeus. Perhaps on his upright rival, Aristeides, rested the responsibility of the decision to use marble instead of poros for the Parthenon, introducing a second period in the history of that structure (p. 273).

Thus by the time of the Persian Wars Athens had begun to be a city of beauty, — even if it was still so little known abroad that Darius, the Persian king, after the burning of Sardis could ask (Herodotus, 5, 105): "The Athenians! Who are they?" The first Persian invasion, which ended disastrously for the invader at Marathon, in 490 B.C., brought only glory to Athens; but ten years later Xerxes, after his costly victory at Thermopylae, moved with all his host on the devoted city. A handful of Athenians, not persuaded by the plea of Themistocles that the Delphic advice to protect themselves behind a wooden wall referred to ships, barricaded the Acropolis, but the Persians soon found an ascent, and both Acropolis and city were at their savage mercy (p. 157). Walls, temples, houses, were almost completely destroyed. What Xerxes spared, his general, Mardonius, the following year, razed to the ground. The old temple of Athena was laid low, the partly finished Parthenon was burnt in scaffold, statues were demolished or, as in the case of the Tyrannicides, carried off to Susa. Athens was in ruins.

As soon, however, as the invaders had been driven from the land, the Athenians returned and began, with what we are wont to think occidental vigor, to rebuild their desolated city. Themistocles, who had been responsible for the success at Salamis, took the lead. To meet the rising jealousy of Sparta, the first necessity was the reconstruction of the wall. While Themistocles, by clever diplomacy, held off the Spartans, the Athenians, men, women, and children, labored feverishly at the wall, using whatever material came to hand. This task accomplished, Themistocles could turn to his cherished scheme of fortifying Peiraeus and her excellent harbors, which were to accommodate the new Athenian navy. That project and the construction of the Long Walls, which should bind the city to its port, progressed rapidly.

Time did not suffice to lay out a new plan for the city, nor had a Hippodamus (p. 21) yet arisen; so the new Athens followed the lines of the old, but with far greater magnificence. On the Acropolis the Hecatompedum, or "hundred-foot" temple, was partially rebuilt, without the peristyle, for a treasury; the Propylum was restored; the broken statues were cleared away and were used with other material as rubbish to level the surface of the hill; the wall was rebuilt outside of the old Pelargicum, and in its sides were inserted architectural remnants of the Hecatompedum and the Parthenon; and to commemorate the victory a colossal bronze image of Athena was erected from Persian spoils. In the Agora and other parts of the lower city similar work went forward. Old buildings, the Royal Stoa, the temple of Paternal Apollo, the theater, and others were repaired; new buildings, such as the Stoa of the Zeus of Freedom, were erected. To replace the group by Antenor, new statues of the Tyrannicides were set up beside the ancient Orchestra.

Under Cimon, who succeeded to the primacy about 472 B.C., the work of building continued. Cimon carried forward vigorously the construction of the Long Walls and rebuilt or reënforced the south wall of the Acropolis. He planted plane trees about the Agora and laid out the Academy as a shaded park; his own magnificent gardens he threw open for public use. The supposed bones of Theseus, which Cimon brought back from Scyros, were laid with ceremony in the Theseum near the east side of the Agora (p. 151). At the north edge of the Agora rows of herms, probably also a Hall of Herms, were set up by Cimon near the spot where his brother-in-law Peisianax built his own stoa, which later was adorned with paintings and came to be known as the Painted Porch.

Athens reached the zenith of her majesty under the administration of Pericles, during approximately the third quarter of the fifth century B.C. The administrative center of the Delian Confederacy, which was formed after the war, in order to resist Persia, was, in 454 B.C., transferred from Delos to Athens, and Pericles found a way to make its funds available for beautifying the new capital.

The defensive policy of Themistocles and Cimon was approved and continued. The harbor of Peiraeus was supplied with an elaborate and costly system of shipsheds (pp. 391 ff), and the seaport town itself was laid out regularly by Hippodamus of Miletus. The Long Walls connecting Peiraeus with Athens were finally completed, a new South Wall, parallel with the North Wall being erected in place of the less direct Phaleric Wall.

The earliest of the splendid buildings of this period seems to have been the Odeum, or Music Hall, of Pericles, on the southeast slope of the Acropolis. Its conical roof is said to have been made of masts from the ruined ships of Xerxes (p. 201). The gymnasium of the Lyceum was also constructed, and numerous other buildings in the lower city, to say nothing of scores of statues and paintings, of which we have only scanty knowledge, or have even lost the names. But the buildings of the Acropolis are the glory of the age. Whether or not at the outset Pericles had conceived a systematic plan for adorning the sacred hill, is still a moot question.

At about the middle of the century, perhaps after the battle of Oenophyta, in 457 B.C., when Athens first triumphed over her old rival, Sparta, a decree was passed providing for the construction of the little temple of Athena Victory on the high bastion beside the entrance to the sacred inclosure. Some doubt has been entertained as to its immediate erection (pp. 242 ff.), but this seems most likely. The Parthenon, as a worthy home of the city's protectress Athena, was probably begun in 447 B.C. on the site of the building destroyed by the Persians. In 438 B.C. the temple was ready for the great gold and ivory statue of Athena, by Pheidias, and five or six years later it was completed. Built entirely of white Pentelic marble, like the majority of the buildings of this age, it was executed throughout with extraordinary painstaking, and was richly decorated with sculptures, as it would seem by several of the leading artists of the day. On the south the wall of the Acropolis was increased in height to support the terrace, which was thus brought to a level with the rock on the north side and afforded a wide promenade about the temple.

The Propylaea, designed to extend quite across the west end of the hill, were begun in 437 B.C., and were brought almost to completion at a cost, so it is said, of 2012 talents, or about $2,400,000, in only five years; the opposition of the priests of Athena Victory and of Artemis Brauronia, and perhaps the troublous times preceding the Peloponnesian

War, effected a curtailment of the plan, so that the Propylaea were never wholly finished (p. 236).

Still, serious as was the effect of the war, building operations were by no means wholly suspended. Some work continued, and the peace of Nicias, commencing in 421 B.C., seems to have been accompanied by a special revival of building interest. The Erechtheum, not improbably also a conception of Pericles, was apparently begun on the cessation of hostilities. Work proceeded somewhat slowly, and the building was still unfinished, though near completion, in 409 B.C. On Colonus Agoraeus the Hephaesteum, or "Theseum," as for several centuries it has wrongly been called, seems to have been ready in 421 B.C. for the statues of Hephaestus and Athena, by Alcamenes. In 420 B.C. a private citizen, Telemachus, founded on the south slope of the Acropolis a sanctuary of Asclepius and Hygieia. At about the same time a new temple of Dionysus was built, perhaps by the famous general Nicias, near the theater, and provided with a gold and ivory statue, by Alcamenes. Numerous minor buildings and statues belong to the same period.

Eventually, however, the war sapped the strength of the city. The plague which followed the overcrowding of the first years of the contest so reduced the population that Cleon secured the contraction of the wall on the southwest. Meanwhile came the erection of new fortifications at Peiraeus and on Museum Hill, soon followed by their overthrow. The mutilation of the herms before the Sicilian Expedition was an augury of the later destruction, by Athenians themselves, of many votive offerings of metal, and the transformation of them into bullion. Finally, the Peloponnesian War and the fifth century closed with the demolition, by the Spartans, of the wall of Peiraeus and a large part of the Long Walls, and with the ruin of the shipsheds, the remains of which were later sold by the Thirty for three talents.

The restoration of the democracy, as the fourth century was about to begin, was again accompanied by the impulse to rebuild and improve. As early as 395 B.C. work began on the walls, and it was carried forward with fresh vigor after the return of Conon with spoils from his victory at Cnidus. Rebuilt of solid stone, these are in the main the walls which survive to-day. At Peiraeus Conon reared a temple of Cnidian Aphrodite in honor of his victory, and in the upper city his services, and those of his son, were rewarded with statues in the Agora and on the Acropolis. Presently the fleet was strengthened and the shipsheds reconstructed in much their former condition. No extensive building operations were undertaken in the first half of the century, but sculptors and painters, Cephisodotus, Praxiteles, Scopas, Euphranor, Parrhasius, and others, vied with one another in the beautifying of former buildings. Statues and other memorials were set up of divinities, of distinguished Athenians, and of foreign patrons of the city.

During the brilliant régime of the orator Lycurgus, from 338 to about 325 B.C., a new revival of building commenced. The walls were again repaired, the shipsheds were increased in number, and the magnificent Arsenal of Philo (p. 393) was erected in Peiraeus. In Athens the Dionysiac Theater (pp. 192 ff.) was completely rebuilt in stone; the Stadium was laid out and excavated (p. 175) south of the Ilissus; a new double gate, the Dipylum, took the place of the old Thriasian Gate, at the end of the thoroughfare from Peiraeus (pp. 63 f.); the Lyceum was furnished with a palaestra and planted anew with trees. Besides larger works, Lycurgus is said to have "embellished the whole city with many other structures."

After the battle of Granicus, in 334 B.C., Alexander the Great sent to Athens three hundred sets of Persian armor, in which were included the shields afterwards used to adorn the architrave of the Parthenon; and he and his wife and mother made other gifts to the city.

Meanwhile, though the population was depleted, increasing commerce had augmented individual fortunes and encouraged luxury. Private houses became more magnificent (p. 23), and display more common. The entire street of Tripods, about the east end of the Acropolis, was lined with private monuments for the exhibition of tripods set up by men who had won choragic victories (p. 180). Cemeteries, too, were adorned with elaborate gravestones. Indeed, this species of luxury was carried so far that in 317 B.C. Demetrius of Phalerum issued an order to limit such display (p. 23). On the whole the period of Lycurgus must have surpassed in splendor, if not in dignity, even the Age of Pericles.

In 322 B.C. Athens was forced to bow her neck to the yoke of Macedon, and received the garrison of Antipater into the fort on Munychia. The long period which follows is in the main one of reminiscent glory. The alternate repair and decay of the walls bear witness to the vacillating and declining spirit of the Athenians, now fast approaching servility; the fact that room could be found within the walls for extensive gymnasia and spacious gardens, like those of Epicurus, indicates a decline in population. Now subject, now nominally free, the city was politically insignificant, though increasingly renowned as a center of culture.

Athens was soon involved in the struggle between Cassander and Polyperchon; and in honor of the victory of

Pleistarchus, Cassander's brother and proxy, a trophy was erected upon a gateway in the Agora (p. 125). Cassander put the city into the hands of Demetrius of Phalerum, who maintained a status of peace, but contributed little to the city's material growth. The obsequious people set up no fewer than three hundred and sixty statues of Demetrius in Athens and Attica, but after his withdrawal all save one of these were destroyed. In 307 B.C. Demetrius Poliorcetes (Sacker of Cities) was set over the city by his father Antigonus. Both father and son were promptly enrolled as Namesake Heroes of new tribes and their statues erected beside those of the other Eponymi (p. 98). Gilded statues of the two men were also set up near the Tyrannicides, a place long held almost sacred. Five years later the city's despot was the impecunious Lachares, who robbed the Parthenon of all available gold and silver, even trying, apparently without success, to carry off the gold sheathing of the great statue of Pheidias.

Ptolemy Philadelphus (285–247 B.C.) was the first of the so-called foreign benefactors of the city. The Ptolemaeum which he built near the Agora was the earliest extensive gymnasium erected within the walls. Under Egyptian influence a temple of the divinity Serapis was built north of the Acropolis. In return for his favors Ptolemy also was made the eponymous hero of another new tribe, and his statue was set up with the other Eponymi. In 229 B.C. the Diogeneum, in honor of Diogenes, another Macedonian lord, was built east of the Agora. The interest of other Egyptian and Macedonian benefactors followed.

During the same period the Pergamene monarchs also began to do homage to the ancient city. Attalus I (241–197 B.C.) dedicated several groups of statues on the Acropolis (pp. 308 f.) and was made a Namesake Hero. Eumenes, his brother (197–159 B.C.), erected the long and elaborate stoa west of the theater. Attalus II (159–138 B.C.) reared a magnificent stoa in the form of a bazaar on the east edge of the Agora. As thank offerings the Athenians raised for Eumenes and Attalus two colossal statues.

In 200 B.C. Philip V of Macedon attempted to force his way into the city, but was resisted successfully (p. 64). In revenge he devastated Cynosarges, the Lyceum, the Academy, and other places outside the walls; and the Athenians fatuously retaliated by destroying all the statues of Philip and his ancestors which were in the city.

The Syrian king Antiochus IV Epiphanes (175–164 B.C.) undertook to complete the temple of Olympian Zeus, which had stood unfinished for several centuries, but he died before his task was done (p. 163). He also presented the city with a gilded head of Medusa, which was affixed to the south wall of the Acropolis as an "averter of evil."

Athens had come under the pervading influence of Rome long before the crushing blow dealt by Mummius, in 146 B.C., brought Greece finally under Roman sway. The city's ready submission gave her half a century of peace. Of this period we know little. A bema for Roman orators in front of the Stoa of Attalus is mentioned; and to this time may perhaps be ascribed the removal of the Prytaneum to its new site north of the Acropolis.

Unfortunately, however, the city was soon inveigled into taking part in the war waged by Mithridates, king of Pontus, against the Romans. Sulla, ruthless avenger, appeared before the gates. The siege, during which the Academy and Lyceum were again laid waste, ended on March 1, 86 B.C., when Sulla succeeded in making a breach in the wall between the Sacred and Peiraic gates. The devastation which followed was surpassed only by that of Xerxes four centuries earlier. For a time the Acropolis held out under the leadership of the demagogue Aristion, but it was taken and plundered. Either Sulla or Aristion burned the Odeum of Pericles; several columns of the unfinished Olympieum and numerous works of art were taken away for shipment to Rome; many public buildings were looted and demolished. Peiraeus, which soon yielded, suffered a fate even worse. Much of the city, including the Arsenal of Philo, the docks, and the shipsheds, was burned. The walls of Peiraeus and the Long Walls were laid in ruins.

Henceforward Athens became more and more Roman in character. She did not lack later benefactors, but most of them were Romans. Pompey gave the city fifty talents for the restoration of public buildings. The Cappadocian king Ariobarzanes rebuilt the Odeum of Pericles. Cicero's wealthy friend Atticus made the city his home and enriched it with gifts, but seems to have made no additions to its buildings. Cicero himself planned to build a festal gateway to the Academy, but did not execute his design. When Brutus visited the city after the assassination of Caesar, the people enthusiastically dedicated statues of Brutus and Cassius beside those of the old Tyrannicides; but these cannot have stood long, for Antony's arrival a little later was the signal for a transfer of obsequious homage. The colossi of Eumenes and Attalus were reinscribed as statues of Antony, and even cult statues of Antony and Cleopatra were erected on the Acropolis. The colossi were blown down by a tempest just before the battle of Actium — an evil omen!

Augustus was very friendly to Athens, and his reign brought many new buildings to the city. The most important of these was the large and ornate market built to the east of the Agora and adorned with statues of the Julian family (pp. 136 ff.). The emperor's general, Agrippa, was honored with a lofty equestrian monument at the entrance to the Acropolis (p. 238), and east of the Parthenon a small round temple was reared to Rome and Augustus (pp. 310 f.). A plan was formed by various eastern kings to finish the Olympieum in honor of Augustus, but it came to naught.

The first century and a half of the Christian era were marked by the continued good-will of Rome and the erection of countless statues in the honor of distinguished Romans, but only a few buildings were constructed. Nero's stay at Athens was accompanied by a rebuilding of the stage of the theater (p. 198), by the placing of a long inscription on the front of the Parthenon (p. 303), and by various dedicatory offerings. A certain Diocles repaired the temple and precinct of Asclepius. A conspicuous monument was erected (114–116 A.D.) on Museum Hill to Gaius Julius Antiochus Philopappus of Commagene in Syria. And at some time during the period a broad flight of marble steps was constructed leading up to the entrance of the Acropolis.

Of all the kingly or imperial patrons of Athens, however, Hadrian was the most beneficent and the most lavish. He showed his favor by repeated and protracted residence in the city. His reign was "a last bright gleam from the west after a murky afternoon and before the descent of the long twilight and the still longer hopeless night." [1] An entire new quarter, New Athens or the Athens of Hadrian, was laid out on the east side of the city and filled with villas, baths, and dwellings. The wall was extended to surround this area, and a triumphal gateway erected on the line between the old city and the new. At last the great temple begun by Peisistratus seven centuries before was completed

[1] Wachsmuth, *Die Stadt Athen*, I, 686.

and dedicated by the emperor himself, in 130 A.D., to Olympian Zeus; while the large area about the temple was leveled, walled, and filled with altars and statues. North of the Acropolis were built the spacious Stoa and Library of Hadrian (pp. 145 ff.); elsewhere were erected a temple of Hera and Panhellenian Zeus, a Pantheon, and a gymnasium; but of these we know little more than the names. In the theater (p. 199) an imperial box was made, and statues were set up in each of the wedge-shaped divisions of seats.

The work of restoration and improvement continued under Antoninus Pius and Marcus Aurelius; the former completed the aqueduct begun by Hadrian to supply the city with water from Pentelicus. Under the Antonines the most generous benefactor was Tiberius Claudius Herodes Atticus of Marathon. In addition to various minor structures he rebuilt the Stadium and seated it with white marble (p. 175); and, in honor of his wife Regilla, who died about 161 A.D., he erected the magnificent Odeum at the southwest corner of the Acropolis. On the hill at one side of the Stadium Herodes dedicated a temple of Fortune. His tomb is said to have been "in the Stadium."

The buildings of Herodes Atticus were the last of importance erected in the ancient city. We read of a fort and of a new statue of Pallas in the Palladium on the Acropolis, of two new pylons, and of some last repairs to the stage of the theater by a man named Phaedrus, but of no conspicuous buildings. The city became still more popular, however, as a university town, a *gymnasium Musarum*, as Symmachus calls it, to which came throngs of youths from all parts of the world. The professors are said to have lectured in small theaters, some of which were adorned with marble, but whether or not these were new buildings, we do not know. Of the schools, such men as Julian were enthusiastic supporters. Sentiment and ratiocination, rather than progress, marked the age.

After the period of stagnation came decay. A horde of Costobocs, which invaded Greece, seems not to have reached the city, but in 267 A.D. the barbarian Heruli captured Athens and Peiraeus; apparently they withdrew without doing serious damage. Near the end of the fourth century of our era a proconsul removed the pictures of the Painted Porch, and in 396 A.D. Alaric and the Goths occupied the city, though again without great harm. But to Constantinople, the new capital of the eastern empire, Athens began to yield up her works of art in increasing numbers. About the time of Theodosius II (408–450 A.D.) even the chryselephantine statue of the Parthenon was among the spoils. The great bronze statue of Athena Promachus (pp. 343 ff.) must have been carried off about the time of Justinian (527–565 A.D.), who took much other booty for his new church of Hagia Sophia (Holy Wisdom). The attitude of the world toward heathendom was changing, and the edict of Theodosius I forbidding sacrifices to heathen gods had been only the expression of a general revolt against the old religion and its votaries. In 529 A.D. Justinian finally closed the schools of philosophy. The temples had previously begun to be changed into Christian churches; the Parthenon, for example, into the shrine of Holy Wisdom (p. 303), the Hephaesteum into that of Saint George (p. 119). Athens itself became a provincial bishopric, and from the sixth to the twelfth centuries almost disappears from history. The decay of the ancient buildings continued unchecked, and letters of the twelfth century written by Archbishop Michael Akominatos speak of the city as being in a sad state of ruin.

In 1204 the Crusaders captured Constantinople; Athens was at once turned over to Otho de la Roche, and it remained under the Dukes for the next century. In 1311 the duchy fell into the hands of the Catalan mercenaries. The Florentine Nerio Acciajuoli became duke in 1387, and he and his successors ruled until 1456, when Athens was captured, after a desperate struggle, by Omar and the Turks. Turkish rule continued with slight interruptions for nearly four hundred years, or until the revolution, which began in 1821. By the end of the sixteenth century the population was reduced to 12,000, and at the close of the Turkish régime to a few hundreds.

Under the Turks the devastation grew ever worse. In 1656, according to Spon, the Propylaea were struck by lightning and blown up by powder stored there. The Erechtheum had been turned into a harem, and was partially built over with rough walls. The temple of Wingless Victory was torn down, that its blocks might be used to strengthen the fortification of the Acropolis. In 1687 the Venetian bombardment laid in ruins the Parthenon. The angry Turks, returning the following year, burned the city around the Acropolis. At the opening of the nineteenth century Lord Elgin carried away many of the remaining sculptures of the Parthenon and some other marbles. And during all these centuries the buildings of the ancient city had served as stone quarries, while the statues, of bronze or marble, save the few that the friendly earth concealed, were thrown into the melting furnace or the limekiln.

In 1833 the Turks finally withdrew, and the next year Athens became the capital of the new kingdom of Greece. The mournful era of destruction was at an end; the period of conservation of ancient monuments soon began.

FIG. 19. — Building of the wall of the Pelargicum; vase painting.

# CHAPTER III

## WALLS AND GATES

### THE PELARGICUM

THE earliest settlement of Athens on the summit of the Acropolis was surmounted by a defensive wall, the Pelasgicum, or Pelargicum. The name Pelasgicum probably has reference to the "Pelasgian" settlers. Indeed, we are informed by Herodotus (6, 137) and others that this people constructed the wall (Fig. 19), while Pausanias (1, 28, 3) adds the names of the builders, Agrolas and Hyperbius (and Euryalus?). But we cannot place much credence in the story; the resemblance of names may have inspired the tradition. At any rate, the form Pelargicum is preferred in inscriptions of the fifth century and is found in the best manuscripts of Thucydides and Aristophanes. Its derivation is uncertain. In his *Birds* (v. 832) Aristophanes plays upon the likeness of the name to pelargos, or "crane," and it may be that "Crane's Nest" was the original name of the citadel.

Portions of this primitive wall are still extant in various parts of the Acropolis, and from these and the literary references we are enabled to learn its structure and to trace much of its course (Fig. 20). The most conspicuous section now remaining is just south of the Propylaea (Fig. 21). This is nearly 60 feet long and 20 feet thick. It is of Cyclopean style, having an outer and an inner face of Acropolis limestone, the space between being filled with rubble and earth. The stones vary greatly in size; some of them

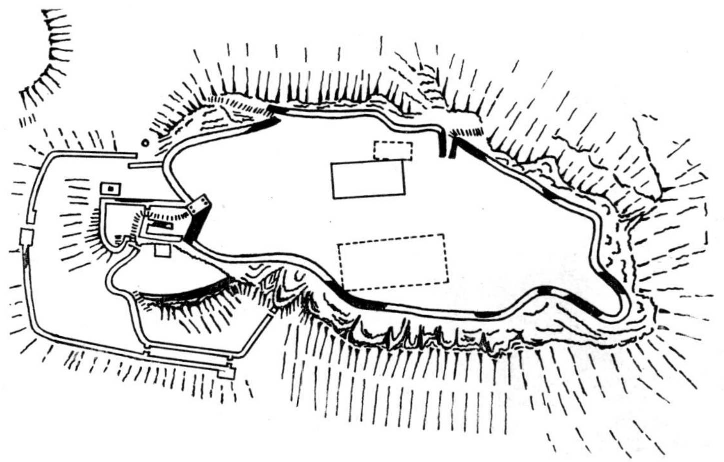

FIG. 20. — Map of the Pelargicum and Enneapylum.

The restoration of the Enneapylum, or out-work at the west of the Acropolis, is almost wholly conjectural.

are enormous. They are rough-hewn, with the smoother face outside, the interstices being filled with the smaller stones. The greatest height at present is about 10 feet, on the west face; the east face has almost disappeared. Where it abuts on this wall, the corner of the Propylaea has been cut off diagonally, to the top of the building; this suggests the inference that the wall here was more than 30 feet high (*cf.* pp. 57 f.).

Turning abruptly toward the east (Fig. 20), the wall

followed the contour of the rock, but considerably inside the later wall, so as to avoid certain clefts. The short stretch before the turn may be of later construction, and the next portion is near the southwest corner of the Parthenon. This latter piece was discovered by the excavators of the hill and is still visible in a pit left open for the purpose.

From this point fragments of the wall are found up to the front of the Acropolis Museum, where begins a great loop that extends under the museum and then about the south-

FIG. 21. — Portion of the wall of the Pelargicum at the west end of the Acropolis.

In the rear is the Parthenon.

east corner (Fig. 2) of the Acropolis. From this point the course is conjectural. The north side of the Acropolis is precipitous, however, and we may assume that the wall followed approximately the course of the later wall to the west end of the hill.

Later constructions have obliterated almost every trace of the wall at the west. A small piece is buried in the bastion on which stands the temple of Wingless Victory, but further than this we are reduced to inferences from the character of the site, from the study of similar walls at Mycenae, Tiryns, and other places, and from the literary evidence.

We are told that this end of the Acropolis, which was most open to assault, was defended by a great fortress, the Enneapylum, or "Nine-gates;" this may be restored conjecturally from analogy with Mycenaean fortifications, but with no certainty of correctness (Fig. 20).

Whether or not the highest opening in the fortress had thus early an ornamental gateway cannot be determined; judging from contemporary cities, we may guess that it had. Though the view is questioned, the probability is that the principal approach was always here. Other entrances were few. A postern gate stood at the northeast corner, where rude rock-hewn steps descend from the ancient palace. Possibly an entrance may have existed near the middle of the north wall, where steps ascending from without meet a flight of steps built in the later wall. A passage may have led from the northwest corner to the spring Clepsydra, but, from the dearth of water suffered by Cylon when he was besieged in the Acropolis, this seems doubtful. The pretender Aristion, in Sulla's time, experienced the same difficulty; and a passage in the *Lysistrata* of Aristophanes implies that the Clepsydra was outside the inclosure.

How far the wall extended eastward along the southern slope of the hill is uncertain; fragments here which some have assigned to the Pelargicum seem hardly substantial enough, but the question is still open.

When the Pelargicum is mentioned in later times, the lower wall is meant. The portion which survived the Persian Wars had fallen into decay, and various laws were passed to prevent the removal of stones from the inclosure and the mowing of grass there. The lower wall is doubtless meant also in the oracle mentioned by Thucydides (2, 17) in connection with the crowding at the beginning of the Peloponnesian War. The advice of the oracle was, "the Pelargicum would better lie idle;" the historian adds, however, "Nevertheless, under stress of the sudden necessity it was settled." But the questions connected with the Pelargicum are complicated, and cannot be examined at greater length here.

### THE CIRCULAR WALL

How long the Pelargicum was the sole fortification of Athens we have no means of knowing. The view has been held by some that the city which spread out about the Acropolis had no defensive wall before the Persian Wars. No remains are extant of a city wall before that of Themistocles, and we have no direct information as to its building; that none existed, however, seems inherently improbable. Fortunately some scattered hints are found in the historians which afford circumstantial evidence as to its existence.

Thucydides's statement (1, 126, 6) that a feast of Zeus in Cylon's time was held "outside of the city" perhaps is not to be pressed, though it is suggestive of definite city limits; but this historian gives us clearer information (6, 57, 1–3) in connection with the conspiracy against the tyrants, Hippias and Hipparchus. The plot was to be executed at the great Panathenaic festival, and Hippias was "outside in the Cerameicus," arranging the details of the procession. Harmodius and Aristogeiton, seeing one of the conspirators conversing with Hippias, supposed their plot betrayed; they "rushed inside the gates" and slew Hipparchus near the Leocorium. The gates can scarcely be other than those of the city, and were probably near the north end of the later Agora.

We next hear of the wall at the time of the Persian Wars. The Delphic oracle delivered to the city's envoys before the battle of Salamis speaks (Hdt. 7, 140) of the "wheel-shaped city," an appropriate epithet of a walled town with the Acropolis at its hub. We are not told directly that a city wall was destroyed by Xerxes, but such a calamity is implied in the statement of Herodotus (9, 13) that Mardonius, the general of Xerxes, returned to Athens the following year and razed to the ground "whatever was left standing anywhere of the walls or the houses or the sanctuaries." Furthermore, several remarks of Thucydides indicate that the wall of Themistocles was regarded as a reconstruction. When the Athenians returned to their city, "they prepared," he says (1, 89, 3), "to rebuild the city and the walls; for small portions of the inclosure were standing and the majority of the houses had fallen;" and elsewhere (1, 93, 2) he informs us that the new "inclosure of the city was extended larger on all sides." These statements would be meaningless, if the only preceding inclosure were the wall of the Acropolis. Again, a remark of Pausanias (1, 25, 6) that the Museum Hill lay "inside the ancient inclosure" can with difficulty be explained of the wall that existed in his own day, though the statement, to be sure, would also have been true of that. And lastly, the law forbidding burial in the city, a law that without much doubt goes back to the days of Cylon, seems to imply that the city was walled.

No sure remains of the Circular Wall are left, and for its course the last remark quoted from Thucydides and the oracle chronicled by Herodotus constitute our principal data; it was wheel-shaped and of less extent than the Themistoclean Wall, the course of which can be traced. On the west and southwest the summits of the hills were probably followed nearly in the course of the later wall. The term "wheel-shaped" and the view of Plato (*Critias*

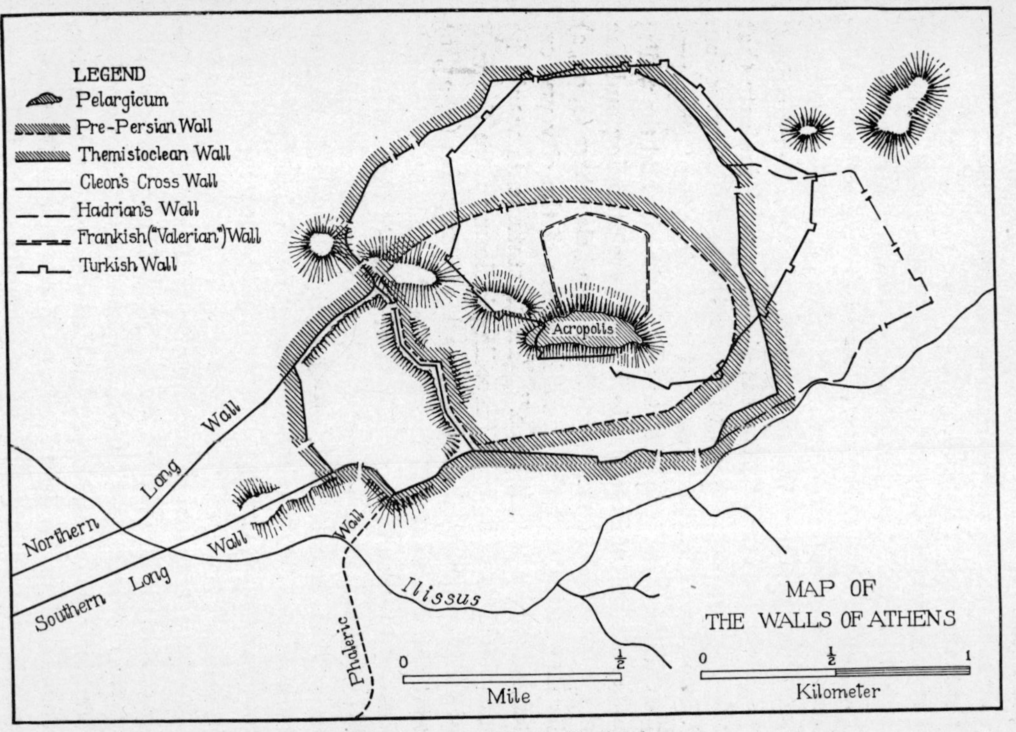


FIG. 22. — Map of the walls of Athens.

112 A) that the old city lay between the Ilissus and Eridanus rivers help us to outline the remainder of the circuit (Fig. 22).

In the southeast corner of the city one point of the wall may perhaps be fixed. Here the Roman emperor Hadrian built an elaborate gateway (Fig. 23). Over the arch on the west face is the inscription: "This is the Athens of Theseus, the former city;" on the other face a corresponding inscription reads: "This is the city of Hadrian, not of Theseus." The hypothesis is reasonable that Hadrian built the gateway on the line of the old wall, parts of which may have been left in his day, although some think that the gate was in line with the Themistoclean Wall. A gate at the north end of the Agora has been mentioned (p. 41). The suggestion that this still existed in the time of Pausanias and was identical with a triumphal arch which he names is plausible, but cannot be proved.

FIG. 23. — Arch of Hadrian, from the east.
A view of the arch from the west is given in Figure 92.

Nothing is known of the construction of the Circular Wall. Very likely it was made of sun-dried bricks with a stone foundation, as was the wall of Themistocles. As we have already seen, it must have been utterly destroyed by the Persians.

### WALLS OF THE ACROPOLIS

The massive walls of the Acropolis have been so often reconstructed and repaired that at present only a tentative history of them can be written. Large portions of the walls as they stand to-day, including the buttresses along the south side, are mediaeval; when these additions shall have been removed, many puzzling questions will doubtless be brought nearer solution.

A large part of the Pelargicum fell at the hands of the Persians. On the south side of the hill the filling in the rear partially preserved it, but along the north side, where the Persians had found it possible to clamber up, the wall almost completely disappeared. Under the leadership, no doubt, of Themistocles, the north wall was rebuilt and probably the south wall repaired. The new north wall was of ashlar masonry for the most part, but into it and facing the homes of the city, as a perpetual reminder of Persian impiety, were inserted drums of columns (Fig. 24) from the early Parthenon, which was burnt in scaffold, blocks and drums from the old temple of Athena, and in one place a section, in its normal relations, of the triglyph frieze and cornice from the same structure.

No general reconstruction was attempted until the return of Cimon from the battle of Eurymedon (465 B.C.) with ample spoils, the sale of which afforded funds for the undertaking. To Cimon, Plutarch and others attribute the south wall, also known as the Cimonium. This, as we now know, was increased in height and strengthened by Pericles, so as to support the terrace along the side of the Parthenon.

Unlike the Pelargicum, the wall of Cimon did not follow the variations of contour, but struck boldly across the edge of the hill from the southwest to the southeast corner in two straight lines which meet in an obtuse angle south of the west end of the Parthenon (Fig. 133). From the south-east corner the same construction continued northward to the modern "belvedere."

The Cimonium was built of squared blocks of poros laid as headers and stretchers (p. 9), but not clamped together.

FIG. 24. — Drums of columns of the old Parthenon built into the north wall of the Acropolis.

The rubble wall at the top is mediaeval and modern.

The exterior was plain, without buttresses. On the south-east side are still as many as twenty-nine courses, arising to a height of nearly 50 feet; here the thickness at the bottom is about 21 feet, at the top about 8 feet. Above the first few courses it batters, inclining inward some two feet before reaching the summit.

In describing the temple of Wingless Victory, Pausanias makes the remark (1, 22, 5), "From this point the sea is visible." Hence it has been inferred that the sea was not visible from within the wall; in other words, that the wall was so high that one could not look over it. Such is still the case with part of the north wall, upon which Lucian makes one of the characters in his *Fisherman* climb, in

FIG. 25. — Relief in the front of the Roman stage of the Dionysiac theater.

Over the head of the seated Dionysus at the right the columns of the Parthenon appear above the cliff.

order to look down into the city. A relief under the later stage of the theater seems to show the Parthenon partly visible above the wall (at the right-hand upper corner in Fig. 25). In a sense the Acropolis was a secret precinct.

## THE THEMISTOCLEAN WALL

The cleverness of Themistocles in outwitting the Spartans and in rebuilding the wall against their opposition has been mentioned (p. 35). The haste with which the construction was carried forward, even the women and children assisting in the work, had an effect on the nature of the structure; its foundations were made, as Thucydides says (1, 93, 2), "of all sorts of stones," even of tombstones and stones wrought for other buildings. But the wall built under such stress fixed the outline of the city throughout most of its later history. The circuit extended on all sides beyond the former wall (p. 53); and from portions still to be seen or else attested by earlier investigators, with the help of literary references, its course can be traced with tolerable certainty over most of its extent.

The most important piece of the wall which remains is at the northwest side of the city (Figs. 26 and 27). Here is an

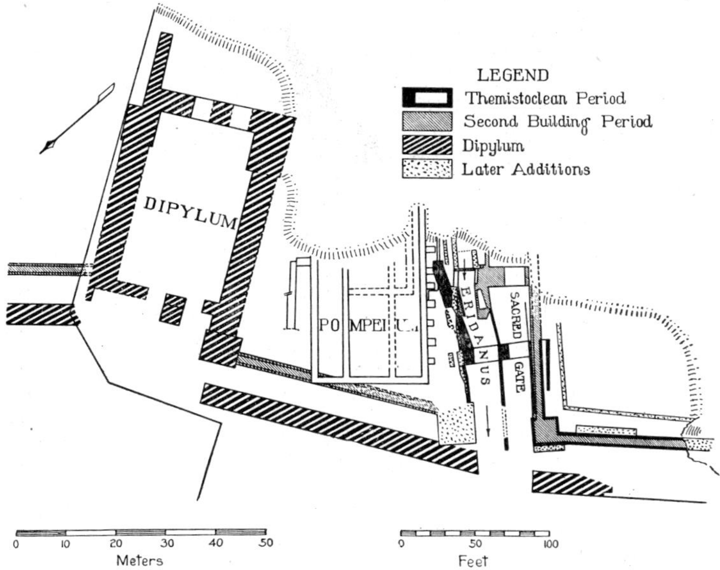


FIG. 26. — Plan of the Dipylum and adjacent walls.

angle measuring about 100 feet on one side, and more than 100 on the other, with a great tower at the apex. It has been repeatedly repaired, and only the lowest courses (below the arrows in Fig. 27) are Themistoclean; at the very bottom of these, recent investigators have discovered stuccoed blocks from other buildings, fragments of carved tombstones (Fig. 28), and other sculptures, — an interesting verification of Thucydides's statement. Only the foundation of the original wall was of stone; the outer and inner faces were of polygonal masonry, the middle of rubble and earth. Above this rose sun-dried brick to a height that cannot now be determined.

Outside of the old wall and running off toward the northeast, another wall, entirely of masonry, was built in the

FIG. 27. — Fragment of the Themistoclean wall, near the Dipylum.

The portion below the arrows is the foundation of the wall of Themistocles; the wall above it was originally of sun-dried brick. The course of large stones above the Themistoclean foundation belongs to the second building period. The upper courses are later repairs.

fourth century B.C., to strengthen the defenses (Fig. 29). During the Middle Ages all these walls were covered deeply with earth, and so were not carried off for building stones, as was most of the circuit.

The southerly course of the wall (Fig. 262) can be traced by extant or known remnants over the high ground from the Dipylum to the Hill of the Nymphs and along the brink of the Barathrum, whence it made an abrupt detour to the southwest, thus affording protection to the populous Hollow (Coele, p. 23), and connecting with the Long Walls which ran to Peiraeus. Skirting the precipitous edge of the Museum Hill, above the modern stone quarries, to the summit, it then descended the steep eastern side and stretched across the level ground to the vicinity of the Olympieum.

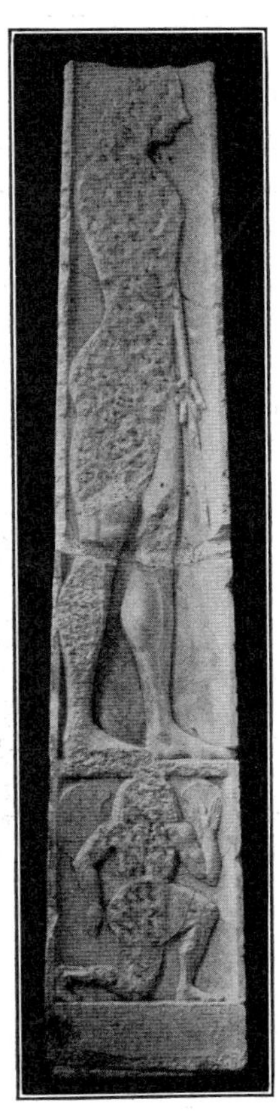

Fig. 28. — Grave stele from beneath the Themistoclean wall (Athens Museum).

Thus far the evidence is in the main secure, abundant fragments of the wall being known, although nearly all of them have now perished. For the east side of the city the evidence is scanty, particularly for the section beyond the Olympieum. Some are inclined to believe that the wall ran straight north, leaving the Olympieum outside the city and connecting with the Arch of Hadrian (p. 55). But the Olympieum seems to have been in the city; the house of Morychus in Plato's *Phaedrus* (p. 227) was "in the city near the Olympieum," whence Phaedrus comes for a walk "outside the wall." Furthermore we learn from the geographer Strabo (p. 404) that certain priests had the duty of watching for the lightnings over Mt. Parnes from the altar of Lightning Zeus, which was "on the wall between the Olympieum and the Pythium." The Pythium (p. 168) was just south of the Olympieum, and the wall in question was apparently that of the city, which must, accordingly, have made a slight detour so as to inclose the temple.

For the remainder of the wall, as for all parts of the circuit, we have another sort of evidence, of a safe though negative character. Speaking of the death of Marcus Marcellus, Cicero says (*Ad fam.* 4, 12, 3): "I could not secure from the Athenians the grant of a place of burial

FIG. 29.—Looking northwest from the Sacred Gate.

On either side are walls of different periods, and in the distance is the Dipylum cemetery.

within the city, which they said was forbidden by their religious scruples, and which, moreover, they had hitherto granted to no one." This prohibition of burial within the city may have had its origin in the purification of Athens by Epimenides, about 600 B.C., after the murder of Cylon; it continued in force, with only a few exceptions, into the second century of our era. Classical Greek or early Roman graves, therefore, we should not expect to find inside the walls. A large series of tombs has been found in and near the present Constitution Square; the wall must have lain west of these. Bending northwestward, the general course is established by graves, and by some remains, to the most northerly point, where are the foundations of the towers of a gate. Again, west of this point, the line is fixed in the same manner around to the Dipylum, whence we started.

Thucydides says (2, 13, 7), according to our manuscripts, that the circumference of the wall, exclusive of the unguarded section between the ends of the Long Walls, was forty-three stades, approximately 4.7 miles. As traced above, however, the circuit, including the section which Thucydides excepts, is a mile short of his figure. While some small errors in our study are possible, the total can in no way be reconciled with the historian's statement. His figures must be wrong, or else wrongly handed down in our manuscripts; the latter alternative is the more probable. Comparisons made by other writers with the Servian Wall of Rome and with the wall of Syracuse are of no value.

The strip of cross-wall, of which small portions remain, between the Hill of the Nymphs and the Hill of the Muses was built by the demagogue Cleon, notwithstanding the gibes of Aristophanes in the *Knights*, about 420 B.C., in order to contract the space which must be guarded.

The Themistoclean Wall was pierced by a dozen principal gates. The most ornate and important of these was the Dipylum, of which the remains are found in the northwest part of the city, a few hundred feet from the best preserved piece of the wall. As the name indicates, this was a double gate, closed at either end of a court by two pairs of doors with intervening piers (Fig. 26). In front of the northwest pier a large base, perhaps of a quadriga, is still in situ (Fig. 30); while before the southeast pier is an altar dedicated to Zeus, Hermes, and Acamas (Fig. 31). The court of the Dipylum measures about 127 by 70 feet, making a spacious "pocket" through which an enemy must fight his way while attacked from above, as Philip of Macedon discovered to his sorrow (p. 42). The Dipylum is constructed of squared blocks of poros, breccia, and Hymettian marble; it was probably built toward the end of the fourth century B.C. (though some fix its date even later), under the administration of Lycurgus, and so was contemporaneous with the outer line of walls mentioned above

FIG. 30. — Front of the Dipylum, with quadriga base on the left.

(p. 60). It took the place of an earlier gate named the Thriasian.

A short distance southwest of the Dipylum is a smaller gate, beside which the stream of the Eridanus issued. This is probably the Sacred Gate, from which the Sacred Way led to Eleusis. In front of it lies the famous Dipylum cemetery (pp. 372 ff.).

Three or four hundred yards south of the Sacred Gate lay the Peiraic Gate, which, before the building of the Dipylum, was the chief exit in the direction of Peiraeus. Portions of wall and towers have been found at either side of the gate, as well as wheel-tracks worn in the rock.

Near the edge of the Hill of the Nymphs lay another gate, and in the southwest detour of the wall two more, one of them the Melitan Gate. Outside of this gate are said to have been the Cimonian tombs, and close at hand was the grave of Thucydides. An elaborate rock-hewn tomb still extant in the end of a hill south of this point may belong to this group of burial places.

In the level ground east of Museum Hill was the Itonian Gate; the precise spot is not known (p. 76). Some scholars look for the Diomean Gate close by the Itonian. That another gate was near is almost certain, but the evidence points to the situation of the Diomean farther on, perhaps a little north or south of the Olympieum (p. 172).

Fig. 31. — Altar dedicated to Zeus, Hermes, and Acamas, at the east end of the Dipylum.

The site of the Gate of Diochares is reasonably sure. Strabo says (9, 397) that the river Eridanus had its sources "outside the so-called Gate of Diochares near the Lyceum" (p. 173). We know that the Eridanus rose on the side of Mt. Lycabettus (pp. 18, 173), and that the Lyceum was east of the city between Lycabettus and the Ilissus; so the Gate of Diochares must have been in this region, probably in the vicinity of the present Hermes Street, a little to the west of the extensive cemetery found here.

The next important opening was the Acharnian Gate, from which a road led to Acharnae, the largest deme, or village, in Attica, seven miles north of Athens. Between this gate and the Dipylum was one other gate, of which ruins have been found.

Besides these, one or two more gates may have existed. We have the name of a Cavalry Gate, but this may be one of those mentioned. Small doorways pierced the wall at various points.

### THE PEIRAIC WALL

The tyrant Hippias is said to have begun a stronghold on the hill of Munychia at Peiraeus, but of his work we have no certain remains. The first to appreciate the advantage to Athens of fortifying Peiraeus was Themistocles, in whose first archonship (493/2 B.C.) the circuit wall was planned and partially constructed. The fortification was not completed until a decade or so after the Persian Wars. This wall was built more deliberately and more strongly than that about Athens itself; its foundation was of massive masonry, so wide, if we correctly interpret Thucydides (1, 93, 4), that two wagons could meet and pass on it.

At the end of the Peloponnesian War a large part of the wall was torn down, but it was not to remain long in ruins. In 395 B.C., the rebuilding began, and in the nick of time Conon arrived with spoils from the battle of Cnidus to give the undertaking impetus. In general the present remains are of the wall of Conon.

Ruins of the wall almost surround the city (Fig. 251). From the land side the chief entrance was the Asty Gate at the north, whence ran the main road to Athens. From this point the wall runs eastward, past the juncture with the Long Walls and two other gates, nearly to the summit of Munychia. Thence it turns to the coast, which it follows throughout the rest of its course, to the west side of the city.

The harbor of Munychia is almost closed by spurs of the hill and a small island. Over these the wall pushes out from either side with moles and towers, until it leaves a passage of only 120 feet, which in times of emergency could be completely closed by a chain or rope boom. On the hill at the south end of the harbor the wall was reënforced by a fort. At Zea Harbor the wall bends in to protect the throat and ends in moles and towers, the open space being about 200 feet.

Around the peninsula of Acte (Fig. 32) the wall follows the high bank, 60 to 130 feet from the water. At the

FIG. 32. — Section of the Peiraic wall about Acte and one of the towers, from within.

northwest corner of the peninsula, Cape Alcimus, is a massive round tower; lower down, at the water's edge, is a square tower. No remains are extant of a wall from this point to the southern mole, which projects across the mouth of the harbor, but one must be assumed, to dominate the entrance of the harbor, as at Zea. The open space between moles was about 180 feet.

From the northern mole the wall leads back to the great northwest gate; it then probably passed across the mouth of Dumb Harbor and northeastward to the Asty Gate. But from the mouth of the harbor the course is conjectural.

West of the peninsula of Eëtioneia a great loop surrounded the bay of Krommydaru, which is now filled and occupied by dry-docks. The suggestion has been made that this was the original wall of Themistocles, and that it went around rather than across Dumb Harbor. This is doubtful, however; it may be even of a later date than that of Conon. The conjecture has also been made that a piece of wall which starts from the east side of Acte and continues across the peninsula was the wall of Themistocles. The suggestion is tempting, for the wall as traced above exceeds the sixty stades given by Thucydides (2, 13, 7) as the length of the Peiraic circuit.

The early wall was probably like that of the upper city, of sun-baked brick with a foundation of stone. The existing wall is constructed of inner and outer faces of ashlar masonry, the space between being filled with rubble and earth. It varies in thickness from about 26 feet along its exposed north side to 10 and 12 feet about Acte and 6.5 to 8 feet on Eëtioneia. For much of its course it was reënforced at intervals on the outside by towers which jut out 12 to 20 feet from the intervening curtain; nearly sixty of these protected the wall about Acte (Fig. 33).

FIG. 33. — Exterior of one of the towers of the wall about Acte.

FIG. 34. — East tower of Asty Gate.

Asty Gate was the principal gate at the north of Peiraeus communicating with Athens outside the Long Walls.

Near the Asty Gate was a small shrine of Hermes, erected by the archons when the construction of the wall was beginning. The gate itself was flanked by two strong towers (Figs. 34 and 35). Whether or not it had a court like the Dipylum is uncertain. Such, at any rate, was the construction of the gate five hundred feet to the east; here, however, were no towers, the gate being flanked by the North

FIG. 35. — West tower of Asty Gate.

FIG. 36. — Peiraic wall and gate near juncture of the North Long Wall.

Long Wall (Fig. 36). Two other gates have been traced to the east of this, and one must be assumed west of Asty Gate. The two imposing round towers of the northwest gate, on Eëtioneia, are still admirably preserved (Fig. 37). Several smaller portals require no mention here.

FIG. 37. — Towers and wall on Eëtioneia, from the southwest.

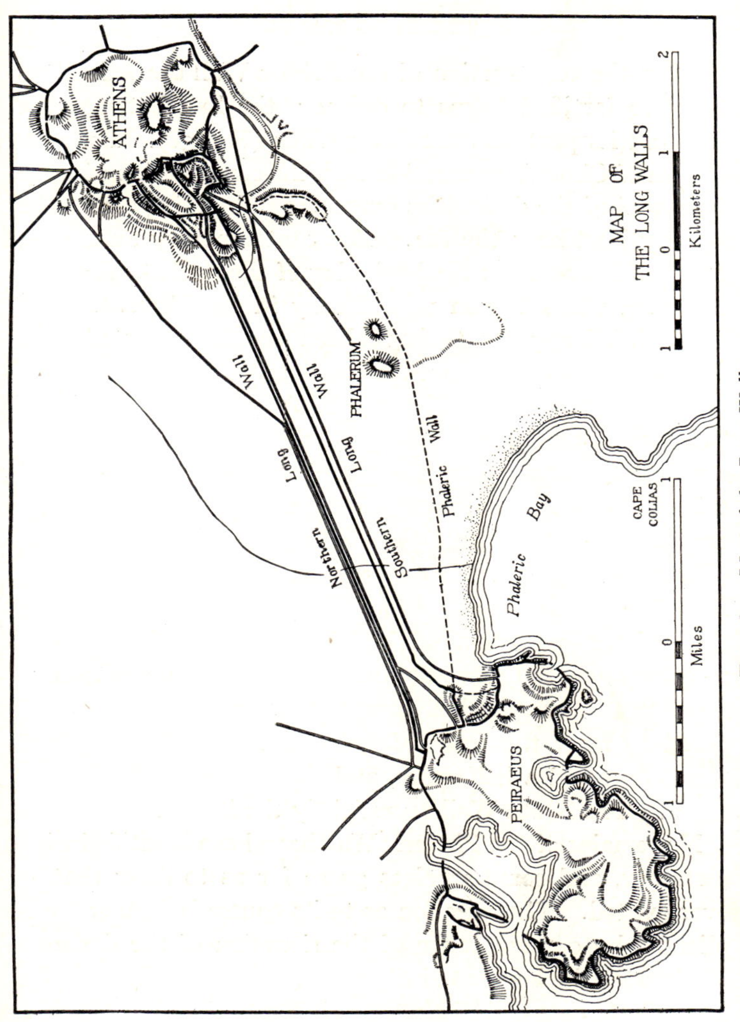


FIG. 38. — Map of the Long Walls.

### THE LONG WALLS

After the construction of the Peiraic Wall the Athenians had two fortified towns to defend; the link between the city and its port was the Long Walls (Fig. 38). Plutarch tells us of Cimon's connection with the construction of these walls and of the difficulties overcome in building across the marshy land near the sea. The contemporary authority, Thucydides, ascribes the beginning of the walls to the year 460 B.C., when Cimon was already in banishment. The North Wall appears to have been the first erected, but the Phaleric Wall followed immediately. Then under the advice of Pericles the Phaleric Wall was abandoned, and "the wall through the middle" was constructed. At the end of the Peloponnesian War the Spartans and the restored exiles "tore down the walls with much enthusiasm, to the accompaniment of flute-players," as Xenophon tells us (*Hellenica* 2, 2, 23). Conon rebuilt the two "legs;" the Phaleric Wall is not again mentioned.

Considerable portions of the Long Walls were in existence a century ago, but now they have nearly disappeared. The two "legs" were parallel, except at their ends, where they flared to meet the walls of the cities. Their length was about four and a half miles, and they were about 550 feet apart. The South Wall was slightly the longer.

No remains of the Phaleric Wall have been identified with certainty, and some scholars go so far as to deny that it ever existed. The question as to its course is further complicated by our ignorance of the situation of the deme of Phalerum, which gave to it its name; Phalerum has usually been placed near Old Phaleron, as it is now called, at the east end of the Phaleric Bay. To the theory that the wall ran to this point, the objection is made that Phalerum was but twenty stades from Athens, whereas Old Phaleron is nearly thirty-five; and that a wall from the Asty to Old Phaleron would leave the long stretch of coast between Old Phaleron and Peiraeus open to an attack of a hostile fleet. Hence Phalerum may more reasonably be sought nearer to Peiraeus, possibly by the chapel of St. Savior (Fig. 38), and the wall (variously said to have been thirty and thirty-five stades in length) connected through Phalerum to Peiraeus; the matter is still uncertain. The coast line has undoubtedly changed since ancient times, and the present distance of St. Savior from the sea is not necessarily an objection to the theory indicated.

The Long Walls had a stone foundation surmounted by

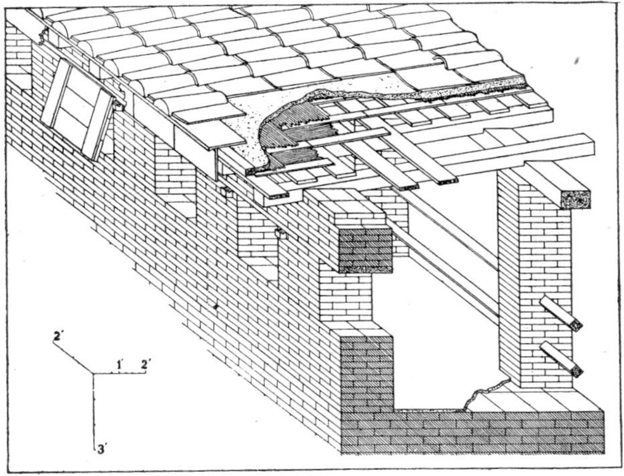


FIG. 39. — Reconstruction of the gallery of the walls of Athens.

sun-dried bricks, and at the top a covered passage, with crenelations and a roof of tiles. From an extant inscription the details of construction can be accurately determined (Fig. 39). Probably the walls were penetrated by several small gates; they had openings also for the Cephissus, whose stream they crossed.

### LATER WALLS OF ATHENS

The emperor Hadrian surrounded his new quarter of the city at the east with a new wall. The foundation of a tower south of the Olympieum, fragments in the present palace gardens, and other remains near the royal stables and elsewhere, make the course of this addition reasonably sure (Fig. 262). The foundations are of large blocks of poros; regarding the superstructure we have no information.

A wall north of the Acropolis formerly called the Valerian Wall is now known to be mediaeval. Other late walls and repairs it is not necessary to mention.

# CHAPTER IV

## The Hellenic Agora

Since the extant ruins represent only small and disconnected portions of the ancient city of the Athenians, we are fortunate in having so many details preserved in the account of Pausanias (p. 2) to supplement our knowledge derived from the monuments. In our survey of the city henceforth his narrative will be followed as a logical and convenient guide.[1]

At the present day the visitor to Athens will usually choose one or the other of two routes leading from Peiraeus up to the city: the electric tramway passing New Phaleron and entering the city at the south near the Olympieum; or the "third-rail" road entering at the northwest. Pausanias describes almost identically the same routes.

"On the road from Phalerum to Athens is a temple of Hera without doors or roof. They say that Mardonius, son of Gobryas, set it on fire. The existing statue, so they say, is by Alcamenes; this the Mede cannot have defiled," because the period of Alcamenes was after the Persian Wars; but which of the two traditions cited by Pausanias is cor-

[1] That is, for Chapters IV to IX. Pausanias's historical and mythological digressions, which are irrelevant for our present purposes, will in most cases be omitted, often without special indication of the place of omission. His description of Athens is comprised in the first thirty chapters of his first book; in general, passages from this portion of his work will be quoted without references being given. In some instances, where no doubt as to authorship can arise, the quotations will be introduced without specific mention of Pausanias's name.

rect, we can determine no better than he. "When one has entered the city there is a monument of the Amazon Antiope." Since this monument, as is known from other sources, was just inside the Itonian Gate (p. 167), the road from Phalerum must have ended at this point.

"On the way up from Peiraeus are ruins of the walls which Conon erected after the sea-fight off Cnidus; for those built by Themistocles after the withdrawal of the Medes were demolished at the time of the rule of the Thirty, as they are called. Along the road are graves, the most famous being that of Menander son of Diopeithes and a cenotaph of Euripides; but Euripides is buried in Macedonia, having gone thither to the court of King Archelaus." The epitaphs on the monuments mentioned by Pausanias are preserved in the Palatine Anthology. "Not far from the gate is a grave surmounted by a warrior standing by a horse. I do not know who he is, but Praxiteles made both the horse and the warrior."

## FROM THE DIPYLUM TO THE AGORA

Unfortunately Pausanias neglected to state at which one of the gates he entered the city, an omission which has been productive of long discussion, with vehement advocates for the Peiraic Gate (p. 65) and for the Dipylum (pp. 63 f.), respectively. Certainty is not yet attainable, but the weight of evidence and of opinion inclines decidedly toward the Dipylum, the usual entrance from Peiraeus.

"When one has entered the city, there is a building for the preparation of the processions which they conduct, some every year, some at intervals of time," those at intervals doubtless being the great Panathenaic processions, which were organized every four years. The building which Pausanias mentions is known in literature and inscriptions as the Pompeum; it probably stood on the large three-aisled foundation which has been uncovered north of the Dipylum (pp. 63 f. and Fig. 26). The foundation is of large blocks of poros, and is about 77 feet wide; its length cannot be determined until the excavation is carried farther toward the east. When the Pompeum was constructed, is not known; our first reference to it is in an oration of Demosthenes in connection with its use for the distribution of grain. The building appears to have been decorated with paintings and statues; we hear of a bronze statue of Socrates by Lysippus, painted portraits of writers of comedy by Craterus, and a painted portrait of Isocrates. Diogenes the Cynic is said to have declared that the Pompeum and the Stoa of Zeus were built for him to live in, which implies nothing more than that these were frequented as public lounging places.

"Near by," continues Pausanias, "is a temple of Demeter, with statues of herself and her daughter, and Iacchus holding a torch; and on the wall is written in Attic letters the fact that they are the works of Praxiteles." "Near by" gives little help in locating the temple. It must have been on one side or the other of the Dipylum, where it may have had an important connection with the sacred embassies to Demeter's greater shrine at Eleusis. Clement of Alexandria (*Protrept.* 4, 18) also speaks of "the Demeter of Praxiteles and Cora and Iacchus the mystic," but the Iacchus had the greatest fame. Cicero asks (*In Verrem* 4, 60): "What would the Athenians take for their marble Iacchus?" Plutarch tells us of an Iaccheum, at which the grandson of Aristeides the Just made a living by interpreting dreams, probably at the sanctuary under consideration.

Here our discussion of the sanctuary might end but for the statement of Pausanias that the inscription was "in

Attic letters." The old Attic alphabet was officially superseded by the Ionic, which had long been coming into private use, in the archonship of Eucleides, 403/2 B.C., while Praxiteles began his work thirty or forty years later. The discrepancy presents a serious difficulty, which some scholars have tried to solve by supposing an elder Praxiteles, the grandfather of the famous artist. But no ancient author tells us of an elder sculptor of this name, and an easier explanation is that the inscription was an archaizing supplement of Roman times. Such imitations are known, and the fact that the inscription was "on the wall," rather than on the base of the statue, favors this view. None of the statues of the group has been preserved, but a superb head from Eleusis, heretofore called Eubuleus, has recently been identified, with much plausibility, as a copy of the famous Iacchus (Fig. 40).

FIG. 40. — Head of Iacchus, by Praxiteles, restored.

The restoration is from the head usually known as Eubuleus, in the National Museum at Athens.

"Not far from the temple is Poseidon, on horseback, hurling a spear at the giant Polybotes (Fig. 168), respecting whom the Coans have the myth about Cape Chelone; but the inscription in my time assigns the statue to another, and not to Poseidon." The Coan myth, however, had it that Poseidon tore off a fragment of the island of Cos as a missile, and this is the version more often represented in existing works of art. An attempt has been made to show that the rededication was to the Roman emperor Caligula, but this is doubtful.

Apparently the monuments thus far mentioned were clustered near the Dipylum, for Pausanias now remarks for the first time that "There are stoae from the gate to the Cerameicus, and bronze images before them of men and women who have risen to fame." These stoae, or colonnades, are mentioned also by Himerius, a sophist of the time of Julian, in his description of the Panathenaic procession. According to him (*Or.* 3, 12) the avenue which ran between them was "straight and smooth and sloping down from above;" that is, from the Agora. Traces of the higher end of this road have been found near the Hephaesteum, and with little doubt the road descended thence in a direct line to the gate. When Athens was sacked by Sulla, the blood shed in the Agora is said to have flowed down to the Dipylum and through it. The Long Stoa, or Alphitopolis, where grain and flour were sold, was probably along the south side of the street near the present railroad station, but the ground on the north side is more level and better suited for the buildings next mentioned by Pausanias.

"One of the stoae contains sanctuaries of the gods and a gymnasium called the Gymnasium of Hermes." Of these we know nothing more. Pausanias continues: "In it is also Pulytion's house, where, they say, not the least distinguished of the Athenians travestied the mysteries of Eleusis; in my time it was dedicated to Dionysus, whom they here call the Minstrel (Melpomenus), in the same way as they call Apollo the Leader of the Muses (Musegetes)." Pausanias refers, of course, to the famous profanation of the Eleusinian mysteries, before the Sicilian Expedition, by Alcibiades, Pulytion, and others. The house, which Plato tells us was distinguished for its magnificence, was apparently confiscated by the state and dedicated to Dionysus.

"Here is a statue of Athena the Healer (Paeonia) and Zeus and Mnemosyne and the Muses, Apollo too, the offering and work of Eubulides, and Acratus, one of Dionysus's attendant divinities; this last is merely a face built into the wall."

At length we have a site that can be identified with much probability. In 1837 in excavating for the foundation of a dwelling north of the railroad station (Fig. 262), a base was found about 26 feet long, with two steps, surmounted by two blocks of the pedestal of a statue, or statues. A large block of Hymettian marble was also found bearing an inscription which has been restored to read: "Eubulides son of Eucheir of Cronia made it." Eubulides lived in the second century B.C. The inscribed block, several marble heads, and a torso, found at the same time, are in the Athens Museum, but the base was covered up and the house built over it. The connection of the base with the statues named by Pausanias could scarcely be doubted but for two things: his declaration that Eubulides offered as well as made them; and the further fact that the text of Pausanias may be understood as saying that Eubulides made not the group but only the Apollo, while the base discovered is too large for a single figure. To reconcile these apparent discrepancies is not easy, but the balance of evidence leans toward the identification of the base with that of the monument which Pausanias mentions. A blank space at the right of the existing inscription forbids our thinking that the words "and dedicated it" can have been broken off, but the dedicatory notice may have been on another block, while the uncertainty in the interpretation of the text of Pausanias is not without parallel; similar ambiguities have been pointed out in other parts of his work. A colossal head found in the same locality in 1874 may be that of Athena the Healer.

The "face built into the wall" was probably a mask of Acratus (drinker of unmixed wine). Such a mask is represented on an ancient crater, now in Glasgow, with the name *Akratos* painted beside it (Fig. 41).

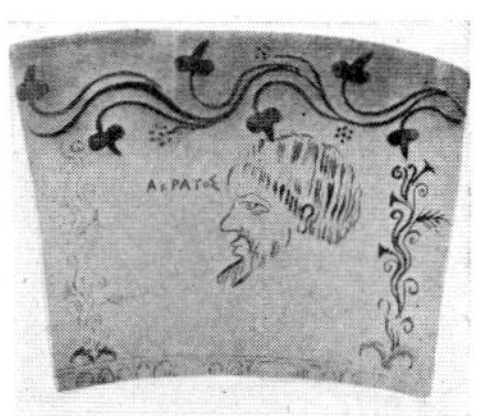


FIG. 41. — Vase painting with the face of *Akratos*.

"After the precinct of Dionysus is a building with statues of clay, Amphictyon, king of the Athenians, feasting Dionysus and other gods. Here too is Pegasus of Eleutherae, who introduced the god among the Athenians." The stoa containing the house of Pulytion, the statues of Eubulides, and the mask of Acratus must have been of considerable extent. Perhaps it had connected with it an inclosure, which Pausanias here calls a precinct. But, while we are not outside the precinct, we are still in a region sacred to Dionysus. Amphictyon and Pegasus are connected in literature with the introduction of the worship of Dionysus into Athens, but how the scene was represented in the "statues of clay" we do not know. We have similar groups portrayed as reliefs, but the figures here mentioned seem to have been in the round.

A small precinct which Pausanias fails to mention has been uncovered in the railroad-cutting at the north end of Colonus Agoraeus, the precinct of Demus and the Graces, together with an altar of Leader Aphrodite (Hegemone). Here, too, Roma was at one time worshiped. The base of a statue by the sculptor Bryaxis was found near by, and we know from literary references that various bronze statues stood here, notably one of the Jewish priest and prince Hyrcanus, mentioned by Josephus as being in this precinct. The road probably turned here to enter the Agora.

## THE AGORA

We now come to the Agora. Pausanias begins his description of it by saying: "Now this place, the Cerameicus, has its name from the hero Ceramus, who is also said to be the son of Dionysus and Ariadne." This derivation is merely an example of popular etymologizing, for the deme Cerameicus (pp. 26 f.) undoubtedly owed its name to the fact that it was the quarter of the potters (kerameis). To Pausanias and other writers of his time the Cerameicus was not a deme, but a place; the name was used as a synonym of Agora, and in consequence many of the sites that these writers speak of as being in the Cerameicus are mentioned by others as in the Agora.

The name Agora, with its double meaning of "market" and "meeting-place," is a more accurate designation for the quarter that we are about to enter than Market-place or Market; while originally the space set apart sufficed for commercial purposes as well as for the transaction of public business, the two uses naturally came in time to be more or less clearly differentiated. The two parts of the Agora, however, were probably not distinctly divided, though that opinion is held by some scholars. In shape, apparently it was not a perfect rectangle, but a somewhat irregular area, which was extended as the city grew; and while trade was gradually exiled from the space devoted to civic and religious affairs, it hovered closely about and sometimes intruded on this area (p. 149).

In order to understand the growth and appearance of the Agora, we shall do well at the outset to go to the south of the Areopagus where was the Ancient Agora; for, as we have seen (pp. 30 f.), when the early settlement outgrew the confines of the Acropolis, it extended at first toward the south, though the particular space with which we are now concerned is nearly west of the citadel. That the Ancient Agora lay in this region we conclude from a quotation from Apollodorus by Harpocration to the effect that the worship of Aphrodite Pandemus was "established near the Ancient Agora." Now from another passage of Pausanias we infer (p. 221) that this sanctuary of Aphrodite was southwest of the Acropolis; the inference is borne out by the discovery, in excavations in this vicinity, of some forty statuettes of Aphrodite, and several inscriptions bearing her name with the title Pandemus. Within narrow limits, therefore, this sanctuary can be located, and near it the Ancient Agora must have been, where we should expect to find it, close to the entrance to the Acropolis. The precise situation cannot yet be determined.

A large portion of the area adjacent to the Ancient Agora, however, has been uncovered through excavations begun in 1887, and with extraordinarily interesting results. The excavations were made on both sides of the modern carriage road as it passes between the Areopagus and the Pnyx Hill (Figs. 42 and 43), but chiefly to the east. Here was found an ancient street with a system of drainage pipes beneath it and walls of sanctuaries and other buildings on either side (p. 22). The street seems to us narrow and crooked, but without much doubt it was the regular ascent from the city to the Acropolis and the course of the great Panathenaic procession.

On the east side of the carriage road, under the slope of the Pnyx Hill, is the fountain Enneacrunus, with an elaborate system of reservoirs and conduits; as the site is mentioned later by Pausanias, the description may be deferred (pp. 108 ff.).

Directly across from the fountain is a trapezoidal inclosure,

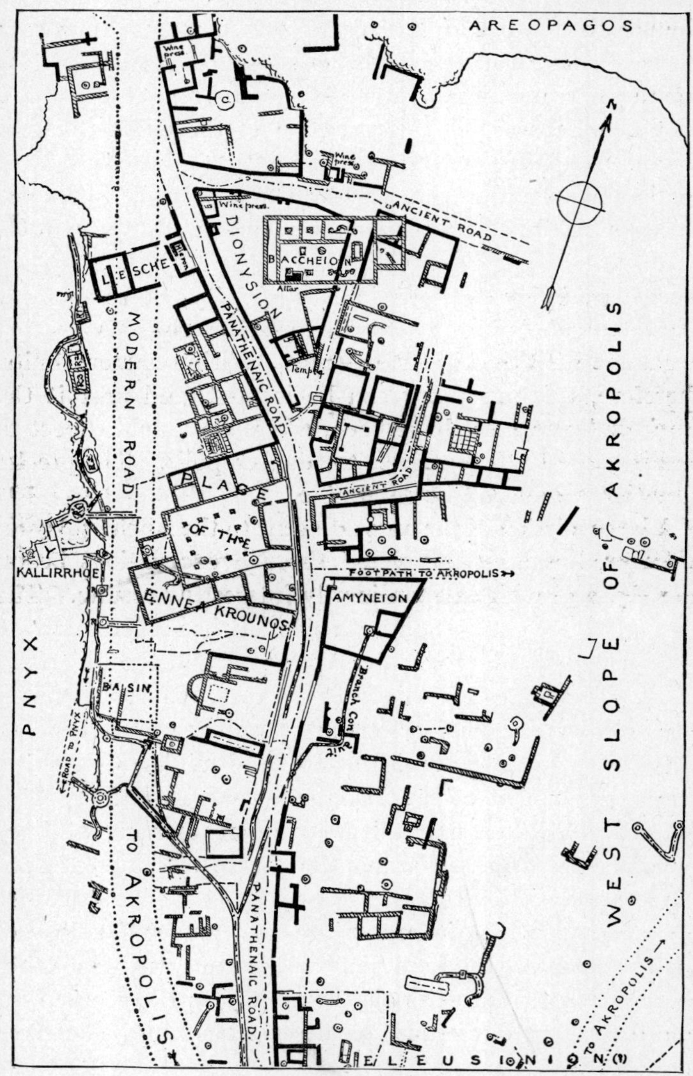


FIG. 42. — Map of excavations south of Areopagus.

about 60 by 55 feet in greatest length and breadth, which has been identified by inscriptions found within it as the Amyneum. The character of the walls shows that the precinct is at least as early as the era of Peisistratus. The entrance is at the northwest corner, and on the east side is a small room containing a marble sacrificial table. At one corner of this room is a deep well partially fed by a branch

FIG. 43.—View of excavations south of Areopagus.

In the background, at the right, is the Acropolis.

from the conduit which supplies the fountain. Amynus is not known in literature, but the inscriptions and votive offerings found in the shrine indicate that he was a healing divinity allied with Asclepius, by whose worship in later times that of Amynus was displaced.

On the same side of the street, some forty paces farther north, is a larger inclosure, triangular in shape, about 148 feet in extreme length and 82 feet in width (Fig. 43). The walls are made of Acropolis limestone and vary in construction from Cyclopean to almost quadrangular polygonal masonry. The precinct is divided by a cross-wall into two sections, and in the smaller southern division is the foundation of a small temple, about 17 by 13 feet in size, facing the southeast. The polygonal walls of the temple, which has no steps, are earlier than the period of Peisistratus, and underneath them are the remains of a temple yet older. Beside the temple is the only entrance into the larger division of the precinct. Near the center of this section is a large base with holes, supposed to have been for the legs of a sacrificial table, and grooves for the reception of inscribed slabs; while in the northwest corner of the precinct is a fairly well preserved winepress, with a paved floor sloping toward one corner where the grape-juice could be received in a jar.

By a somewhat extended course of reasoning, which cannot be outlined here, the precinct has been identified as the celebrated Dionysium in the Marshes (Limnae). This sanctuary was opened only once a year, during the Anthesteria, when at the "feast of pitchers" the people presented their garlands in the sanctuary and offered sacrifices to the god.

The suggestion has recently been made that the precinct is that of Heracles in Melite, or the Heracleum. This identification rests largely upon the theory that the base which has been taken for that of a sacrificial altar is really for a sort of aedicula of Heracles. The hypothesis carries too much else with it to be acceptable at present.

That the spot was sacred to Dionysus in later times is evident from the large rectangular Roman building, with two rows of columns, which was built on a higher level over the old precinct. Here were found an altar bearing emblems of Dionysus, or Bacchus, and several inscriptions, one of considerable length, indicating that this was the Baccheum, the clubhouse of the Iobacchi.

Another large precinct with a winepress lies north of the

Dionysium; while opposite and partly under the carriage road is a shrine with a Lesche, or Clubhouse, of the fourth century B.C. Numerous other buildings of different dates surround those mentioned, but none of them can be identified.

We cannot now determine just when the Ancient Agora was abandoned for the area north of the Areopagus, which

FIG. 44. — Site of the Hellenic Agora, in its present state.
At the left is the east end of the "Theseum," on Market Hill.

for convenience may be called the Hellenic Agora, although, of course, the Ancient Agora was also Hellenic. Certainly the transfer had been completed long before the end of the sixth century B.C. Unfortunately the ground above the Hellenic Agora is now covered with houses (Fig. 44), and the excavations which have been possible in scattered places have thus far yielded no definite returns.[1] In fact, the only

[1] The Greek Archaeological Society has undertaken the enormous task of clearing this area, and in a few years the spade may furnish the key to many baffling problems.

building that can positively be identified both by literary evidence and by the extant remains is the Stoa of Attalus (pp. 130 ff.). As this is a late structure of Hellenistic times, it yields no satisfactory data for the Hellenic Agora, which can scarcely have been so wide as to reach to it, though most scholars have considered the Stoa as situated on the Agora's east boundary. While the Stoa of the Giants (pp. 134 ff.) is a late structure, built of earlier architectural members, it may be conjectured to be nearer the east line.

The south boundary was the Areopagus, some of the buildings of the Agora being well up its slope. Excavations made in 1897 a hundred yards north of the hill, in the inclosure of the chapel of St. Elias, revealed the corner of a large foundation of poros facing the east. This must have been on the Agora, but it has not been identified.

On the west the Agora was limited by the low Colonus Agoraeus, or Market Hill. On its slopes desultory excavations (Fig. 45) begun in 1896, have uncovered a series of

FIG. 45. — Foundations excavated along the west side of the Agora.

foundations of buildings which faced the east and had their fronts on the same north and south line (p. 131). These were small structures; unfortunately none of them can be identified, but without doubt they were either on the west edge of the Agora or along the road of approach from the north; future excavations will probably remove the uncertainty.

The north boundary is still more in doubt. Here the commercial district crowded closest, and, unhappily, Pausanias passes this section without a word.

Probably the Agora was not paved. In it in several places grew trees, chiefly plane trees, many of them planted by Cimon; several small springs furnished water to the throngs of citizens who frequented it. We must regret keenly that the remains of this center of Athenian civic life are so few, while we congratulate ourselves that the literary evidence, together with the general lay of the land, enables us to outline a fairly satisfactory picture.

We now return to the place where we left our guide. Having entered the Cerameicus from the north (Fig. 46), Pausanias says: "First upon the right is the stoa called the Royal Stoa, where the king sits while holding his year of office called the kingship. On the tiled roof of this Stoa are images of terra cotta, Theseus casting Sciron into the sea and Hemera (Day) carrying Cephalus."

Later Pausanias tells us that the temple of Hephaestus, which is probably to be identified with the "Theseum" (p. 116), was "above the Cerameicus and the Royal Stoa." The Royal Stoa, then, must have been on the west side of the Agora and not far from the Hephaesteum. This situation would be met by any of the foundations uncovered on the side of the hill, but none of them has the usual shape of a stoa, a long narrow building with a colonnade in front, and the precise situation cannot yet be determined. The images on the roof would seem to have been acroteria, or ornaments crowning the gables; if so, the Stoa may not

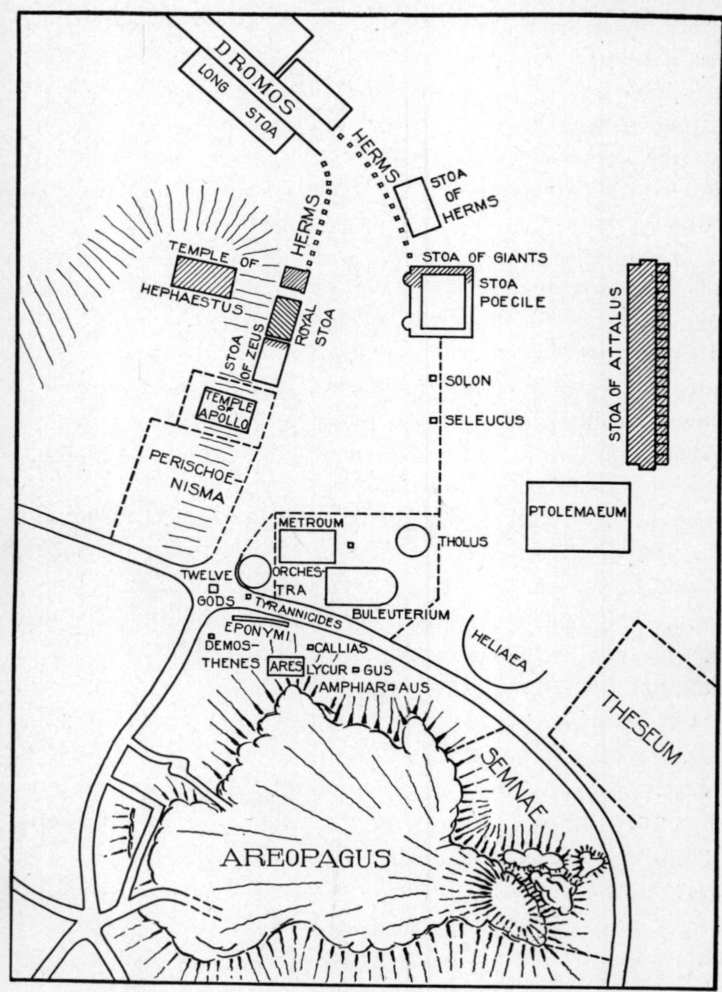


FIG. 46. — Map of the Hellenic Agora.

The boundaries of the Agora and the situation of the majority of the buildings are conjectural.

have been of the customary form. Terra cottas of the type mentioned are archaic, and this is consistent with the probable early date of the Stoa, possibly as early as Solon; either it was one of the few buildings that the Persians spared, or else it was rebuilt after their departure. As late as the fifth century B.C. it was known simply as The Stoa.

In the Royal Stoa were deposited the stone wedges engraved with Solon's laws. In or before it were copies of the lease of the Lelantine Plain, the reënacted laws of Draco, the laws of the restored democracy, and various others. Here the court of the Areopagus is said to have met upon occasion, in a space especially roped off for the purpose; and here the king archon, whose office was a connecting link with the regal period, sat to judge in special cases, particularly cases of impiety. Here, therefore, Euthyphro (in Plato's *Euthyphro*), summoned to meet a charge of unfilial conduct toward his father, meets Socrates, who is present to answer the accusation of infidelity to the religion of the state. In front of the Stoa stood the altar stone on which the archons took their oath, vowing, if faithless, to dedicate a golden statue at Delphi. Here also once stood a statue of Pindar, probably later removed to the vicinity of the temple of Ares (pp. 104 f.).

"Near the stoa," continues Pausanias, "stand Conon and Timotheus son of Conon and Evagoras, king of Cyprus. . . . Here stand Zeus called the Zeus of Freedom (Eleutherius) and King Hadrian, who was the benefactor of many, and especially of the city of the Athenians. And behind these has been built a stoa. . . ." Conon, Timotheus, and Evagoras are naturally brought together because of their illustrious services to Athens after her subjection to Sparta. The statues in their honor were erected while they still lived. That of Conon, at least, was of bronze, as presumably were the others. The statue of Zeus was given the name of Savior as well as Zeus of Freedom; the reason for neither epithet is clear, but probably the tradition that the dedication was in memory of the defeat of the Persians is correct. Near the statue of Hadrian, as we learn from an inscription, stood one of some other Roman emperor; of what emperor we do not know.

The statement of Pausanias, repeated by Eustathius, that the statues were "near the stoa" is indefinite, but from his later statement and the words of other writers we understand that they stood in front of the Stoa of Zeus of Freedom. This and the Royal Stoa are said by Harpocration and others to have been "beside each other," or, as some would translate the phrase, "parallel to each other." Since Pausanias has warned us that he is describing first the buildings on the right, as he proceeds southward, we must look for the site of this stoa south of the Royal Stoa and near it, but the foundation has not yet been discovered, or at any rate identified. The Stoa of Zeus of Freedom, known also as the Stoa of Zeus the Savior, or simply as the Stoa of Zeus, was, like the Royal Stoa, the repository of important law tablets, as well as of the shields of citizens who had distinguished themselves in battle; later the shields were carried off by Sulla. Seats were set about the walls of the building, and loiterers made it their rendezvous. Here Socrates found Ischomachus waiting by appointment for some strangers, and held the conversation related in Xenophon's *Economicus*.

Pausanias's account continues: "And behind these has been built a stoa having paintings of the Twelve Gods, as they are called; on the wall opposite them Theseus is depicted, and Democracy and the People (Demus). The painting makes it clear that Theseus was the one who established equal political rights for the Athenians. . . . Here is portrayed also the action near Mantineia of the Athenians who were sent to aid the Lacedaemonians. . . . And in the painting is a battle of the cavalry, in which the most conspicuous participants are Grylus son of Xenophon on the Athenian side and Epameinondas the Theban amid the Boeotian horse. Euphranor painted these pictures for the Athenians." The paintings of Euphranor were among the most famous in Athens. From the order in which Pausanias names them, the picture of the Twelve Gods would seem to have been on the shorter north end of the Stoa, and the Theseus, Democracy, and Demus on the opposite or south end, while the battle of Mantineia occupied the long rear wall fronting the colonnade. Eustathius tells us that the figure of Zeus was inspired by the famous lines in the first book of the Iliad (vv. 528–530): —

"Thus spake the dread son of Cronus and nodded his dark brows, assenting;
Then the ambrosial locks flowed down from the head of the father,
From his immortal head, and he made great Olympus to tremble."

But this is probably an echo of the story told of the statue of Zeus, by Pheidias, at Olympia. Valerius Maximus says that the figure of Poseidon was more majestic than that of Zeus, while Lucian speaks with particular admiration of the coloring of the hair of Hera. Euphranor himself is reported by Pliny and Plutarch to have declared that his Theseus was fed on meat, while the Theseus of Parrhasius was fed on roses. The cavalry battle Pausanias mentions again elsewhere and says that a copy of the painting was at Mantineia; but he was misinformed as to the history, for Epameinondas had no part in the engagement.

Continuing the last sentence, Pausanias adds: "And near by he [Euphranor] made in the temple the Apollo surnamed Paternal (Patroüs). One Apollo in front of the temple was made by Leochares, while Calamis made the other, which they call the Averter of Evil (Alexicacus). They say that the god got this name because by an oracle from Delphi he ended the pestilential malady which oppressed them at the time of the Peloponnesian War." We have no other topographical reference to the temple of Paternal Apollo, save that it was in the Agora, but apparently it was just south of the Stoa of Zeus, where, like most Greek temples, it could face the east. The sanctuary of Paternal Apollo is singled out by Demosthenes among the shrines to which a certain lad was led upon being introduced into his father's phratry. A representation of Paternal Apollo holding a lyre is found on an altar at Athens; whether or not this is copied from the statue of Euphranor cannot be told. Pausanias's association of the Apollo Averter of Evil with the famous plague of 430 B.C. is questionable, if the statue was made by the elder Calamis, who belonged to the previous generation; the artist may have been the younger Calamis, whose identity is now fairly well established. With the statues in front of the temple was an altar which in the time of Lycurgus was gilded by a certain Neoptolemus.

Without designation of locality Pausanias now speaks of three buildings which were grouped together, the Metroum, or sanctuary of the Mother of the Gods, the Buleuterium, or Senate House, and the Tholus, or Rotunda. "A sanctuary has also been built of the Mother of the Gods, whose statue was made by Pheidias; and near it the Buleuterium of the Five Hundred, as they are called, who are the annual senators of the Athenians. In the Buleuterium are a wooden image of Zeus the Councilor, an Apollo by Peisias, and a Demus by Lyson. The Thesmothetae [the six minor archons] were painted by Protogenes the Caunian; Olbiades painted the portrait of Callipus, who led the Athenians to Thermopylae to beat back the invasion of the Galatians into Greece. . . . Near the Buleuterium of the Five Hundred is the Tholus, as it is called. Here the presidents of the senate sacrifice, and here are certain images made of silver, not of large size." Though Pausanias's words are not explicit, we have no reason to think that he has changed his order of description, and we may look for these buildings at the south end of the Agora.

Some inscriptions mentioning the Metroum have recently been found, but no foundations have been discovered. Other evidence leads to the same conclusion regarding the site. A story is related by Aeschines (*Timarchus* 60 ff.) of a certain man who flees for refuge to the Agora and takes his seat on the altar of the Mother of the Gods just as the people are hurrying to an assembly on the Pnyx; whereupon his pursuers, fearing that their misdeeds will be found out, run to the altar and beg him to retire. From this we infer that the altar, which was doubtless before the shrine, was plainly visible to persons passing along the road which rounds the west end of the Areopagus and leads directly to the Pnyx. Furthermore, Arrian, the biographer of Alexander the Great, in speaking of the Tyrannicides, says (*Anab.* 3, 16, 8) that they "stood in the Cerameicus where we go up to the Acropolis, just about opposite the Metroum and not far from the altar of the Eudanemi." Again, Pausanias in a later passage (p. 98) speaks of the statues of the Namesake Heroes as "higher up" than the group of buildings under consideration, and we know from other sources that these statues were "in a conspicuous place," and that public notices were posted near them; while Aristotle mentions a certain pillar as at once "near the Namesake Heroes" and "in front of the Buleuterium." Arrian's contemporaries doubtless knew what he meant when he said, "where we go up to the Acropolis;" unfortunately we cannot tell whether he means the Panathenaic Road or the shorter path ascending to the east of the Areopagus. Nor do we know the precise situation of the Tyrannicides (p. 105) or of the altar of the Eudanemi. The Namesake Heroes (p. 98) were evidently well up the slope of the Areopagus, where they could easily be seen. So the network of evidence is frail, but we cannot go far astray in looking for the site of the group, as has been stated, at the south end of the Agora, possibly to the west of the road. This situation is consistent with Pausanias's order of treatment, and here the altar would be in view of persons passing from the Agora to the Pnyx. Then "just about opposite the Metroum" we should find the Tyrannicides, near the branching of the path to the Acropolis, while the Namesake Heroes will be higher up, so that the pillar near them will be in front of the Buleuterium.

The Metroum seems to have included in its precinct the Buleuterium, and possibly also the Tholus, thus bringing the entire group under divine protection, though a scholiast (on Aeschines, *Ctesiph.* 187) declares that "the Athenians made the Metroum a part of the Buleuterium." Knowing that he was near death, Lycurgus (*Vit. X or.* 842 F) "ordered that he be brought into the Metroum and the Buleuterium," that he might render account of his transactions with the state. Somewhere in the precinct was the famous "tub" of Diogenes; and here stood a statue of a certain magician with whom a Byzantine writer, oddly enough, connects the founding of the precinct.

A temple of the Mother of the Gods is not directly attested, but the statue made by Pheidias, or his pupil Agoracritus, probably was a cult statue and implies a temple. The goddess was represented as seated and holding a tympanum in her hand, with a lion beneath her chair. Numerous reliefs of this type have been found, which may have been inspired directly or indirectly by the statue of the Metroum. Apparently the Mother worshiped here was originally Demeter, but later she was identified with the Asiatic Rhea Cybele.

Somewhere in the sanctuary were preserved the important documents of the state. Here were the original papyri of decrees of both senate and assembly, financial and other records, as well as valuable papers concerning individuals, such as Meletus's charge and the court's finding against Socrates, the will of Epicurus, and official copies of the tragedies of Aeschylus, Sophocles, and Euripides. All these were under the charge of successive chairmen selected from the presidents of the senate, each of them holding the key for a single day.

The Buleuterium must have been a large building. Probably near the entrance was the xoanon, or wooden image, of Zeus Bulaeus (Councilor), and another of Athena Bulaea, together with the public hearth and altar. On this altar Theramenes took refuge, and from it he was dragged, at the command of Critias, by the Eleven under Satyrus. The main hall was provided with a bema for speakers and with seats, numbered either individually or by tribes, for the Five Hundred, and special seats for the presidents; the spectators were barred out by a wooden railing. Pausanias mentions some of the decorations of the building, the statues and paintings. Numerous important law tablets were set up outside, notably the edict against traitors, and copies of Solon's laws.

The official name for the Tholus was Skias (Umbrella). The building was circular and bore a conical roof of stone; in general appearance it may have resembled the Tholus of Epidaurus. In the Tholus the fifty presidents of the senate dined each day at the state's expense during their term of office; they even spent the night there in times of public stress. Here were kept the standards of weights and measures under the care of a slave of the state, who was guarded by the chairman of the presidents. In the Tholus Socrates and four others were ordered by the Thirty to arrest Leon the Salaminian, that he might be put to death — and dared to disobey.

We pass on from this group of buildings, "and higher up stand statues of Heroes from whom the tribes of the Athenians later got their names." These Heroes, who gave their names to the ten tribes established by Cleisthenes, were Erechtheus, Aegeus, Pandion, Leos, Acamas, Oeneus, Cecrops, Hippothoön, Ajax, and Antiochus. In addition to these, Pausanias names the statues of Attalus, Ptolemy, and Hadrian, Namesake Heroes of the tribes afterward formed (p. 41). The tribes named in honor of Demetrius and Antigonus had been abolished before Pausanias's time, and beyond doubt their statues had been destroyed. Other statues were not allowed near the Namesake Heroes, and the site was one of great honor. The "conspicuous place" where the Eponymi stood served, as has been stated, for the publication of bulletins, such as the list of men drafted for military service and copies of proposed laws. The names of benefactors of the state, of ephebi, and of traitors were posted here on stone tablets.

Beyond the Namesake Heroes stood several important statues. Of these Pausanias says: "After the figures of the Eponymi are statues of gods, Amphiaraus and Peace carrying the child Wealth. Here too is a bronze statue of Lycurgus son of Lycophron and a statue of Callias, who, as most of the Athenians say, brought about the peace between the Greeks and Artaxerxes son of Xerxes. There is also a statue of Demosthenes." Our evidence for the location of these statues is very slight. The statue of Demosthenes is said by the author of the *Lives of the Ten Orators* to have been "near the Roped-in-space (Perischoenisma) and the altar of the Twelve Gods" (p. 32); that is, near the southwest corner of the Agora. Since Amphiaraus, like the Semnae, was a subterraneous deity, the plausible suggestion has been made that his statue and cult may have been situated near the sanctuary of the Semnae at the northeast corner of the Areopagus (p. 361). These data, together with Pausanias's statement that they were "after the figures of the Eponymi," may suffice to locate the group along the north slope of the Areopagus.

Amphiaraus was really a Theban rather than an Attic divinity. The Amphiareum at Oropus came into Athenian control at the beginning of the Peloponnesian War, and the statue at Athens may have been set up at that time; but this is only a conjecture.

The statue of Peace carrying Wealth is happily better known. An Athenian coin of the time of Hadrian represents a female figure with long robes and staff in her right hand, while on her left arm she bears a child holding a cornucopia. The same motive has been identified in a marble statue now in the Glyptothek at Munich, without doubt a replica of the statue of the Agora (Fig. 47). Other copies of both figures have since been found, notably a fine torso of Peace in the Metropolitan Museum at New York (Fig. 48) and a copy of the child discovered at Peiraeus (Fig. 49). The stately figure of Peace rests on the left foot and is clothed in a full chiton girded high and folded over to the waist; her flowing hair falls upon her shoulders. Her right hand, as the coin bears witness, held a scepter, while the left arm supported a cornucopia, not a vase, as has been restored in the Munich copy.

FIG. 47. — Copy of the statue of Eirene and Plutus, by Cephisodotus (Glyptothek, Munich).

The original statue may have been discovered and destroyed in 1672. The letter of that year written by Babin (p. 3) narrates the finding, in the ruins of an old church, of "a statue of marble, which represents the Holy Virgin holding her son in her arms." With iconoclastic ardor the "idol" was at once broken in pieces. If, however, as some think, the original was of bronze, the one destroyed must have been a copy.

Pausanias mentions the statue of Peace and Wealth again in a later book (9, 16, 2), and there says that it was the work of Cephisodotus, a successor of Pheidias and probably the father of Praxiteles. The style of the extant copies is consistent with its attribution to a sculptor of this period, and the statue is accordingly a valuable document in the study of the history of art. Cephisodotus flourished at the end of the fifth century B.C.

The beneficent works of Lycurgus entitled him to the grateful memory of Athens (pp. 39 f.). This statue in the Agora was set up in 307/6 B.C. in accordance with a decree proposed by a certain Stratocles. A piece of Hymettian marble which probably is a part of the base has been found. It bears an inscription which, as restored, reads: "Lycurgus son of Lycophron, a Butad." Fragments of the base of another statue of Lycurgus have also been found.

FIG. 48. — Eirene (Metropolitan Museum, New York).

Whether any such peace between Athens and Persia as is attributed to Callias was ever made, is doubtful, but the tradition dates from the fourth century B.C. Callias's statue is not otherwise known; not accidental, perhaps, was its erection near the statue of Peace, or, since he was the earlier, the statue of Peace near his.

FIG. 49. — Plutus; a copy found in Peiraeus (National Museum, Athens).

We have a little more information about the statue of the great orator. The sculptor was Polyeuctus, and the statue was set up in 280/279 B.C. according to a decree proposed by Demochares, Demosthenes's nephew. In his life of the orator Plutarch tells us that he was represented with clasped hands, and that a plane tree stood near by. A soldier, on leaving the city, hid his money in the hands of the statue, and the leaves from the tree helped to conceal the treasure. This statue was probably the original of extant statues and heads of Demosthenes, which have some differences, but agree in the general features, particularly the expression of the stammering lips (Fig. 50). Very suggestive is Lord Macaulay's characterization of the Vatican copy.[1] "The Demosthenes is very noble. There can be no doubt about the face of Demosthenes. There are two busts of him in the Vatican, besides this statue. They are all exactly alike, being distinguished by the strong projection of the upper lip. The face is lean, wrinkled, and haggard; the expression singularly stern and intense. You see that he was no trifler, no jester, no voluptuary; but a man whose soul was devoured by ambition, and constantly on the stretch." The restored hands of the Vatican copy hold a scroll; the correct restoration has recently been made, on a cast, from hands found in the garden of the Barberini palace at Rome. Another copy, almost like that of the Vatican, is in England.

Fig. 50. — Demosthenes; from a cast after the Vatican copy, restored with clasped hands instead of scroll.

[1] Quoted by Frazer, *Pausanias*, II, 90, from Trevelyan's *Life and Letters of Lord Macaulay*.

"Near the image of Demosthenes is a sanctuary of Ares. Here are set up two statues of Aphrodite. The statue of Ares is by Alcamenes; the Athena, by a Parian named Locrus. Here is also a statue of Enyo, made by the sons of Praxiteles. About the temple stand Heracles and Theseus and Apollo binding his hair with a fillet. Other statues are Calades, who is said to have written laws [nomes?] for the Athenians, and Pindar, who received the statue and other honors at the hands of the Athenians for his praise of their city in his poetry." Only one other literary reference to the temple of Ares exists, a passage of a Byzantine writer (Georgios Kodinos, *De orig. Constant.* 47, 14), who mentions "the columns of the elephants of the Golden Gate brought from Athens, from the temple of Ares, by Theodosius the Little." This has no topographical value, and in addition we have only Pausanias's statements that the sanctuary was "near the statue of Demosthenes," and that the Tyrannicides were "not far" from it; we are perhaps justified in assuming that the precinct was near the Areopagus, which was often, rightly or wrongly, called the Hill of Ares (pp. 357 f.). Possibly it stood on or near the site of the church of St. Athanasius.

The suggestion has been made that the Borghese Ares (Fig. 51) is a copy of the statue of Alcamenes. Various other replicas are known of this type, the original of which must have been famous, but the evidence to support the identification with the statue of the temple is not strong.

Of the other statues in and about the temple of Ares little can be said. Aphrodite is often associated with Ares, as with Hephaestus. Neither the Athena of Locrus the Parian nor the sculptor himself is otherwise known.

Enyo, the personification of the horror of war, is named with Ares and Zeus Geleon on a base found on the Acropolis. The sculptors of the statue of Enyo, the "sons of Praxiteles," were Cephisodotus and Timarchus, who made

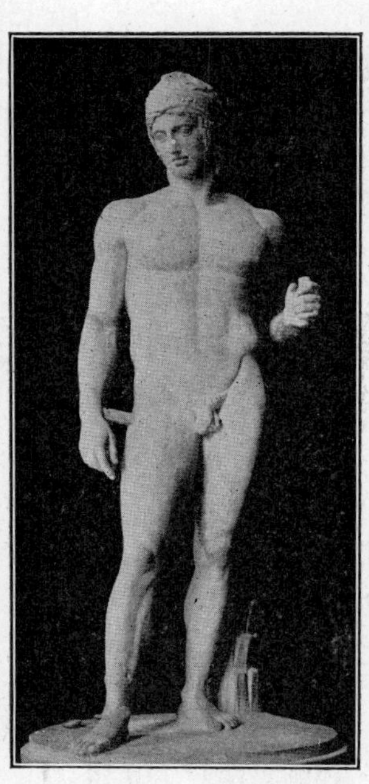

FIG. 51. — Borghese Ares (Louvre Museum, Paris).

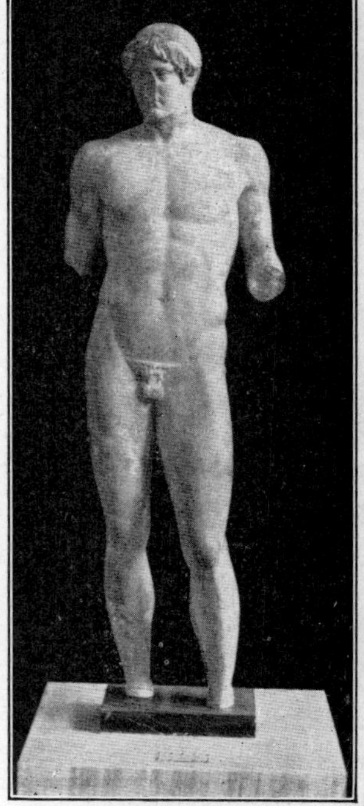

FIG. 52. — Theseus, commonly known as "Apollo of the Omphalos" (National Museum, Athens).

statues also in other parts of Greece. Calades is otherwise quite unknown. A valuable suggestion as to the identification of the Theseus has lately been made (Fig. 52).

Of the statue of Pindar the Pseudo-Aeschines says (*Ep.* 4, 3) that the poet was represented as a "draped and seated figure with a lyre and diadem and a book unrolled on his knees." He further tells us that this famous statue was "in front of the Royal Stoa" (p. 91). At present no consistent arrangement of the buildings can be found that will admit of the placing of the statue near both the Royal Stoa and the temple of Ares. Either the statue must have been moved to the new site before Pausanias's time, or else one or the other of the statements must be wrong. By the "other honors" which Pindar enjoyed, Pausanias doubtless means the double payment by the Athenians of the fine imposed on Pindar by the jealous Thebans for his praise of Athens as, "O, resplendent, violet-crowned, glorious Athens, famous in song and story, pillar of Greece, city divine."

"Not far away," Pausanias goes on, "stand Harmodius and Aristogeiton, who slew Hipparchus; the reason for their deed and the manner of the doing of it have been told by others. The one pair is by Critius; the archaic pair is by Antenor. When the Athenians deserted Athens and Xerxes took the city, he carried off the latter as spoils, and Antiochus sent them back afterwards to the Athenians." The assassination of Hipparchus took place in 514 B.C. (p. 33), and the first group of the Tyrannicides, by Antenor, must have been set up soon after that date, or certainly before 480 B.C., when it was carried off by Xerxes. The lost statues were at once replaced by Critius and Nesiotes — not Critius alone, as Pausanias says — and stood throughout the classic period. The original group was restored by Alexander, or Seleucus, or Antiochus; ancient authorities differ. The situation of the statues has already been discussed. The Orchestra near which they stood was probably the place where, according to Plato's *Apology*, the activities of the booksellers were centered; perhaps it was the scene of musical and dramatic contests before the construction of the great theater (p. 192).

Several representations of the Tyrannicides have been preserved. They appear, for example, as the blazon of Athena's shield on a Panathenaic vase (Fig. 53), on the arm of a marble throne, on coins, and on vase-fragments from the tomb of Dexileos (p. 374). Usually they are represented as advancing, side by side, with outstretched arms and brandished swords to the attack. From these minor copies have been identified two statues of the Naples Museum, which had been posed as duelists (Fig. 54). These represent, fairly accurately, the ancient statues, which, however, being of bronze, dispensed with the supporting tree-trunks, necessary in the more fragile marble, and were on one base. The present head of Aristogeiton on the copy at Naples has been added from a statue of a much later period, and is obviously inconsistent both with the dry rendering of the body and with the archaic head of Harmodius; the arms, too, are wrongly restored. When these errors have been corrected, we gain a very clear notion of the ancient statues (Fig. 55). Whether the extant reproductions are from the group of Antenor or from that of Critius and Nesiotes has been much discussed; in all probability they portray the later group. From the fourth century B.C., the two groups stood side by side.

FIG. 53. — Tyrannicides, as blazon on Athena's shield on a Panathenaic vase.

After leaving the Tyrannicides, Pausanias names the next point of interest with no clew as to its situation. "In front of the entrance to the theater which they call the

Odeum are statues of Egyptian kings." These he mentions, in what is for us a long digression, as Ptolemy Philometor and his daughter Berenice, Ptolemy Philadelphus and his sister Arsinoë, Ptolemy Lagus and his son Ptolemy Soter. He adds, "Beyond the Egyptians are Philip and Alexander the son of Philip," and beside these the statues of Lysimachus and Pyrrhus. Finally he says, "As you enter the Odeum at Athens, among other things is a Dionysus worth seeing; and near by is a fountain. . . ." This Odeum, or Music Hall, is thought by some to be identical with the Agrippeum spoken of by Philostratus (*Vit. soph.* 2, 5, 3) as "in the Cerameicus," but we do not know its history or its situation, save that it was near the fountain whose site we are soon to visit. To the identification suggested the objections may be raised that a building near the fountain, that is, at the southwest corner of the Areopagus, would not be "in the Cerameicus," and that the statues at its entrance are of an earlier date than Agrippa (*cf.* p. 238); but Philostratus may be using the name Cerameicus as a general term synonymous with Agora, and this

FIG. 54. — Tyrannicides (Naples Museum).

may not be the original site of the statues. Agrippa may have built over an earlier structure and have given it his own name.

To continue with Pausanias: "And near by is a fountain; they call it Enneacrunus, since it was adorned with nine spouts by Peisistratus. Wells exist throughout all the city, but this is the only fountain." No point in Athenian topography has been more discussed than the "Enneacrunus episode." We have already seen (p. 30) that Thucydides mentions the fountain as having been reconstructed "by the tyrants" and renamed Enneacrunus, or Nine-spouts, instead of Callirrhoë, or Fair-flowing. In the bed of the Ilissus just south of the Olympieum is a Callirrhoë (Fig. 56) whose name is well attested, and many have thought that this is the spring in question, the alleged break in Pausanias's narrative being explained in various ways. But the supposition is far easier that the spring which the excavations uncovered (p. 83) between the Areopagus and the Pnyx is the Enneacrunus of Pausanias and Thucydides.

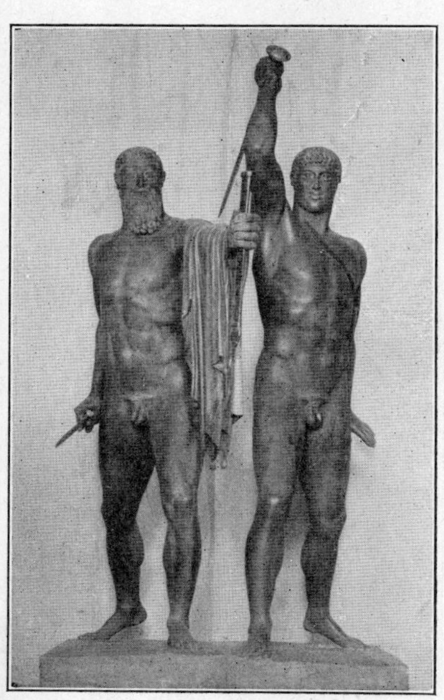

FIG. 55. — Tyrannicides; the Naples group restored and corrected (Brunswick Museum).

At this spot are the remains of an extensive system of waterworks. The original spring, Callirrhoë, comprised a large rock-hewn chamber, to which steps descended through a corridor (now closed to the public by an iron gate), a well at the rear of this chamber with a parapet in

FIG. 56. — Callirrhoë and rock ridge in the bed of the Ilissus.

The Ilissus in summer when the stream has shrunk to a mere thread; in freshets the flow passes over the ridge of rock.

front, and a large cistern connecting with the chamber and with the outside by corridors and steps (Fig. 57). The additions of Peisistratus lay in front of Callirrhoë and consisted of a series of reservoirs, a main storage basin, whence water was drawn in jars by a rope, and another basin, whose water flowed through nine lions' heads into the jars set beneath, quite as portrayed in ancient vase paintings (Fig. 58). The last is the Nine-spouts. The fountain was adorned with columns; in front was a large square which opened on the road. To reënforce the natural supply of water a large conduit with various branches was constructed, leading from the valley of Ilissus in the foothills of Mt.

Hymettus. In the city this conduit passes through the present palace gardens and along the southern slope of the Acropolis to the valley of the Ancient Agora. The tunnel is sometimes high enough to allow a man to stand upright in it, and through it run the clay pipes, joined with lead, to

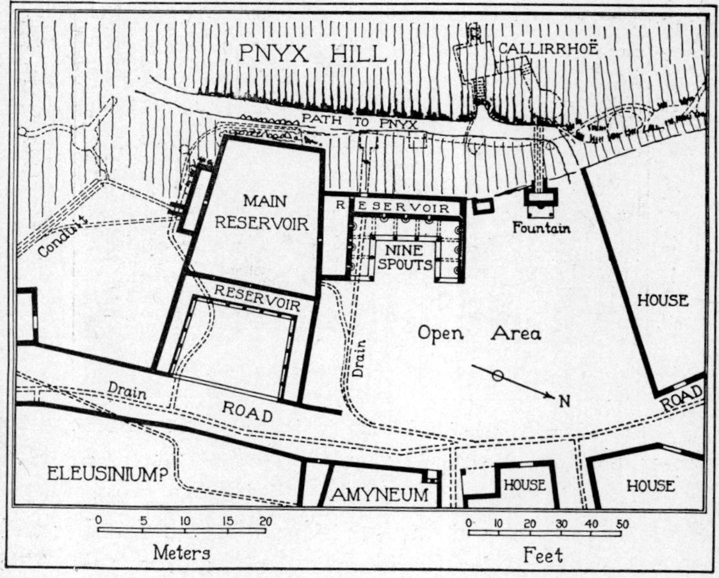


FIG. 57. — Plan of Enneacrunus and adjacent sites, restored.

carry the water to Enneacrunus. In Roman times the conduit was extended to supply other sites in this region.

The system is undoubtedly of the time of Peisistratus, and rivals the similar aqueducts made in this period by other tyrants, Periander of Corinth, Polycrates of Samos, and Theagenes of Megara.

Before leaving this region we must visit a site probably identified correctly as the Pnyx, which Pausanias fails to mention. It lies on the side of the hill (Fig. 59) of the same name and commands a wide view over this section of the city. Here seems to have been a meeting place of the

FIG. 58. — Callirrhoë-Enneacrunus; vase painting.

Athenian assembly, although the view that this was the Pnyx has met, and still meets, vigorous opposition. The present construction dates from the fourth century B.C., but the existence of an earlier wall and of rock-hewn steps beneath the area point to its use for the same or some other purpose prior to that period.

The Pnyx, as we now have it, consists of an irregularly semicircular space nearly 400 feet in its longitudinal diameter and about 230 feet wide (Fig. 60). The ground here by nature slopes toward the north, and the area was raised on its curved side by a supporting wall of carefully joined stones, some of them of enormous size. By means of this wall the slope in ancient times was probably turned toward the south, or rather southwest. In the obtuse angle at the middle of the south side lies the bema, or orators'

FIG. 59. — Pnyx, at the left, and Hill of the Nymphs, at the right, as seen from the Areopagus.

The national observatory stands on the summit of the Hill of the Nymphs.

platform (Fig. 61). The rock has been hewn down vertically along this side of the area, a portion at the east corner never having been removed, and the bema with its steps is cut from a projection of the solid rock. Niches for

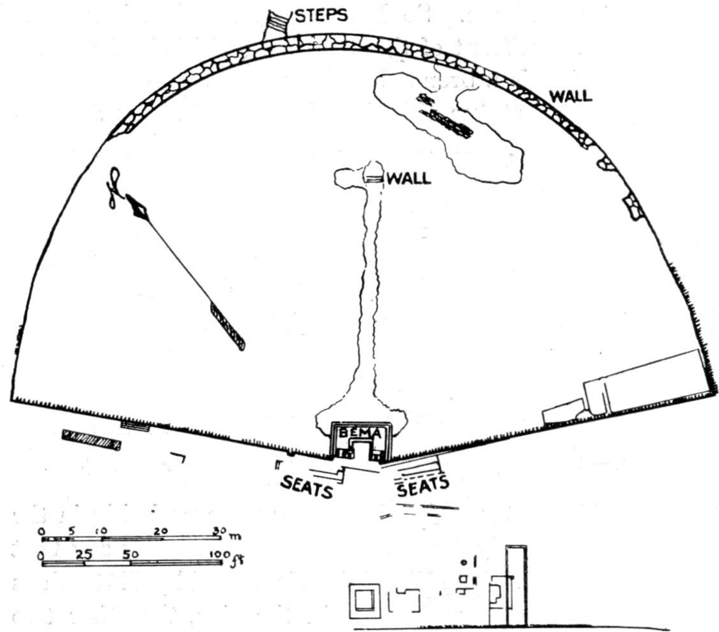


FIG. 60. — Plan of the Pnyx.

votive offerings are cut in the scarped rock at one side of the bema, and inscriptions referring to Most High Zeus indicate that a sanctuary of Zeus was at some time located here. Above and behind the bema are seats, probably seats of honor, cut from the rock and facing the assembly, while back of these are remains of an altar and various bases belonging to some shrine.

Returning again to Pausanias, we read: "Temples are

built beyond [above?] the fountain; one of Demeter and Cora, while in that of Triptolemus is a statue. . . . As I was about to continue this narrative and state the explanation for the sanctuary at Athens called the Eleusinium, a vision prevented me. So I will turn to what is holy to write to all. In front of this temple in which is the statue of Triptolemus is a bronze bull being led to sacrifice; and here is a seated statue of Epimenides the Cnossian." The

FIG. 61. — Orators' platform on the Pnyx; in the rear the Acropolis.

temples of Demeter and Triptolemus were probably in the Eleusinium, though Pausanias does not expressly say that this was the case. The Eleusinium is named by Plutarch as one of three most sacred spots in the city, the other two being the Acropolis and the Theseum; his view seems to be in part an inference from the statement of Thucydides that these were the most notable inclosures not occupied by the crowds of Attic countrymen who thronged the city during the second year of the Peloponnesian War. Clement of Alexandria, whose word is supported by inscriptions, says (*Protrept.* 13) that the Eleusinium lay "at the foot of the Acropolis." The order of mention by Pausanias seems to limit this vague statement to the western foot, and this is amply proved by other evidence. Xenophon, for example, advises (*Hipparch.* 3, 2) his ideal cavalry leader to display his squadron by making the round of the shrines in the Agora and then "to ride up at full speed by tribes to the Eleusinium;" and Philostratus, in describing the course of the ship used in the great Panathenaic procession, says (*Vit. soph.* 2, 1, 5) that it started from the Cerameicus — meaning the Outer Cerameicus, beyond the Dipylum — and advanced "to the Eleusinium, and, rounding that, passed by the Pelargicum" (p. 363). The situation suggested, south of the Areopagus (*cf.* Fig. 42), manifestly satisfies the requirements of these passages; a recent investigator would put it on the south slope of the Acropolis, which is doubtful.

Pausanias's "vision" has deprived us of much that we should like to know about the Eleusinium; ancient writers rarely slip in the matter of the Eleusinian secrets. The great Eleusinium was, of course, at Eleusis. Triptolemus is often associated with the Eleusinian Demeter and Persephone; he is usually represented by the vase painters as riding on a winged car drawn by serpents (Fig. 62). Pausanias identifies the Epimenides whose statue he saw with the Cnossian, "the Greek Rip Van Winkle," who purified Athens from the guilt of the Alcmaeonids, but more probably this was the statue of the Attic Epimenides, who was said to have been the first ox-driver and who was allied with Triptolemus, a divinity of agriculture.

"And still farther on is a temple of Fair Fame (Eucleia); this too is a votive offering from the Medes who landed at Marathon." Eucleia is probably an epithet of Artemis. In inscriptions Eucleia is usually associated with Fair Order (Eunomia). If Pausanias is correct, the temple must have been erected soon after the Persian Wars, but its history and location are little known. In various other Greek cities a temple of Artemis Eucleia was in the Agora; perhaps the temple was on Pausanias's way as he now returned to the Agora at Athens.

From the temple of Fair Fame, then, Pausanias comes back toward the north end of the Agora. "Above the

FIG. 62. — Persephone, Triptolemus, and Demeter; vase painting.

Cerameicus," he says, "and the so-called Royal Stoa is a temple of Hephaestus. I was not surprised that the statue of Athena stands near him, as I knew the story of Erichthonius. Observing that the statue of Athena had gray eyes, . . ." We have already seen that the Royal Stoa was on the west side of the Agora and on the slope of Colonus Agoraeus, or Market Hill (p. 89), the only elevation of importance in the region north of the Areopagus. That the temple of Hephaestus stood on this hill can scarcely be doubted. Harpocration speaks of hired slaves who were called Colonetae, "because they stood by Colonus near the Agora where are the Hephaesteum and the Eurysaceum." Andocides mentions (1, 40) a certain Euphemus, who was seen in the braziers' quarter and "led up to the Hephaesteum;" Hephaestus, the god of the forge, would appropriately have his temple near the smithies, a supposition which is confirmed by the remark of another writer (Bekker, *Anec. gr.* 1, 316, 23) that "bronze is sold where the Hephaesteum is." At the present time Colonus Agoraeus is for the most part singularly bare of ancient remains; but at its northern end, "above the Royal Stoa," stands the best preserved of Greek temples (Fig. 63).

The name "Theseum" was first applied to this building in the Middle Ages, probably because on some of its metopes and a part of its frieze deeds of Theseus are depicted. But inference from the sculptural decoration of a temple has been shown to be hazardous. On such grounds, for example, the temple of Zeus at Olympia might be attributed to Heracles and the Parthenon at Athens to Theseus. The true Theseum was certainly on the east side of the Agora near the foot of the Acropolis (p. 152); it may not have contained a temple at all, and it was built at a much earlier date than the structure before us. The Theseum, then, this building cannot be. In recent years it has been ascribed variously to Ares, Apollo, Heracles, Aphrodite, the Amazons, and Hephaestus; but on the topographical grounds outlined above, as well as certain interpretations of the sculptural remains, the claim of Hephaestus seems most conclusive, though complete agreement of scholars has not been reached.

The temple measures 104 by 45 feet on the stylobate, or upper step. It is built of Pentelic and Parian marble, save the lowest of the three steps, which is of poros. The build-

FIG. 63. — Hephaesteum, from the northeast.

In the background is the Hill of the Nymph.

ing is hexastyle peripteral; in front are six, on the sides thirteen, Doric columns, 19.3 feet high, 3.3 feet in diameter at the base, and tapering to 2.6 feet at the top of the shaft. The intercolumniations are 5.3 feet, except at the corners, where the space between columns is nearly a foot less, the usual device to adjust the triglyphs over the corner columns. Above the colonnade is the customary entablature, consisting of architrave, triglyph frieze, and cornice.

The cella is 40 feet long by 20 feet wide, the side walls terminating in square antae, between which at either end were two smaller Doric columns; of these the east pair was removed to make an apse in later days when the temple was transformed into a Christian church. At the same time the east cross-wall was torn down and a large door cut in the west cross-wall; but this was later closed, to prevent the Turks from riding in on horseback, and the two small doors, by one of which the temple is now entered, were cut in the sides. On the interior the walls have been covered with a coat of stucco, probably for Christian paintings. The original wooden roof has perished, and the present vaulted roof over the cella, of stone and concrete, dates from Christian times; over the aisles many panels of the ceiling are still in place.

The temple was richly decorated with sculptures. Of the pedimental groups only the traces remain, unfortunately not enough to indicate clearly their motive. A plausible argument has been offered to show that the east pediment represented the birth of Erichthonius, the west, Hephaestus with Thetis and Eurynome.

The ten metopes on the front or east end and the adjacent four on each side of the temple are sculptured. The reliefs of these, of Parian marble, are much battered. Those across the front represent the labors of Heracles: (1)

the Nemean lion, (2) the Lernaean hydra, (3) the Cerynaean stag, (4) the Erymanthian boar, (5) the mare of Diomede, (6) Cerberus, (7) the Amazon queen, (8, 9) Geryon, and (10) the apples of the Hesperides. The metopes on the sides represent the deeds of Theseus: those

Fig. 64. — Southeast corner of the Hephaesteum, showing four of the sculptured metopes.

on the south side (Fig. 64), from east to west, portray the hero with (1) the Minotaur, (2) the Marathonian bull, (3) Sinis, and (4) Periphetes; those on the north side, Theseus with (1) Procrustes, (2) Cercyon, (3) Sciron, and (4) the Crommyonian sow.

Above the columns at either end of the cella is an Ionic frieze; the eastern section extends across the side-aisles and is about 37 feet long; the western terminates above the antae and is about 25 feet long. The former depicts six seated gods, three grouped over each anta, watching a battle, perhaps Erichthonius and Amphictyon and their followers fighting for the kingship of Attica; the latter represents the battle of Lapiths and Centaurs. The friezes are also of Parian marble.

On stylistic grounds the Hephaesteum seems to be somewhat later than the Parthenon; it may have been completed, or nearly so, before the Peloponnesian War. An inscription tells us of a festival held every four years in honor of Hephaestus and Athena which was inaugurated during the peace of Nicias (421/20 B.C.), when bronze statues of the divinities on a common base were begun. The statues were completed at the next celebration of the festival, four years later, and probably were those seen by Pausanias in the temple. The sculptor seems to have been Alcamenes, and the Hephaestus may be identical with a statue of that artist praised by Cicero and Valerius Maximus for the skill with which the god's lameness was treated as an attribute rather than as a defect. The type of the Athena has recently been identified (Fig. 65).

The temple has a romantic later history which we cannot now follow. We owe its comparatively excellent preservation to its early dedication to St. George and its long use as a Christian church. In the last century it was used as a general museum; at present it contains a Byzantine collection.

The Eurysaceum, or sanctuary of Eurysaces, son of Ajax, stood in the vicinity of the Hephaesteum. It is said to have been in the deme of Melite, and it included an

FIG. 65. — Copy of Athena Hephaestia, by Alcamenes (Museo Chiaramonti, Rome).

A more faithful, but less complete copy is in the museum of Cherchell, Algeria. The cult-statues of the Hephaesteum were of Hephaestus and Athena together.

altar which is mentioned elsewhere by Pausanias. Not far away were the Amazonium, the graves of the Amazons, and the Chalcodon, the latter near the Peiraic Gate. Pausanias does not mention these, but says, "Near by is a sanctuary of Heavenly Aphrodite." Of this we have no further knowledge, save for his added remark that "the image still remaining in our time is of Parian marble, and the work of Pheidias." Various efforts have been made to identify it.

We entered the Agora with Pausanias from the north and first visited the buildings on the right hand, or west side, continuing thence along the Panathenaic road and around the end of the Areopagus to the very foot of the Acropolis. Thence we retraced our steps to the Hephaesteum on Market Hill, and now accompany Pausanias across the north side of the Agora. "As you go toward the stoa which from its paintings they call the Painted Porch (Stoa Poecile), there is a bronze Hermes called Agoraeus, and near by a gate; on this is a trophy of the Athenians who conquered Pleistarchus in a cavalry battle; for, being the brother of Cassander, Pleistarchus had been intrusted with the command of his cavalry and mercenary force.

"This stoa has in the first place a painting of the Athenians who have been marshalled at Oenoe in Argolis against the Lacedaemonians. The battle has been painted not as already coming to the acme of the fray and as a display of daring deeds, but rather as the beginning of the fight, while the men are still gathering for the hand-to-hand conflict. In the middle of the walls Theseus and the Athenians are fighting the Amazons. . . . Next to the Amazons is the scene when the Greeks have captured Ilium, and the kings have assembled on account of the assault of Ajax on Cassandra; the painting shows Ajax himself, and Cassandra with other captive women. Last is the painting of the combatants at Marathon. The Boeotians of Plataea and all the Attic force are entering into hand-to-hand engagement with the Barbarians. Over here both parties are on equal terms in the action; in the heart of the mêlée the Barbarians are in flight and are pushing one another into the marsh; on the farther side of the picture are the Phoenician ships and the Greeks slaughtering those of the Barbarians who are tumbling into them. Here, too, is depicted the hero Marathon, from whom the plain got its name, and Theseus in the guise of one rising out of the ground, and Athena, and Heracles. . . . Of the warriors the most conspicuous in the painting are Callimachus, whom the Athenians chose as polemarch, Miltiades, one of the generals, and the hero Echetlus, of whom I shall make mention later.

"Here have been dedicated some shields of bronze; part of them have an inscription to the effect that they are from the Scionians and their allies; others, smeared with pitch to defy the erosion of rust and time, are said to have been taken from the Lacedaemonians who were captured on the island of Sphacteria.

"Bronze statues are set up before the stoa: Solon, who wrote laws for the Athenians, and a little farther on Seleucus."

The location of the Painted Porch is a vexed problem. From the description of Pausanias we should infer that it was at the north end of the Agora, and this conclusion is quite consistent with a quotation of Harpocration from "Menecles or Callicrates," saying that "out from the Stoa Poecile and the Stoa of the King [the Royal Stoa] are the so-called Herms." Some have understood that these herms crossed in a straight line from stoa to stoa, dividing the Agora into two sections, the civic and the commercial; but the language of the passage is satisfied better by supposing that they ran in nearly parallel lines, perhaps extending along the road which entered the Agora from the Dipylum. From the herms Xenophon would have his cavalry leader (p. 115) begin his circuit of the shrines of the Agora. Near them was a Stoa of the Herms, named by a scholiast on Demosthenes along with the Stoa Poecile and the Royal Stoa as one of the three most important stoae of Athens. In it were set up, according to Aeschines, three stone herms in honor of the generals who were victorious on the Strymon.

On the way from Market Hill to the Stoa Poecile stood the statue of Hermes Agoraeus. Most Attic herms were square pillars surmounted by the head of the god (Fig. 150); but this was a complete figure and of so graceful lines that it served constantly as a sculptor's model. In Lucian's *Zeus the Tragedian* (§ 33) Hermes Agoraeus is represented as rushing up to an assembly of the gods, to tell them of the impious things he has heard in the Agora. Zeus exclaims: "But who is this coming in such haste, this bronze figure of goodly lines and contour, his hair tied back in the old-fashioned style? Why, Hermes, it is your brother from the Agora, he who stands by the Painted Porch! Anyway he's smeared with pitch from the statue-makers taking casts of him every day." Evidently the Hermes in question was of archaic style, but we do not know who the sculptor was. We hear of an altar dedicated to the god; and the sausage seller in Aristophanes's *Knights* swears "by Hermes Agoraeus."

The gate "near by" surmounted by a trophy is puzzling. The victory which the trophy commemorated took place about 317 B.C.; but the triumphal arch as an architectural type is Roman rather than Greek. Possibly the gate was an old one put to a new use (p. 55).

All things considered, the requirements of extant evidence seem best to be met by the location of the Painted Porch at or near the Stoa of the Giants (p. 136); the later building may even have been placed upon the site of the renowned Poecile, but this is a conjecture the accuracy of which cannot now be verified.

Like one at least of the stoae along the avenue from the Dipylum, the Stoa Poecile would seem to have had an open court, or peristyle, perhaps in the rear; for Lucian in the work just mentioned speaks of a time when the Stoa was crowded, and some, while apparently still in the Stoa, were walking about under the open sky. The Stoa was built at about the middle of the fifth century by Peisianax, son-in-law of Cimon and uncle of Alcibiades; accordingly it was at first called the Stoa of Peisianax. Benches were provided in the Stoa where poet, or philosopher, or fishmonger might loiter at will; but its greatest fame arose from its being the meeting place of Zeno and his followers, who in consequence were called Stoics. It was used sometimes for informal assemblies, and for the selection of the quota of citizens; also for the sittings of courts of justice, and, in the reign of the Thirty, for a criminal court. Lucian frequently places here the scenes of his amusing dialogues, and we learn that jugglers found the crowded Stoa a favorable place for their performances. Apuleius tells us of a mountebank who swallows a sword and a hunting spear and of a youthful acrobat who performs before the throngs. That the Stoa stood on the edge of the Agora is evident from the dwellings said to have been near it, including that of the famous astronomer Meton.

The paintings that gave the Stoa its later name are fully described by Pausanias. Various conjectures have been made as to the arrangement on the walls. The most plausible suggestion is that the Battle of Oenoe was at the north end, the Battle of the Amazons and the Capture of Troy on the middle wall parallel to the colonnade, and the Battle of Marathon at the south end, though some would reverse this order. The paintings were probably frescoes, though the statement of Synesius, a Christian writer of the fifth century (*Ep.* 54; 135), that a Roman proconsul "removed the boards on which Polygnotus of Thasos expended his art" has given rise to much discussion.

The Battle of Oenoe is known only from this and another passage of Pausanias; why it was deemed worthy of portrayal here and who was the artist is undetermined. Of the

Battle of the Amazons we learn in addition that the Amazons were mounted and that the painting was by Micon. The picture of the Capture of Troy was by the epoch-making Thasian painter Polygnotus, who came to Athens about 460 B.C. Plutarch says that among the pictures of captive women that of Laodice, daughter of Priam, was a portrait of Cimon's sister Elpinice.

The Battle of Marathon was one of the most famous of all Greek paintings. The artist is said elsewhere by Pausanias to have been Panaenus, the brother of Pheidias. Others name Micon and Polygnotus; perhaps all three had a share in it. From the description of Pausanias we see that the battle was represented in three scenes, the attack, the rout, and the carnage by the ships. Pausanias specifies two gods, three heroes, and two mortals as delineated in the painting. From other descriptions we may add the hero Butes, who was hidden behind a hill as far as his eyes. Echetlus was depicted as slaying the Persians with his plowshare. To the men Pausanias elsewhere adds Aeschylus, the tragic poet; and Pliny adds Cynaegeirus, Aeschylus's brother, who, according to Herodotus, had his hand hewn off while clinging to a Persian ship, and the two Persian officers, Datis and Artaphernes. Miltiades was conspicuous among the ten generals, "extending his hand to point out the Barbarians to the Greeks, and urging on his men" (Schol. Aristeid. 46, 174). As a touch of humor a dog was painted in the picture (Aelian, *De nat. animal.* 7, 38) as the "fellow-soldier" of one of the men.

After mentioning the shields preserved in the Painted Porch and the statues of Solon and Seleucus, which stood near it, Pausanias passes to the altar of Pity and incidentally speaks of other evidences of Athenian piety, the altars of Modesty, Rumor, and Impulse. The mention of the several altars collectively shows that the passage is a digression and without topographical value; some of the altars at least seem not to have been in the Agora. As the spot which Pausanias names is "a short distance from the Agora," his description of the Agora evidently ceases here. Apparently he has selected from his notes only the sites that seemed to him most important. Several sites regarding which we have information from other sources may be considered before we leave the Hellenic Agora.

A precinct frequently mentioned by ancient authors, one evidently of no small moment, is the Leocorium. The story went that the sanctuary was dedicated to the three daughters of Leos, who were devoted to death in a time of famine, another example of popular etymology; the truth we do not know. The precinct was an heroum, and probably contained no temple. From its connection with the assassination of Hipparchus (p. 52) and its proximity to the mercantile booths of Pythodorus (p. 149) we may judge that it was on the edge of the Agora, at the north; a statement of a scholiast (on Demos. 54, 7) that it was "in the middle of Cerameicus" may refer to the deme of that name. Demosthenes mentions it (*l.c.*) as the terminus of a promenade taken by two men who pass from the Leocorium "through the Agora" and back, turning at the Pherephattium, or sanctuary of Persephone, which accordingly, as we should expect, must be placed near the Metroum (pp. 94 ff.).

The state's Prison, often euphemistically termed the Dwelling, must also have been placed near the north end of the Agora; for Theramenes, having been torn away from the altar of the Senate House at the south end of the Agora (Xenophon, *Hellen.* 2, 3, 56), was dragged "through the Agora" to the prison, where he was to drink the fatal hemlock. Here too Socrates died, and from the events related by Plato in connection with his death, we learn that the "Dwelling" contained several rooms, one of them a bath. Near the prison was the court in which Socrates was condemned (p. 23).

The lesser buildings of the Agora need not detain us; for most of them, Strategium, Thesmothesium, Poleterium, Agoranomium, and the like, are little more than names to us.

# CHAPTER V

## The Hellenistic and Roman Agora and Other Sites

### HELLENISTIC AND ROMAN AGORA

If the characterization were taken to imply a distinct or different area, the phrase "Hellenistic and Roman Agora" would not be justifiable. What we have called the Hellenic Agora was also the Agora throughout the rest of Athenian history; but in the later days its bounds were extended, particularly toward the east and north, since the hills hemmed it in on the other sides; for the sake of clearness this enlarged Agora deserves a distinguishing appellation. The Hellenistic and Roman Agora is not described by Pausanias, an antiquarian by nature, and its imposing buildings are rarely mentioned by any author; but the remains are extensive, and among the most interesting in the city to-day.

Near the north end of the added area is the Stoa of Attalus. This Stoa is mentioned only once in extant literature, and then only casually in connection with the experiences of a certain man named Athenion, who enjoyed a brief period of despotic power at Athens on his return from an embassy to Mithridates, about 88 B.C. Excitement in the city was intense. "The Cerameicus was filled with citizens and strangers, and the crowds ran unsummoned to the assembly. Athenion advanced with difficulty, and . . . mounting the bema which was built in front of the Stoa of Attalus for the generals of the Romans, he stood upon it; and, casting his eyes around over the throng," he addressed the people. The first part of this passage, from Athenaeus (5, 212 f.), has been taken as evidence for the location of the Stoa on the Hellenic Agora. But the term "Cerameicus" refers properly to the entire deme (pp. 26 f.), within and without the Dipylum, and, even were it granted that the Agora only is meant, the passage would still be insufficient to prove that the Agora of Hellenic times extended so far eastwards. As we have seen (pp. 88 f.), the buildings excavated just east of the Hephaesteum, though north of the civic Agora, determine its western limits; to make the earlier Agora include the entire space between this and the Stoa of Attalus is to disregard the gradual growth of the area and to give it extraordinary dimensions, four or five times as great, for example, as the Roman Forum.

The identification of the Stoa of Attalus is made certain by the discovery of the fragments of an inscription which originally stood above the lower colonnade on the front of the building, and which now has been fitted together and stands in the midst of the ruins. It reads: "King Attalus son of King Attalus and of Queen Apollonis." The founder of the Stoa was, therefore, Attalus II, king of Pergamum from 159 to 138 B.C., and the building was patterned after Pergamene colonnades.

The Stoa (Fig. 66) was built on sloping ground, an excavation being made for the foundation at the south end (Fig. 67), while the north end was elevated on a high podium; a ramp at the southwest corner gave access to the building. The façade, facing the west, was mostly of Pentelic marble, but nearly all of the remainder was of poros; the foundation was of breccia. Originally the Stoa, including the exedrae at the ends, was about 331 feet long and 65 feet wide, but later its length was increased to about 380 feet by an addition toward the north. It had two stories connected by a stairway at the south end. Each floor comprehended a broad open portico fronting a row of twenty-one (originally eighteen) shops, or magazines; the ceilings were of wood. Before the lower portico ran a colonnade of forty-five Doric columns resting on a three-stepped stereobate; the lower portion of the columns was unfluted so as to prevent breakage. The open space was divided into two aisles by a row of twenty-two Ionic columns. At either end of the front aisle was a small door; at either end of the second aisle, a marble exedra (Fig. 68). The shops were uniformly about 16 feet deep, but varied slightly in width (Fig. 69). A large door opened from each shop into the portico, and the shops were also lighted by narrow windows in the rear wall. Sockets were cut in the sides of the rooms for the insertion of shelves to accommodate the wares of merchants. The second story was fronted by forty-five shorter Ionic columns resting on pilasters, between which ran a marble balustrade; but this story had no inner row of columns. The roof of the building was of wood.

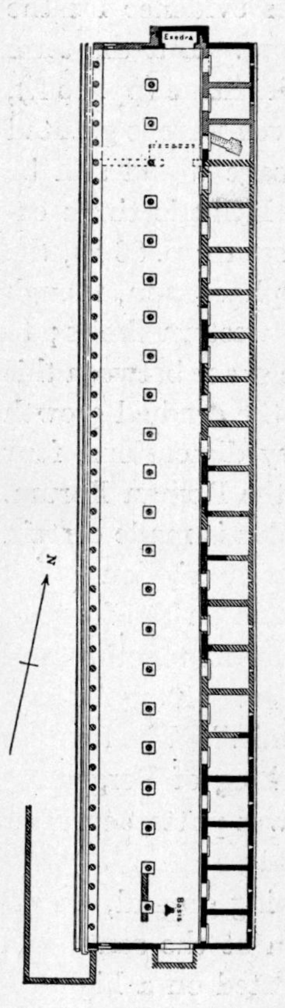

Fig. 66. — Plan of the Stoa of Attalus.

The Stoa of Attalus owes its preservation in part to its having been built into the "Valerian Wall" (p. 74); this has now been taken down and the building fully excavated.

Fig. 67. — South end of the Stoa of Attalus.

The doorways at the left communicate with the shops of the Stoa. The wall at the rear is modern.

Fig. 68. — North end of the Stoa of Attalus; at the left a marble exedra.

At some depth below the level of the third room from the north the excavators came upon a spring-house of an earlier date, which may have limited the length of the Stoa when first constructed. The building must have seemed a magnificent addition to the mercantile quarters of the

FIG. 69. — Stoa of Attalus, looking south; at the left the foundations of shops.

city, and many a close bargain, we may surmise, was struck beneath its roof.

Some two hundred feet west of the Stoa of Attalus is the Stoa of the Giants, as it is now called because of its colossal figures (Fig. 70). The foundation is of late Roman construction, composed of stones from various sources; only part of it has been uncovered. At either end of the excavated portion are parallel walls running north and south, apparently belonging to colonnades, one of which opened into an apse. In a small room at the end of one colonnade are ruins of a stairway leading to an upper story; in the room on the opposite side are remains of a bath.

Projecting from the ends of the side walls are broad stylobates with two independent bases in line between them, leaving room for three wide entrances. Here stood the

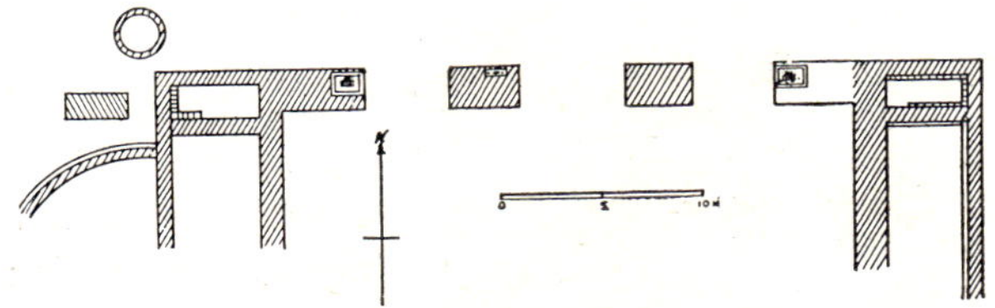

FIG. 70.—Plan of the excavated portion of the Stoa of the Giants.

marble Atlantes which rested against pilasters and supported the entablature. These statues, of which three are fairly well preserved (Fig. 71), seem to have been taken from a building of about the time of Hadrian. They re-

FIG. 71.—Remains of the Stoa of the Giants, from the northwest.

semble in style the crouching Sileni beneath the stage built by Phaedrus in the great theater (p. 200). The upper part of each statue is that of a man, while below they pass, one into the form of a serpent, the others into the form of a fish.

Each rests on a square marble basis of later and cruder workmanship, adorned in front with an olive tree about which a serpent entwines (Fig. 72). Though of degenerate type, the façade may not have been wholly ignoble. Whether or not the Stoa stood on the site of an earlier building is uncertain; we have seen reason to believe that here may have been the site of the Painted Porch, on the east side of the Hellenic Agora (p. 88).

FIG. 72. — East figure of the Stoa of the Giants.

About a hundred yards east of the southern end of the Stoa of Attalus stands the conspicuous gateway of the great Market of Caesar and Augustus, usually called the Roman Market. This structure (Fig. 73) extended northwest by southeast and was of immense size, measuring about 367 by 315 feet over all. It was inclosed by a high wall of stone, lined with colonnades and shops; whether or not the wall was faced with marble, we do not know.

The main entrance was an elaborate propylum (Fig. 74), having a front of four fluted Doric columns about 26 feet high and 4 feet thick at the base; the central intercolumniation is especially wide, in order to admit vehicles. The architrave bears the city's dedicatory inscription to Athena Archegetis (Foundress), the names of the donors, Julius Caesar and Augustus, and of the officers responsible for the construction. Instead of an acroterium the summit

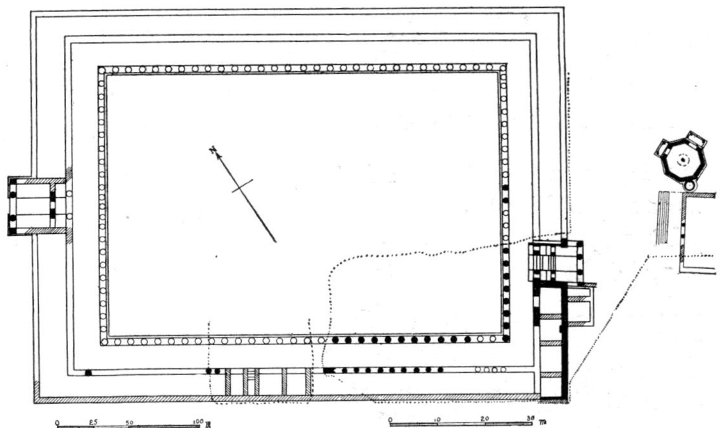

FIG. 73.—Plan of the Market of Caesar and Augustus; at the right the Tower of the Winds and the Agoranomium.

The rooms at the middle of the south side are conjecturally added from memory and the published description; no plan of this newly excavated portion of the Market has been published.

of the gable was surmounted by a statue, whose base alone survives, of the grandson of Augustus, Lucius Caesar. This young man was adopted by the emperor in 17 B.C. and died in 2 A.D. Within this period the building probably was erected. Near the propylum stood a statue of Julia, Augustus's profligate daughter, the mother of Lucius.

The actual gateway was about 25 feet east of the columns and had three entrances corresponding with their intercolumniations. The marble jamb of the central doorway, on the north side, still stands, and on its inner face is in-

FIG. 74. — Gate of Athena Archegetis, or propylum of the Market of Caesar and Augustus.

scribed a long decree of Hadrian containing regulations for the sale of oil. Behind the doorways were two columns facing the interior.

The greater part of the Market is still covered with streets and buildings, but the construction is fairly clear from a study of the excavated southeast corner. Here is found a second gateway much like the eastern, but in a very ruinous condition. Its paved floor is elevated by three steps above the interior, showing that it was used only by visitors on foot; the four columns which front it are unfluted (Fig. 75). This entrance lies obliquely to the wall and is so far south that a corresponding gateway farther north may be assumed. South of the second propylum are foundations of four shops, somewhat like those of the Stoa of Attalus. The inclosure may have had doors also on the north side; the spade alone can determine. Excavations are being continued near the middle of the south side, and here a series of rooms, a spring, which still affords a rill of water, and a stairway leading down from above have already been brought to light.

In front of the extant east shops was a row of unfluted Ionic columns, of which numerous bases and stumps remain. These columns supported a covered portico, which continued along the south side; only here, at least up to a point near the middle, was a central row of columns without bases, instead of shops. The arrangement on the other sides is conjectural; so, too, is the treatment of the paved central area, which alone covers more than an acre of ground.

The decree concerning the sale of oil, the standard measures of length cut in the extant anta, tables found in the inclosure with hollows giving the standard measures of volume, and inscriptions relating to overseers of the Market, make the use of the structure certain. We should be glad to know if the oil-market of classic times also stood here; such locations are persistent. The building as we know it is an impressive testimony to the favor of the early Caesars, as well as to the comparatively good taste still prevailing in Athens in their day.

FIG. 75. — East propylum of the Market of Caesar and Augustus, from the west.

On the left is the Tower of the Winds and near the middle the arches of the Agoranomium.

Some fifty feet east of the second gateway of the Market, and nearly parallel with it, was a flight of eight or ten steps, of which portions of four remain, leading up to some sort of a public building. Two and a half arches of an entrance way (Fig. 76), and part of the foundation, survive.

FIG. 76. — Steps and arches belonging to the Roman "Agoranomium."

These together with fragmentary inscriptions make it likely that here was the Agoranomium, or office of the overseers of the Market. The building was dedicated, like the Market, to Athena Archegetis and to the "August Gods," that is, to Roman emperors. The building is certainly later than the Tower of the Winds, for its corner rests partly upon the corner of that structure; and considerations of style make it probable that it was also later than the Market of Caesar and Augustus, though the peculiar orientation of the east gateway of the Market may have some relation to the Agoranomium. At a still later date additions were made at the east end.

Just north of the Agoranomium is the Horologium, which is popularly known as the Tower of the Winds (Fig. 77).

This building is mentioned by Varro in his *De re rustica*, composed in 37 B.C., and is described in detail by the Roman architect Vitruvius, who probably wrote during the reign of Augustus. On their authority we know that it was constructed by Andronicus Cyrrhestes, who flourished in

FIG. 77.—Tower of the Winds, or Horologium of Andronicus Cyrrhestes.

the first century B.C., and who took his name from his birthplace, Cyrrhus, in Syria. The building is to be dated, then, somewhere near the middle of the last century of the old era.

The Horologium is built of Pentelic marble, and in plan is a true octagon; it is about 26 feet in greatest diameter, and 42 feet high. Its wall rises above three steps and is composed of squared blocks of varying widths, the sections being divided by narrow string-courses, which correspond to projecting cornices on the interior. The building is oriented a little to the east of due north, and has two entrances, on the northeast and northwest, respectively. Before the doors were small porticoes, whose roofs were supported at the back by pilasters and in front by Corinthian columns of good style but without bases; the lower portions of the columns are in situ. The roof of the building is made of wedge-shaped slabs of marble, topped by a crown-stone which was originally surmounted, as Vitruvius tells us, by a weather-vane in the form of a bronze

FIG. 78.—Reliefs representing the Winds Caecias, Boreas, Sciron, and Zephyrus, on the Horologium.

Triton pointing with a wand at the personifications of the prevailing winds (pp. 20 f.) as portrayed in the reliefs below the cornice (Fig. 78).

These eight reliefs bear inscriptions giving their names. Boreas, the cold north wind, is a bearded man wearing a heavy sleeved robe and buskins, and blowing on a shell; Caecias, the boisterous northeast wind, is also bearded and warmly clad, and carries a vessel containing what seem to be hailstones; Apeliotes, the mild and rainy east wind, is a youth with a bundle of grain and fruits; Eurus, the threatening southeast wind, is a bearded man clad in a chlamys, which he lifts to shield his face; Notus, the showery south wind, is a youth lightly dressed and holding an inverted water jar; Lips, the southwest wind, favorable for sailors, is a youth bearing the aplustre of a ship; Zephyrus, the warm west wind, is almost nude and has his mantle filled with flowers; Sciron, the scorching northwest wind, is a bearded man with an inverted brazier. All the figures are winged; some of their attributes admit of various interpretations, and the forms are somewhat formal and stiff.

Diverging from a gnomon under each relief are the incised lines of a sundial, and inside the building was a clepsydra, or water clock, so that the habitué of the Agora, in fair and cloudy weather alike, might learn the time of day. Engaged structurally with the south wall is a small circular wing, perhaps a cistern to supply the clepsydra, which may have stood in the center of the floor, where complicated cuttings have so far defied efforts at interpretation. The walls inside the building are divided into three "stories" and an attic by cornices, or shelves, the second from the bottom being of ornate Corinthian style (Fig. 79). On the upper cornice and in the corners behind the reliefs are miniature Doric columns, while close under the roof are horizontal slits which probably served for ventilation.

The most pretentious building in this region is the one which has long been called the Stoa of Hadrian, though this name has no ancient authority. The building is probably the Library of Hadrian, which Pausanias mentions in a later passage (p. 162) as a conspicuous edifice erected by the emperor, and to which St. Jerome gave special praise (Eusebius, *Chron. Ol.* 227). It was adorned, Pausanias adds, with a hundred columns of Phrygian marble and with stoae against its marble, or marble-veneered, walls, while its rooms for books were covered with alabaster, with gilded ceilings, and were adorned with statues and paintings.

FIG. 79. — Elevation and section of the Tower of the Winds, restored.

The Library of Hadrian (Fig. 80) lies a little north of the Market of Caesar and Augustus and nearly parallel to it. It was a huge rectangle, 400 feet long and 270 feet wide, with walls of poros. The long northern, and doubtless the southern, wall had three large apses, the middle one rectangular, the others semicircular. Close to the west, or chief, façade of the building (Fig. 81) ran a colonnade of fourteen unfluted Corinthian columns filling the spaces between the antae at the ends of the prolonged side walls and the central propylum. The northern seven of these columns remain; they are said to be of Carystian marble, or cipollino, with capitals of Pentelic marble. Possibly they once bore statues. The propylum at the middle faced the west and was fronted by four fluted Corinthian columns, only one of which remains (visible at the extreme right in Fig. 81). The eastern façade (Fig. 82), facing on the present Aeolus Street, is plain, save for its projection and buttresses at the middle.

Less than half of the interior has been excavated. At the east end have been uncovered the foundations of several

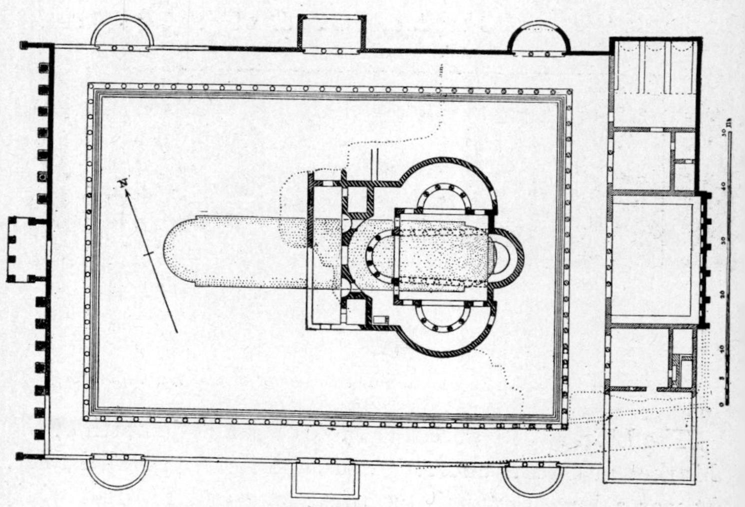

FIG. 80. — Plan of the Library of Hadrian.

large rooms. The middle room may have been the room devoted to the storage of books; near it were found personifications, in marble, of the Iliad and the Odyssey. The corner rooms were covered with barrel vaults and may have been reading or lecture rooms. The other rooms at this end of the building perhaps were cloak rooms; off one of them was a toilet room.

Around the central area ran the portico, about 24 feet wide; the roof was supported by the hundred columns of Phrygian marble, only fragments of which have been found.

Fig. 81. — West end of the Library of Hadrian.

Fig. 82. — East end of the Library of Hadrian.

Originally the space inclosed by the colonnade, some 268 by 196 feet in dimensions, had in its center a long and narrow reservoir, doubtless surrounded by trees, flowers, and statues. But later the reservoir was filled, and an elaborate building, possibly an extension to the library proper, with corridors, apses, and niches, was constructed to take its place (Fig. 83). In the Middle Ages this central structure

Fig. 83. — Interior of the Library of Hadrian; on the left the columns and walls of mediaeval church.

was turned into a church of the Virgin. The palace of the Turkish voivode was afterwards built on the site of the Library, and still later the ruins were made into a bazaar, for which Lord Byron supplied a clock. The bazaar was burned in a great fire in 1886.

In the passage in which Pausanias speaks of the Library (1, 18, 9) he names also several other buildings of Hadrian; a gymnasium with a hundred columns of Libyan marble, a temple of Hera and Zeus Panhellenius (here, Hadrian and his wife Sabina), and a "sanctuary common to all the gods," a Pantheum. Some scholars identify the building described above with the gymnasium, but this is less likely.

Unfortunately Pausanias is not following a topographical order when he names these buildings, and we cannot tell where they are.

### THE MARKET

As in Athens to-day, so in ancient Athens most of the trade was in the hands of the small dealer. In later times such buildings as the Alphitopolis, the Stoa of Attalus, and the Market of Caesar and Augustus provided stalls for various tradesmen, but during the classical period simple booths were erected for the purpose. The localities of trade were "circles" named from the commodities offered for sale. The booths, or "tents," were made of wood or wickerwork; probably they were separated by narrow streets or lanes.

The various circles crowded close about the civic Agora on all sides except the south, but we can locate few of them more definitely. The shops belonging to one Pythodorus were near the Leocorium (p. 128), at the north edge of the Agora; the coppersmiths were adjacent to the temple of Hephaestus (p. 117); the fish market was probably near the Painted Porch (pp. 123 ff.); the dealers in secondhand purloined goods, called the Cercopes from the "thievish and wights" who once robbed Heracles, were near the court of Heliaea (p. 364) at the southeast corner of the Agora. Books were sold in the civic Agora at the old Orchestra (p. 105). We can localize no further, but we know the names of many of the circles; the tables of each were the centers of traffic in the particular kind of merchandise. The consideration of the lively scenes enacted here belongs rather to the study of Greek life than to our present topic. The *Characters* of Theophrastus picture some amusing types of the men who thronged the market.

The circle called "The Fishes," with special booths for the sale of eels, or anchovies, or salted fish, and a score of others, was a quarter much frequented. At "The Meats" one found beef, pork, asses' flesh, game, and other varieties. "The Birds" afforded different fowls, wild and domestic. "The Vegetables" included numerous smaller circles, "The Pulses," "The Cresses," "The Onions," "The Figs," and the rest. Wines, oils, vinegar, honey, of course, had each their circle. "The Cheeses," particularly "The Green Cheese," was a circle much patronized. For all these a generic name seems to have been "The Relishes." Other circles were devoted to prepared and manufactured merchandise, as bread, sausage, and bakestuffs. Still others were for clothing and the various utensils. At the "Women's Agora" were sold articles of women's handiwork and goods made for women's use. A horse market and a slave market were also to be found. Money changers had a special quarter for their "tables." In other places cooks and other workmen waited for employment; flute players and courtesans as well, the latter near the Leocorium. Barbers' shops, shoe-shops, perfumers' shops, and the like were favorite lounging places for idlers. Of these and many others Greek literature makes frequent mention.

## BUILDINGS ON THE NORTH SLOPE OF THE ACROPOLIS

Since leaving the Painted Porch (p. 128) we have been obliged to abandon the guidance of Pausanias; we may now return to his narrative. "In the gymnasium not far distant from the Agora, and called the Gymnasium of Ptolemy from its builder, are some stone herms worth seeing and a bronze image of Ptolemy. A statue of Juba the Libyan and one of Chrysippus of Soli are also here." From the Painted

Porch, or rather the Altar of Pity, which caused him to make a digression on Athenian altars, Pausanias passes southward towards the Acropolis, naming in order the Gymnasium of Ptolemy, the Theseum, the Anaceum, and the Aglaurium.

The Ptolemaeum may be sought southwest of the Stoa of Attalus (Fig. 46). Indeed, a number of inscriptions mentioning it have been found within this Stoa, which probably were carried the short distance to build into the "Valerian Wall." These inscriptions tell us that the ephebi, or lads of from eighteen to twenty years, attended lectures on philosophy in the Ptolemaeum; and Cicero says (*De fin.* 5, 1, 1) that he listened to the philosopher Antiochus "in that gymnasium which is called the Ptolemaeum." The building contained a library to which the ephebi often contributed books; it must also have had spacious rooms and courts for exercise and recreation. If, as is probable, it was constructed by Ptolemy Philadelphus (285–247 B.C.), it was one of the earliest Hellenistic buildings in the city. No sure trace of it has yet been found.

Plutarch tells us on the authority of Philochorus (*Thes.* 36) that the tomb of Theseus lay "in the middle of the city beside the present gymnasium," doubtless the gymnasium of Ptolemy, the statement thus being consistent with Pausanias's words, "Next to the gymnasium is a sanctuary of Theseus." Pausanias also tells us that the sacred close of Theseus was founded when the bones of the hero were buried in it, having been brought back from the island of Scyros by Cimon "later than the Median landing at Marathon," apparently in 469 B.C. Thereafter it became one of the most sacred sites of Athens (p. 114) and an inviolate asylum for all fugitives. The inclosure must have been of considerable extent, for in it troops sometimes marshaled, assemblies met, and certain trials and elections were held. No mention is made of a temple; being a heroum, it probably had none, but it certainly possessed one or more buildings, of which at least one contained paintings.

We have previously noted that the temple long called the Theseum has wrongly been assigned to Theseus (p. 117), and we now see one reason. That the Theseum must have been near the entrance to the Acropolis is evident from a ruse of Peisistratus narrated by Aristotle (*Const. of Athens* 15). "He disarmed the citizens in the following manner: He called an armed assembly to be held in the Theseum and undertook to address the people, but he purposely spoke in a low tone. When they said they could not hear him, he told them to ascend toward the propylum of the Acropolis, in order that he might speak more easily. While he kept on with his harangue, men appointed for the purpose took the weapons and locked them up in the buildings near the Theseum." Polyaenus (1, 21, 2) tells the same story with some variations, particularly that the assembly was held in the Anaceum and that the weapons were put "in the sanctuary of Agraulus." But the "buildings near the Theseum," in Aristotle's story, may have been those of the Agraulium; the Theseum and Anaceum were contiguous, so that the slight confusion is not strange; hence the general argument for the location of the precinct, added to the words of Plutarch and Pausanias, is not invalidated. The period of Peisistratus, so much before the time when the bones of Theseus were brought back to Athens, justifies the assumption that a sanctuary was situated here earlier than the days of Cimon; this does not, however, impair the topographical value of the story of Peisistratus's trick.

Pausanias further adds that in the Theseum "are paintings of the Athenians fighting with the Amazons, the war depicted also on the shield of Athena and on the base of Olympian Zeus. In the sanctuary is painted also the Battle of Centaurs and Lapiths. Theseus has already slain his Centaur, but the battle of the rest is still raging on even terms. The painting on the third of the walls is not clear to those who have not learned the story, partly because of the defacement wrought by time, and partly because Micon did not paint the entire story. When Minos was taking Theseus and the rest of the youths to Crete, he fell enamored of Periboea. As Theseus vehemently protested, Minos in a fury hurled other insults at him and declared that Theseus was not the son of Poseidon, since he could not bring back the seal ring which Minos chanced to be wearing, if he cast it in the sea. With these words Minos is said to have flung the ring into the sea, from which Theseus, they say, emerged both with the ring and with a golden crown given him by Amphitrite."

Pausanias does not state specifically that Micon painted all the pictures of the Theseum, but this is the natural inference. Our interest, like his, is centered on the third painting. The story is repeated by Hyginus, but the fullest and best account is that of a beautiful ode of Bacchylides found a few years ago in Egypt. Representations of the tale are painted on several extant Greek vases, the best of which is the superb cylix signed by Euphronius and now in the Louvre at Paris (Fig. 84). Theseus supported on the hands of Triton is at the bottom of the sea, as the dolphins about him indicate. He reaches out his hand to Amphitrite, who holds a crown. In the background is the goddess Athena.

Without mentioning its situation, Pausanias says: "The sanctuary of the Dioscuri is ancient; they themselves are standing, and their sons are on horseback. Here is a painting by Polygnotus of the marriage of the daughters of Leucippus, which concerned the Dioscuri, and one by Micon of those who sailed with Jason to Colchis. The emphasis in Micon's painting is laid on Acastus and his

FIG. 84.—Theseus, Athena, and Amphitrite, beneath the sea; vase painting by Euphronius.

horses." The situation of the precinct of the Dioscuri, or Anaceum, is indicated by the order of mention by Pausanias, the story of Polyaenus, and the fact that it was lower than the Aglaurium (see below). That it was on the slope of the Acropolis is also clear from the scene depicted by Lucian (*Pisc.* 42) of the needy philosophers climbing up to the Acropolis to receive a proffered dole. "Whew!" cries the donor. "How full the ascent is of crowding men when they have merely heard of the two minae! And others past the Pelargicum, and others down by the Asclepieum, and still more past the Areopagus, and some too down by the tomb of Talus, and others are even planting ladders against the Anaceum and climbing up."

The sanctuary must have been large, for it could accommodate troops of cavalry and infantry. Slaves sometimes stood there waiting to be hired; Demosthenes speaks of a rascally Phormio "from up in the Anaceum." We know nothing of its buildings, but we hear of its having been struck by lightning in the time of Pericles and later undergoing repairs. The paintings of Polygnotus doubtless portrayed Castor and Polydeuces carrying off from Messene the daughters of Leucippus, Hilaeira and Phoebe, who were betrothed to Lynceus and Idas, the sons of Aphareus. The scene is represented in several vase paintings, notably one by Meidias in the British Museum (Fig. 85). Rubens employed the theme for one of his best works, the "Rape of the daughters of Leucippus," at Munich. Evidently the representations of the Dioscuri and their sons, Anaxis and Mnasinus (or Anogon and Mnesileos), were sculptured. At Athens the Dioscuri were called Saviors, and Lords (Anaces), whence the name of their precinct.

"Above the sanctuary of the Dioscuri," Pausanias goes on, "is the precinct of Aglaurus. They say that Athena put Erichthonius in a chest and gave it to Aglaurus and her sisters Herse and Pandrosus, forbidding them to meddle with what she intrusted to them. Pandrosus is said to have obeyed; but the other two opened the chest, and went mad when they saw Erichthonius, and cast themselves down from the Acropolis where it was most precipitous. The Medes went up at this point and slew those of the Athenians who thought that they knew better than Themistocles about the oracle and fortified the Acropolis with timbers and palisades."

FIG. 85.—Rape of the daughters of Leucippus, above; the garden of the Hesperides, below; vase painting by Meidias.

The tale related by Pausanias is only one of various forms of the myth, but we are not concerned with that here. We see from his story that the Aglaurium, or Agraulium, must have been at the foot of the Acropolis. That it was near the Propylaea is clear from the tale told by Aristotle and Polyaenus about Peisistratus (p. 152), and this inference is further justified by the express statement of an ancient commentator on Demosthenes. In speaking of the assault on the Acropolis by the Persians in 480 B.C., Pausanias has in mind the words of Herodotus, who says (8, 53) that the Persians clambered up "in front of the Acropolis"—that is, at its western end, which was adorned with an ornamental gateway and faced the Agora — "but back of the gates and the ascent . . . by the sanctuary of the daughter of Cecrops, Aglaurus, though the place was precipitous." This evidence permits us to locate the precinct at the northwest foot of the Acropolis close to the Clepsydra (Fig. 233), which is also consistent with the connection of the site by Euripides with the Long Rocks and the caves of Pan and Apollo (pp. 353 ff.). The dance of the Aglauridae, of which Euripides sings, may be depicted in certain marble reliefs portraying Pan peeping down from his cave above on the left, while the head of the water god, Achelous, perhaps here a personification of the Clepsydra, is on the right.

The Aglaurium was a sanctuary of importance, for here the ephebi took their oath of allegiance on going forth to war. This may account for one version of the myth, that Aglaurus threw herself from the rock as a voluntary sacrifice in fidelity to the city.

"Near by is the Prytaneum, in which the laws of Solon have been inscribed, and where are statues of the goddesses Peace and Hestia, and of Autolycus, the pancratiast, and others, for they have reinscribed the figures of Miltiades and Themistocles, turning them into a Roman and a Thracian, respectively."

The Prytaneum was the city hall. In it burned a perpetual fire on the common hearth of the state, and here the Athenians entertained at public expense famous citizens and guests of the city; Socrates at his trial demanded that his penalty be life maintenance in the Prytaneum, of which he deemed his services to be worthy.

The situation of the Prytaneum is said by Pausanias to be near the Aglaurium. Since he descends thence "to the lower parts of the city" and turns eastward, and since from the Prytaneum there was a street leading around the east end of the Acropolis (p. 180), the Prytaneum must have lain on the slope, a little to the east of the Aglaurium, somewhere near the ruined chapel of St. Nicholas. Some reason exists for the belief that the building that Pausanias saw was one of Roman date and that the earlier site was by the Ancient Agora (p. 83); the establishment goes back into the regal period of the city.

The laws of Solon, which were preserved in the Prytaneum, were engraved on axones, or revolving stone tablets; whether these were like the wedges set up in the Royal Stoa, or not, we do not know. The Autolycus, whose statue Pausanias saw, was the athletic youth in whose honor the banquet described in the *Symposium* of Xenophon was held; his victory in the pancratium was won in 422 B.C., and the statue was probably the work of Leochares. Besides the statues mentioned above was one of Demochares, the nephew of Demosthenes, and, near the Prytaneum, one of Good Fortune; the latter was so beautiful that, as Aelian states, a certain young man fell violently in love with it.

Behind the Prytaneum, perhaps to the west, since the site was on the slope of the Acropolis, was Hunger Plain (Limoupedion); and near by were the Basileum and the Bucoleum, where in the days of Draco the king archon lived, and where down into the fourth century the symbolic marriage of the wife of the king with Dionysus was celebrated. But these sites, too, may have been near the Ancient Agora.

"As you go hence to the lower parts of the city is a sanctuary of Serapis." Serapis was an Egyptian divinity, whose worship was introduced into Athens in the time of Ptolemy Philadelphus. Inscriptions relating to his worship have been found near the Metropolitan Church and at the northeast corner of the Acropolis. The Serapeum may have been at or near one of these points, or between them.

"Not far from the sanctuary of Serapis is a place where Peirithoüs and Theseus are said to have made a compact before they went to Lacedaemon and afterwards to the Thesprotians." The agreement related to the rape of Helen from Sparta. The place to which Pausanias refers cannot be located.

"Near by is built a temple of Eileithyia," the goddess of childbirth. Various inscriptions of the divinity have been found, but the places of discovery are so scattered that the temple cannot be located.

Before leaving this quarter we must notice the Gymnasium of Diogenes — the Macedonian, not the Cynic, philosopher — where, as Plutarch says (*Quaest. symp.* 9, 1, 1), the ephebi studied "letters and geometry and rhetoric and music," the ordinary routine of ancient education. A large number of ephebic inscriptions have been found near the ruined church of Demetrios Katiphores, but no building; probably the Diogeneum was in the vicinity.

Most of this region was occupied in antiquity, as at the present time, by private houses. Some shrines and niches are to be seen halfway up the slope of the Acropolis, but the whole quarter awaits excavation.

From the vicinity of the Prytaneum two roads ran eastwards. Pausanias first pursues the more northerly of these, and passes to Southeast Athens.

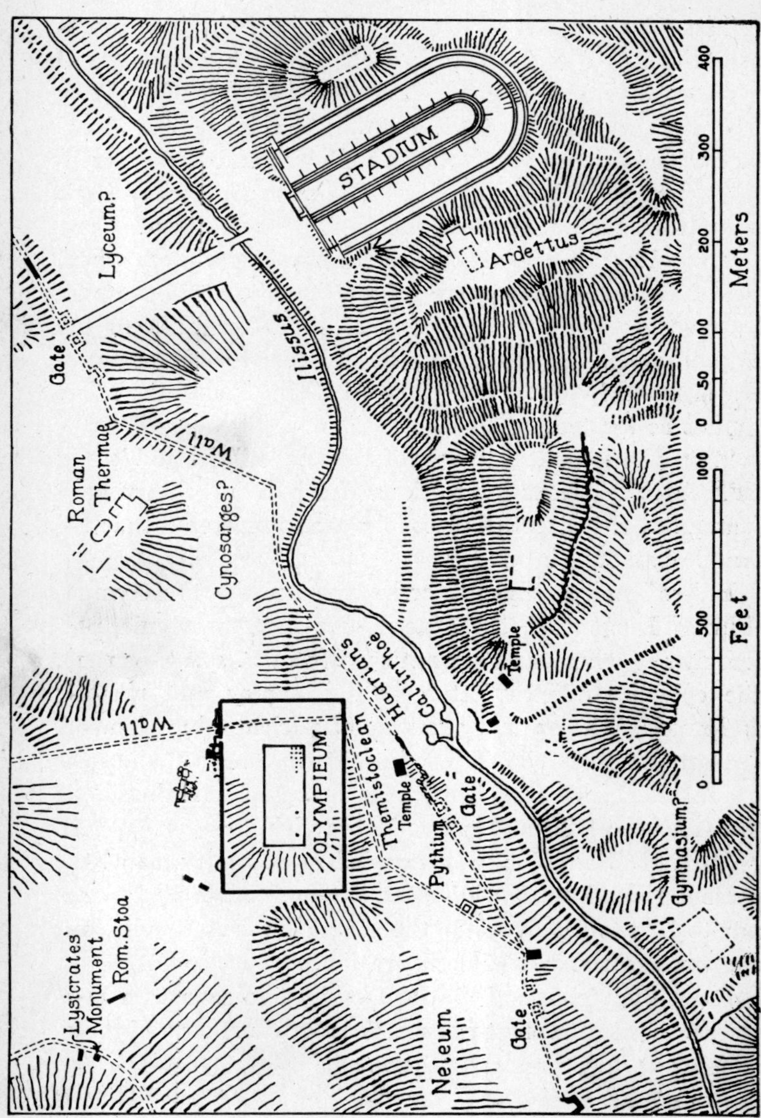


Fig. 86. — Map of Southeast Athens.

# CHAPTER VI

## Southeast Athens

The most notable building of Southeast Athens (Figs. 87 and 88) is the Olympieum, the largest temple in Greece

Fig. 87. — Temple of Olympian Zeus, or Olympieum, from the northeast.

and one of the largest in the ancient world; only a few temples in Magna Graecia and Asia Minor are larger. Pausanias's description is prolix and ill-articulated: "Before coming to the sanctuary of Olympian Zeus (Hadrian, the king of the Romans, dedicated both the temple and the statue, which is worth seeing, since it surpasses in size all other statues alike except the colossi of Rhodes and of Rome, and is made of ivory and gold, and, considering its size, is of good workmanship) there are two statues of

Hadrian in Thasian and two in Egyptian marble; and before the columns are bronze images which the Athenians call 'Colonies.' The entire inclosure is about four stades in circuit and full of statues; for from each city is dedicated an image of King Hadrian, and the Athenians outdid them all by dedicating the colossus, worth seeing, behind the temple. In the inclosure are some ancient works, a bronze Zeus, a temple of Cronus and Rhea, and a precinct of Earth surnamed Olympian. The ground here is cleft for about a cubit, and they say that after the flood, which occurred in the time of Deucalion, the water ran off here, and every year they cast into the chasm wheaten bread kneaded with honey. Upon a column is set up a statue of Isocrates. . . . Here, too, are Persians of Phrygian marble supporting a bronze tripod, both men and tripod worth seeing. They say that Deucalion built the ancient sanctuary of Olympian Zeus, and they point out, as proof of the fact that Deucalion lived at Athens, a grave not far distant from the present temple." Here follows the enumeration of Hadrian's other buildings in Athens, which have been discussed in another connection (pp. 144, 148).

Excavation in the central area of the Olympieum revealed a primitive cross-wall, which may belong to the sanctuary ascribed by tradition to Deucalion. Other walls which were found have been thought to be a part of the great temple begun by Peisistratus about 530 B.C.; this is the work at which, according to Aristotle, Peisistratus kept the people busy for years, after the manner of the builders of the pyramids of Egypt and the works of the tyrants of Corinth and Samos, so as to prevent their murmuring over his rule. The cella of this temple was of a slightly different orientation from that of the later buildings; it is estimated to have been 116 by 50 feet in dimensions. It was doubtless Doric in style; several unfluted drums of the columns have been found, one of them 7.5 feet in diameter. The architects were Antistates, Callaeschrus, Antimachides, and Pormus (or Porinus); this we learn from Vitruvius (7, *praef.* 15).

The end of the tyranny stopped work on the temple, and for nearly seven centuries it stood unfinished. No mention of it, further than the name, is found in literature of the classic period. About 174 B.C. the task was resumed by Antiochus IV Epiphanes, king of Syria, who employed the Roman architect Cossutius to design a temple on a larger scale and of the Corinthian order. Judging from their style, — though not all critics are agreed in the matter, — the extant remains seem to be the work of Cossutius; but again the temple was left unfinished, though well advanced, as the praise of Vitruvius shows. Livy speaks of it (41, 20, 8) as *unum in terris inchoatum pro magnitudine dei*, but Lucian makes Zeus ask impatiently (*Icaromen.* 24) "if the Athenians mean to finish his Olympieum;" and other writers speak of it as half-done. Sulla carried off some of the columns, perhaps from the inside of the cella, to rebuild the Capitoline temple of Jupiter at Rome. A proposal to complete the building was brought forward in the time of Augustus, but abandoned.

The temple was finally finished by the emperor Hadrian and dedicated in 130 or 131 A.D. The sophist Polemo delivered the dedicatory address in the emperor's presence, and a serpent from India was consecrated in the sanctuary. How much of the structure Hadrian built cannot now be determined; probably at least the interior colonnades, the roof and the decorations, perhaps the entire cella, and certainly the enormous statue of the god.

On its upper step the temple (Fig. 88) measured 354 by 135 feet, and its height was upwards of 90 feet. The two lower of its three steps were of poros, but the upper step and, so far as we know, the remainder of the temple was of Pentelic marble. At present only sixteen columns remain, one of these lying prostrate (Fig. 89) as the result of a hurricane in 1852. "There it still lies with its vast drums

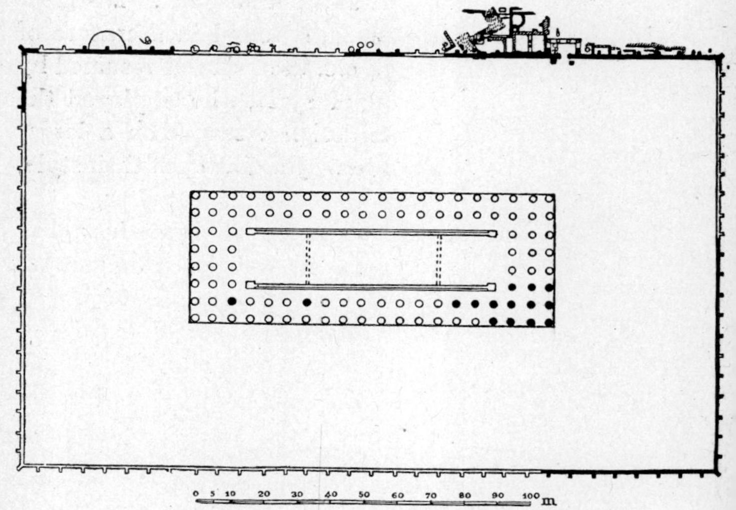


FIG. 88. — Plan of the Olympieum.

of solid Pentelic marble shuffled under one another like so many cards spread to choose a partner; a sight well fitted to excite astonishment in these days of lath and plaster."[1] An American minister,[2] who had an estimate made some years ago of the probable expense of reërecting the column, found that this task alone would cost about $3000, an estimate which affords a slight basis for reckoning the total cost of the temple. A seventeenth column was burned by

[1] Dyer, *Ancient Athens*, p. 276.

[2] Mr. Tuckerman; see his *The Greeks of To-day*, ed. 3, p. 81.

the Turks about 1760, to procure mortar for the building of a new mosque. Near the middle of the fifteenth century a traveler saw twenty-one columns. The thirteen columns grouped at the southeast corner are still surmounted by a part of the architrave. In the Middle Ages a stylite hermit made his lofty abode on the isolated piece of architrave over two of the inner columns; the crude masonry of his retreat remained until recently. In the same period a church of St. John was located here.

FIG. 89. — Upper part of a fallen column of the Olympieum.
The man is a modern Greek soldier, an Evzone.

The temple was octastyle, with eight columns across the front and rear, these being set in three rows; and it was dipteral, with two rows of columns along the sides, twenty in each row, counting corner columns twice. Between the antae at each end of the cella two columns probably stood; these included, there were one hundred and four columns in all. The columns are 56.6 feet high and 5.6 feet in diameter at the base. The shafts have twenty-four flutings, and the capitals are beautifully wrought (Fig. 89). The remains do not permit of a reconstruction of the cella in detail, though its dimensions have been ascertained; it measured 248 feet by 62 feet. The roof, by unusual exception, was probably hypaethral, having an opening in the middle to light the cella. Whether or not the pediments and frieze were sculptured, cannot be determined.

Evidently Pausanias was not altogether satisfied with the

great gold and ivory image of Zeus in the cella of the temple. Coins of Athens (Fig. 90) show that it imitated the Zeus of Pheidias at Olympia — small wonder if it fell short! The god was represented as sitting on an elaborate throne. He was nude to the waist and held a Victory in the outstretched right hand, a scepter in the left.

Fig. 90. — Statue of Olympian Zeus; Athenian coin.

The inclosure in which the temple stood was of the time of Hadrian, and Pausanias's account presents nearly all the information we have about it. It is 674 feet long by 423 feet wide, or 2194 feet, not far from Pausanias's four stades (about 2328 feet) in circuit; its area is more than six and a half acres. This space is surrounded by a massive wall of squared blocks, supported on all sides by buttresses, and highest on the southeast corner (Fig. 4). The inclosure was entered on the north by an ornamental gateway in line with the front of the temple; near the west end of the north wall was a semicircular exedra.

Fig. 91. — Fortune of Antioch, by Eutychides (Vatican Museum, Rome).

The "Colonies" in the precinct were statues showing personifications of the cities which dedicated them, doubtless like the Fortune of Antioch, by Eutychides (Fig. 91). Of the statues of Hadrian numerous bases have been found in the area, but the figures have perished. The statue of Isocrates which Pausanias saw must have been the one that was set up by the adopted son of the orator, Aphareus.

The precinct of Cronus and Rhea seems to have extended down to the Ilissus; it can have had only slight connection with the Olympieum. The small foundation just south of the Olympieum may conceivably be within its area. The precinct of Olympian Earth was also extensive, reaching nearly to the Itonian Gate and the statue of the Amazon Antiope (p. 76).

Near the northwest corner of the Olympieum, but having no direct relation with it, is the Arch of Hadrian, which, on account of its inscriptions and its possible connection

FIG. 92. — Arch of Hadrian, from the west.

A view of the arch from the east is given in Figure 23.

with the pre-Persian wall, has already been mentioned (p. 55). The Arch is of Pentelic marble (Fig. 92); it is 59 feet high, 44 feet wide, and 7.5 feet deep. On either side of the central opening, on each face, was set a Corinthian column. The attic, or second story, is composed of pilasters and columns surmounted by an entablature; over the middle columns are pediments. The "windows" of the attic were originally closed by slabs of marble. The structure is somewhat crude in design, but no good reason exists for attributing it to any one but Hadrian.

"After the temple of Olympian Zeus is a statue, near at hand, of Pythian Apollo; and there is also another sanctuary of Apollo surnamed Delphinian." Thucydides tells us (6, 54, 6 f.) of an altar belonging to the sanctuary of Pythian Apollo and dedicated by the grandson of Peisistratus. The inscription "in dim letters," says the historian, reads: "This memorial of his archonship Peisistratus son of Hippias set up in the precinct of Pythian Apollo." Happily a part of the altar has been found near its original place of dedication with the inscription almost intact (Fig. 93). But the letters are cut fairly deep and do not seem especially dim; doubtless they were once bright with the red color, of which traces have been detected on them. This and other discoveries make the situation of the Pythium certain.

The Delphinium, sacred to both Apollo and Artemis, cannot be located so surely, but it must have been near the Pythium, a little farther to the east. Aegeus, the father of Theseus, is said to have founded it. Pausanias relates an entertaining anecdote in connection with this sanctuary. "They say that when the temple was all finished but the roof, Theseus, still unknown to every one, came to the city, wearing a tunic reaching to his feet and his hair becomingly braided. When he got to the temple of the Delphinium, the men who were building the roof asked in sport: 'Well! Why is this girl just ripe for marriage strolling about alone?' Theseus gave no sign of having heard, so the story runs, but unhitched the oxen from the wagon that stood near and hurled them higher than the roof which the men were building." A sturdy hero!

FIG. 93. — Coping of the altar of the Pythium (National Museum, Athens).
The inscription reads: *μνῆμα τόδε ἧς ἀρχῆς Πεισίστ[ρατος Ἱππίου ]υἱὸς | θῆκεν Ἀπόλλωνος Π[υθί]ου ἐν τεμένει.*

In this region we must notice also the precinct of Neleus and Basile and Codrus, made known by an inscription, of 418 B.C., found in 1884 southwest of the Olympieum, where the precinct must have been located. The inscription records provision for the rental and repair of the precinct and the planting, by the lessee, of not fewer than two hundred olive trees, which should be irrigated by the water draining from the Olympieum and from the Dionysium near the theater. This Neleum was evidently between the two gates here opening in the city wall, and near it were a Bath of Isthmonicus, a "public house," and the Palaestra, or wrestling court, of Taureas.

West of the site of the Neleum stands an isolated column, formerly conspicuous, but now surrounded by houses; it may have formed part of a Roman stoa.

"About the place which they call the Gardens and the temple of Aphrodite no story is told; none either concerning the Aphrodite that stands near the temple. Now this is square in form like the herms, and the inscription sets forth that the Heavenly Aphrodite is the eldest of the Fates, as they are called. The statue of the 'Aphrodite in the Gardens' is the work of Alcamenes and is one of the things most worth seeing in Athens." We learn from Pliny (*Nat. hist.* 36, 5) that the Gardens were *extra muros.* They must have lain along the Ilissus south of the Olympieum, probably on the right bank, since Pausanias seems not yet to have crossed the river (p. 174). Not far away was an inclosure to which maidens brought mystic objects from the Acropolis at the time of a sacred festival (p. 338). The district is still noteworthy for its luxuriant vegetation.

The statue of Aphrodite in the Gardens was apparently the cult statue in the temple and distinct from the Aphrodite herm which Pausanias also mentions; though some think otherwise. Lucian asks in one of his dialogues (*Imagines* 4): "Answer this! Have you seen the Aphrodite by Alcamenes in the Gardens at Athens?" "Of course!" is the reply. "I should be the most stupid of men if I had not seen the fairest of the sculptures of Alcamenes." And for his ideal composite statue he says (*Ibid.* 6) he will take from Alcamenes's figure "the cheeks and the look of the face and, besides, the shape of the hands, the graceful wrists, and the delicately tapering fingers." Many attempts have been made to identify the statue with existing copies. The most favored is the well-known Venus Genetrix (Fig. 94), of which numerous replicas exist; but the identification is by no means certain.

Fig. 94. — "Venus Genetrix," supposed to be a copy of the Aphrodite in the Gardens, by Alcamenes (Louvre Museum, Paris).

"And there is a sanctuary of Heracles which is called Cynosarges; those who have read the oracle will know of the 'white dog.' Here are altars of Heracles and Hebe, the daughter of Zeus, who, they think, was the wife of Heracles. An altar has been made also of Alcmene and Iolaus, the latter of whom assisted Heracles in the majority of his labors." Cynosarges, with its grove and gymnasium, was one of the famous parks of Athens. According to Plutarch (*Themistocles* 1), Themistocles, being the son of an alien mother and so forbidden to use the gymnasia within the walls, in order to lessen his disgrace, persuaded a number of high-born youths to join him in Cynosarges. The founder of the Cynic school of philosophy, Antisthenes, lectured here, and in the fourth century B.C. the park was the rendezvous of a group of wits who called themselves "The Sixty." The park was of considerable size, for in it troops were sometimes quartered; the warriors returning from Marathon encamped here. The story to which Pausanias alludes, that Diomus founded the precinct where the "white dog" dropped a victim stolen from the altar, is doubtless an aetiological explanation of the meaning of the word Cynosarges; whether or not it really means "White Dog" is not easy to determine.

Opinions as to the site of Cynosarges are various. We know that it was outside the Diomean Gate (p. 65), but unfortunately the situation of the gate is not known independently. The place last named by Pausanias was the Gardens; the next to be mentioned is the Lyceum, unquestionably east of the city. We should infer, then, that Cynosarges lay between these points. The opening paragraphs of the Pseudo-Platonic *Axiochus* corroborate this view. Socrates is speaking: "As I was going out to Cynosarges and was down by the Ilissus, I heard the voice of some one crying 'Socrates! Socrates!' When I turned around to discover the source of the sound, I saw Cleinias, the son of Axiochus, running to Callirrhoë with Damon, the musician, and Charmides, the son of Glaucon. . . . So I decided to leave the straight road and meet them, that we might get together most easily." Cleinias begs Socrates to come home with him to comfort his father, who is dying, and Socrates accedes to his request. "And as we went on more rapidly by the road along the wall, we found Axiochus by the Itonian Gate, for he lived near the gate by the pillar of the Amazon." Evidently Cleinias, hurrying from his home by the Itonian Gate (p. 65), calls to Socrates just as he has passed Callirrhoë on his way northeastward to Cynosarges. These conditions are best met by a site near the present Zappeion, northeast of the Olympieum (Fig. 86). On the rise of ground to the left were the tombs of the family of Isocrates, whose own grave was surmounted by a pillar thirty cubits high bearing a Siren seven cubits high, the symbol of the orator's eloquence. The tomb of the Spartan Anchiomolius, who died at Phalerum in the attempt to drive out the Peisistratids, was also near, probably to the east, toward the deme of Alopece. But these had perhaps disappeared before the time of Pausanias, for the sanctuary was laid waste in 200 B.C. by Philip V of Macedon.

"The Lyceum takes its name from Lycus, the son of Pandion, and has been considered sacred to Apollo from the beginning up to our time; the god was first called Lycean here. Behind the Lyceum is a monument of Nisus." Pausanias is wrong in his explanation of the name Lyceum, which doubtless comes from Lycian, or "Wolfish," Apollo. The Lyceum was founded in the sixth or fifth century B.C. and restored by Lycurgus in the fourth century. It was large enough to serve for the evolutions of infantry and cavalry. Socrates liked to loiter here, and the spot is still more famous as the scene of the lectures of Aristotle, founder of the Peripatetics, so named from their custom of walking about in the shady park during his discourses. Philip devasted the Lyceum as well as Cynosarges, and more than a century later Sulla cut down the trees to make siege-engines.

Strabo tells us that the sources of the Eridanus, which rose on the side of Lycabettus and flowed through the city, were "outside of the so-called Gate of Diochares near the Lyceum" (p. 65), and again that the Ilissus flowed from the region "beyond Agra and the Lyceum." The first of these statements indicates that the site of the Lyceum was east of the city and not far from Lycabettus; the second justifies the inference that it was across the Ilissus from Agra. It cannot have been far from the present military barracks. A broad road, nearly identical with the modern Cephissia Street, led from the Lyceum to the Diochares Gate. During the civil war of 403 B.C. this road was blocked by the engineer of the oligarchs against the attempts of the democratic party from Peiraeus to assail the gate with siege-engines.

Before crossing the river Pausanias mentions several lesser sanctuaries, the spot whence the north wind, Boreas, carried off the maid Oreithyia, an altar of the Ilissian Muses, and the place "where the Peloponnesians killed Codrus son of Melanthus, the king of Athens;" but the situation of these we know only approximately. Atticus, the friend of Cicero, had a house in this region.

"After you cross the Ilissus there is a place called Agrae, and a temple of Huntress Artemis (Agrotera). Here Artemis is said to have hunted for the first time on coming from Delos; for this reason her statue holds a bow." The point where Pausanias crossed the river must be just south of the place where we have located the Lyceum, and Agrae, or Agra, included an extensive district beside the left bank of the stream. The temple of Huntress Artemis was a famous one; here was made the annual sacrifice of five hundred she-goats in memory of the battle of Marathon, these being in lieu of the single sacrifice, vowed by the Athenians, of as many goats as were slain of their foes, since the number proved too great for the vow to be paid literally. The annual sacrifice was still in vogue in the first century after Christ, as we learn from Plutarch.

Another important sanctuary in Agrae was that of Demeter, where the lesser mysteries were celebrated every spring, before the greater mysteries at Eleusis. Probably the sanctuary had a temple, but none is mentioned. Somewhere in Agrae there was also a temple of Eileithyia.

"Not equally attractive to hear about but wonderful to behold is a Stadium of white marble. Its size may be realized best in this way: a mountain beginning above the Ilissus in crescent-shape runs straight down in two spurs to the bank of the river. This structure was built by the Athenian Herodes, and in its construction most of the marble of his quarries on Pentelicus was exhausted."

The ground for the Stadium was donated by a certain Deinias, and the Stadium was laid out under the direction of the orator Lycurgus. As Pausanias notes, the contour of the land was favorable for the purpose, and an artificial embankment was necessary only at the rounded end; but the excavation was extensive and an inscription is extant recording the thanks of the state to a man named Eudemus for furnishing a thousand oxen "for the making of the Stadium and the Panathenaic theater." This early Stadium had no seats, and the spectators were ranged along the sloping banks, as always at Olympia. About 140 A.D. Herodes Atticus, who had received a crown at the Great Panathenaea, publicly promised that before the next festival the Stadium should be seated in white marble. He kept his word, "and produced a work," says Philostratus (*Vit. soph.* 2, 1, 5), "beyond all the wonders; no theater vies with it."

The total length of the Stadium (Fig. 95) was about 770 feet; the space inclosed was about a hundred feet shorter and 109 feet wide, but the course proper was 600 Greek feet long and was marked by four double herms, which have been recovered; two of them have been reërected in the Stadium (Fig. 96). A marble parapet separated the course from the spectators, of whom more than 50,000 could be seated. Behind this parapet ran a broad corridor; another ran along inside of the parapet at the top; and a third divided the fifty or more zones of seats horizontally at about the middle of the slope. Vertically the seats were separated into sections by stairways, twelve on each of the straight sides and seven on the curved end. The main

FIG. 95. — Stadium, reconstructed.

entrance appears to have been adorned with a stoa, the rear of the curved end by another. At the southern extremity of the curve a tunnel enters from the rear. This may have been made in the time of Hadrian to admit the wild beasts for the emperor's "hunts," in one of which a

FIG. 96. — View across the Stadium, showing herms and the tunnel.

thousand animals were slain. A metal paling on the top of the lower parapet may date from the same period.

A modern Herodes has been found in the person of the late M. Averoff, of Alexandria, through whose bequest the Stadium has been magnificently reseated in Pentelic marble. The ancient design of Herodes, as revealed by the excavations made in 1869–1870 at the expense of King George, has been followed as closely as possible, and the Stadium is again worthy of Philostratus's praise. The new structure is devoted to modern "Olympic games" and to various large assemblages.

Herodes is said to have been buried "in the Stadium;" some have conjectured, without much reason, that the ruins on the hill to the east of the Stadium belong to his tomb. The higher hill to the west is probably the ancient Ardettus, earlier called Helicon; on its summit are ruins, perhaps of the temple of Fortune erected by Herodes.

A little west of Ardettus is the ruined foundation of a small temple. Much of the building was standing and used as the church of "Our Lady of the Rock" until the end of the eighteenth century, when the Turks destroyed it. Fortunately it had been visited a little earlier by Stuart and Revett (p. 4), and we know it from their drawings (Fig. 97). The temple was small and of the Ionic order, of

FIG. 97.—Ionic temple on the Ilissus. From a drawing by Stuart and Revett.

exceeding delicacy and perfection. We do not know to what divinity it was originally dedicated.

Various other ruins are found in this vicinity. Quite recently a rude shrine of the god Pan was discovered in this vicinity, near the church of St. Photini, and has been linked by the finder with the idyllic scene at the beginning of Plato's *Phaedrus*. Especially noteworthy is a large foundation some distance west of the Ionic temple; this some have associated with the gymnasium of Cynosarges (but see p. 172). In front of the Stadium the Ilissus is now crossed by a bridge which has replaced one built by Herodes Atticus.

Before leaving Southeast Athens we must notice also various Roman buildings of which considerable ruins are left. Among these are baths just north of the Olympieum, and a villa across the modern street from the baths. Larger baths lay in front of the Zappeion, and other Roman buildings in the palace gardens. Several of these have interesting mosaic floors.

## CHAPTER VII

### The South Slope of the Acropolis

We again start from the Prytaneum, whence we set out to visit Southeast Athens (p. 159). "Now a street leads from the Prytaneum called Tripods. The place gets its name from certain temples of suitable size for the purpose, on which stand tripods. These are of bronze and include works of art well worthy of note; for here is a Satyr in which Praxiteles is said to have taken much pride." At the southeast foot of the Acropolis the course of this street is definitely determined by the well-preserved choregic Monument of Lysicrates and the foundations of several more of these diminutive "temples." On the east side of the architrave of the monument is the dedicatory inscription, which undoubtedly faced the street called Tripods. The earlier course from the Prytaneum is uncertain, though it must have followed close to the foot of the Acropolis; and from the Monument of Lysicrates it turned west to the theater. The street was a famous one, and, at least in the time of Demetrius of Phalerum, it was a favorite lounging place.

The Monument of Lysicrates (Fig. 98) was designed to support the tripod which he dedicated in honor of his victory in 335/4 B.C., with a dithyrambic chorus. The inscription reads: "Lysicrates son of Lysitheides of Cicynna was choregus; the tribe Acamantis won with a chorus of boys; Theon played the flute; Lysiades the Athenian taught the chorus; Evaenetus was archon."

This little building is not only the oldest specimen in Athens of the Corinthian order of architecture, but also among the most charming examples of Greek art. It is composed of a podium of poros about 13 feet high and 9.5 feet square, with a cornice of Hymettian marble; and on

FIG. 98. — Choregic Monument of Lysicrates.

this is the round shrine of Pentelic marble about 20 feet high and a little more than 7 feet in diameter. Upon three steps, the upper one modeled, stand six fluted columns, whose intercolumniations are closed by curved marble slabs, making the interior inaccessible; several of the slabs now in place are restorations. Above the columns are the inscribed architrave and sculptured frieze, surmounted by a cornice and conical roof. All the portion above the columns except the cornice is cut from a single block of marble, including the acanthus scrolls and the three-armed finial, which bore the tripod. The frieze, 10 inches high, depicts the punishment of the pirates who attempted to do violence to Dionysus and who are being turned into dolphins (Fig. 99); possibly this was the theme sung by Lysicrates's chorus. The story is told in the Homeric hymn to Dionysus, and was a familiar theme in poetry.

Fig. 99. — Section of the frieze of the Monument of Lysicrates, portraying the pirates transformed into dolphins by Dionysus.

The Monument of Lysicrates was preserved to modern times by being built into a Capuchin convent, burned in 1821. It is now popularly called the "Lantern of Diogenes." Formerly this name was given a similar monument, of which only a portion of the base remains, and the monument before us was called the "Lantern of Demosthenes," the foolish tale being added that Demosthenes used it for his study. Lord Byron is said to have written in the building, one side of which then opened into the convent (Fig. 100).

A little to the north are the fragmentary foundations of two similar structures, one near the Monument of Lysicrates and in the open, another in the cellar of a house. Remains of two others have been found farther west, near the theater.

The legs of the tripods on these diminutive shrines seem to have inclosed the statues of which Pausanias speaks. The Satyr of Praxiteles cannot surely be identified with existing copies. It may be the same as one called by Pliny (*Nat. hist.* 34, 69) the Periboëtus, or Renowned. Replicas

Fig. 100.—Monument of Lysicrates built into the "Hospitium of the Capuchins." From a drawing by Stuart and Revett.

of a superb Praxitelean Satyr are found in various European museums. The copy in the Capitoline Museum at Rome is the most familiar to us through Hawthorne's *Marble Faun* (Fig. 101); possibly it reproduces the type here represented. A torso even more exquisite is in the Louvre. In this connection Pausanias repeats an anecdote: "They say that Phryne once asked Praxiteles what was his finest work. He agreed, they say, to give it to her, but refused to state his choice; whereupon Phryne had one of her servants run in and tell Praxiteles that his studio was on fire and the majority of his works had perished, but not all. Praxiteles started at once to run from the door, crying that nothing was left for all his toil if the flames had reached the Satyr and the Eros. Phryne bade him stay and be of good cheer; that no misfortune had happened, but that this was a ruse to make him confess what were his best works. So Phryne chose the Eros."

FIG. 101. — Satyr of Praxiteles — the "Marble Faun" (Capitoline Museum, Rome).

About a block east of the Monument of Lysicrates in front of a church of St. Catherine are columns and other remains which, as recent excavations have shown, belong to an Ionic stoa of Roman times.

Of the next site which Pausanias mentions we have no definite knowledge. "In the temple near by is a youthful Satyr who is giving a drink to Dionysus; the Eros and Dionysus standing in the same place are the work of Thymilus." Various conjectures have been made as to these

FIG. 102. — Dionysus and Satyr, by Praxiteles, restored.

statues. The most plausible for the first group is the union of two familiar types (Fig. 102), and the view that these figures too were the work of Praxiteles.

Following the street of Tripods to the west, we come to the precinct of Dionysus (Fig. 103) and the great Dionysiac theater. "The oldest sanctuary of Dionysus is near the theater; in the inclosure are two temples and two statues of Dionysus, the Eleutherian and the one that Alcamenes made of ivory and gold. Here too are paintings: Dionysus conducting Hephaestus up to heaven — Now the Greeks

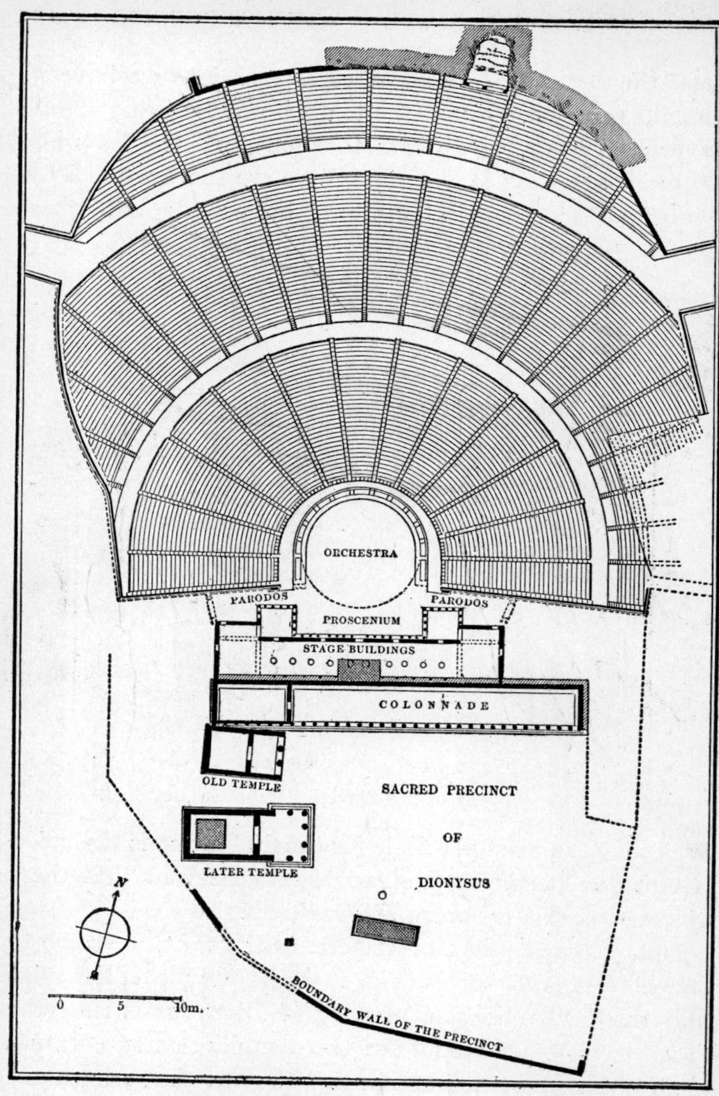


FIG. 103. — Plan of the precinct of Dionysus, and the Dionysiac theater, restored.

say also that Hera cast Hephaestus out at his birth, and that in revenge he sent her as a gift a chair of gold with invisible bonds, and when she sat down in it she was caught; no one else of the gods could prevail on Hephaestus, but Dionysus, who had exchanged many pledges with him, got him drunk and led him back to heaven [Fig. 104] —

FIG. 104. — Hephaestus conducted back to Olympus by Dionysus; vase painting.

Well, this painting is there, and Pentheus and Lycurgus paying the penalty for their insolence to Dionysus; and also Ariadne asleep, with Theseus setting sail and Dionysus coming to steal her away" [Fig. 105].

The boundary wall of the Dionysium can in part be traced, and the foundations of the two temples are still extant (Fig. 106). The foundation of the older temple crowds against the west end of the stoa of the theater. A part of the north wall and small portions of the rear and cross-walls, together with a few fragments of the columns, frieze, and pediment, are all that remain. The material of the foundation, Acropolis and Kará limestones, and the Z-shaped cramps (p. 10) with which the blocks are united, are indicative of construction before the Persian Wars, perhaps in the time of Peisistratus. We have seen that the

FIG. 105 A. — Theseus deserting Ariadne; Pompeian wall painting.

The theme of the picture described by Pausanias is divided into two parts in the Pompeian wall paintings given in this and the accompanying figure.

Dionysium in the Marshes (p. 86) is of a still earlier date; but this had perished and had been covered up before the days of Pausanias; so his statement that here was the oldest precinct of Dionysus was correct for his time.

This temple is to be restored with two columns between pilasters (distyle in antis). It had a square cella and a porch, and was about 44 feet long by 26 feet wide. In the cella must have stood the ancient xoanon, or wooden statue, of Dionysus, which was brought from Eleutherae (p. 81).

A few yards to the south is the second temple; nothing but the foundation, of breccia, is left. This building prob-

FIG. 105 B. — Dionysus coming to the rescue of Ariadne; Pompeian wall painting.

ably dates from the end of the fifth century B.C., and may be the offering of the famous general Nicias, who died in the ill-starred expedition to Sicily in 413 B.C. The temple was about 72 feet long by 30 feet wide; its open portico in front was a little wider than the rest of the temple and surrounded on three sides by columns and steps. The base of the gold and ivory statue by Alcamenes is still partly preserved. A few yards southeast of the temple is the foundation of what appears to have been a large altar.

We do not know where the pictures mentioned by Pausanias were painted. They may have been in the new

FIG. 106. — Foundations of the temples of Dionysus.

The foundation of the earlier temple is in the foreground; that of the later temple is a little beyond it.

temple; or they may have been on the rear wall of the long stoa back of the theater.

Pausanias barely mentions the theater; to him it was merely one of scores with which he was familiar, but to us it is of the deepest interest from its association with the great Attic dramatists. The literary evidence respecting it is so scanty, and time has dealt so harshly with the structure itself, that its tangled history is difficult to unravel, and many questions are still in dispute; a brief sketch must therefore assume much that is not fully settled. Three main periods are reasonably distinct; besides these are various minor periods of repair or alteration. The principal epochs are: (1) the earliest theater of the late sixth or beginning of the fifth century B.C., to which somewhat later was added a stone theatron, or auditorium;

(2) the stone theater of Lycurgus near the end of the fourth century, which was partially rebuilt a generation or so later, that is, in Hellenistic times; (3) the transformation of the Greek into a Roman theater, probably first in the time of Nero and afterwards in the time of Hadrian and later, including the rebuilding of the stage by a certain Phaedrus in the third or fourth century after Christ.

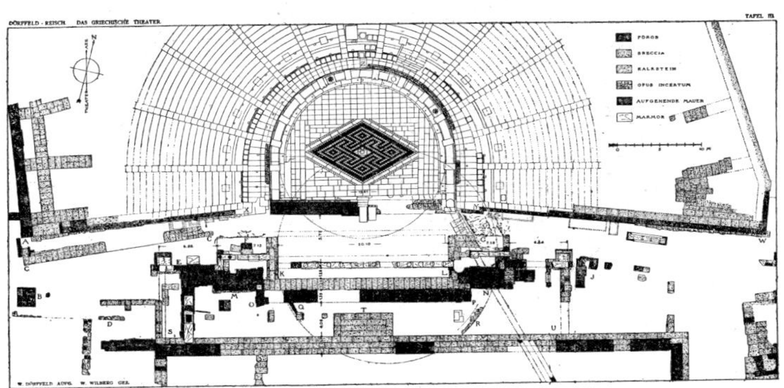


FIG. 107. — Scene-buildings and orchestra of the Dionysiac theater.

The larger circle is that of the orchestra of the fifth century; the only portions of this orchestra remaining are the bits of wall marked *Q* and *R* in the drawing, and the bedding in the rock in the east parodos.

At what date the first theater was built we do not know. As early as 534 B.C. Thespis brought out the first tragedy at the City Dionysia, perhaps in this place. Unfortunately only a fragment of the earliest theater is left. Two pieces of curved wall, and a cutting in the rock in the east entrance (Fig. 107), enable us to reconstruct the circle of the orchestra, which was about 79 feet in diameter. No traces of stage-buildings survive. We recall that plays were first performed in front of the booth or tent (skené, scaena) which served as green room, and we may assume that in the early theater nothing more substantial than a wooden building was constructed for this purpose. The situation of the orchestra, or dancing-floor, was designedly chosen near the front of the old temple of Dionysus, in whose honor the plays were produced. The adjacent slope of the Acropolis made a convenient place for the spectators, who at first stood or sat on the ground; later they sat on wooden seats. Our extant literature does not distinguish these periods, but we cannot be far astray.

In the seventieth Olympiad (500–497 B.C.), during a dramatic contest of Choerilus, Pratinas, and Aeschylus, the wooden scaffolding of the seats is said to have collapsed, and thereafter the first stone theater is said to have been built. Whether this accident took place by the Old Orchestra of the Agora, or here on the side of the Acropolis, is a moot point. If the latter, as on the whole seems more likely, the construction then undertaken must have been the erection of a stone auditorium, or theatron (view-place) proper, in place of what had previously been in use. Notwithstanding the tradition as to the accident, some scholars deny the existence of a stone theatron in this period; but their contention fails to account for surviving portions of supporting walls lying in the parodoi, or entrances, of the present theater, an inscribed block apparently coming from one of the seats, and some few stones of a foundation in the upper part of the auditorium. At any rate, in this simple theater were enacted most of the plays of Aeschylus, Sophocles, Euripides, Aristophanes, and their contemporaries.

The theater is named among the works "half-done" which Lycurgus is said to have completed. The excavation for the building seems to have been in progress, or just finished, about 330 B.C. (p. 39), and as Lycurgus died in 325 B.C., the theater must have been built near the end of his life. His work amounted to a complete reconstruction (Fig. 108). A new orchestra was laid out farther north than the old one, but circular, as before, and about 64 feet in diameter. Its surface was of beaten earth, unpaved, and in the center was the thymele, or altar of Dionysus.

FIG. 108. — Theater and precinct of Dionysus, as seen from the Acropolis.

Running around the orchestra and issuing at the southeast corner was a drain, crossed by slabs opposite the stairways of the auditorium.

The auditorium was horseshoe-shaped. At the top the rock was scarped down to receive the upper seats; the rest of the circuit was surrounded by massive walls of poros and breccia; on the west side, where the height was greatest, were double walls connected and strengthened by buttresses and cross-walls.

The seats were made of poros and were laid out in three

zones, the two lower zones containing each about thirty-two rows, the highest zone probably fourteen. The zones were separated horizontally by belts (diazomata), or aisles. The upper aisle served also as a section of a roadway along the slope; the situation of the central aisle is not certain. About the orchestra and a little above it is another aisle widened at the ends so as to accommodate better the incoming or outgoing crowds.

In each of the three zones the seats were divided vertically by stairways into wedge-shaped sections. The extant seats belong to the lower zone, which had thirteen wedges and fourteen stairways, two stairways adjoining the southern walls. Probably the upper zones had two wedges corresponding with each single wedge below, such being the rule recorded by Vitruvius. The profile of the seats shows a depression along the back and a hollow beneath the front edge (Fig. 109); this device afforded room for the feet of the spectators and decreased the total height of the theater.

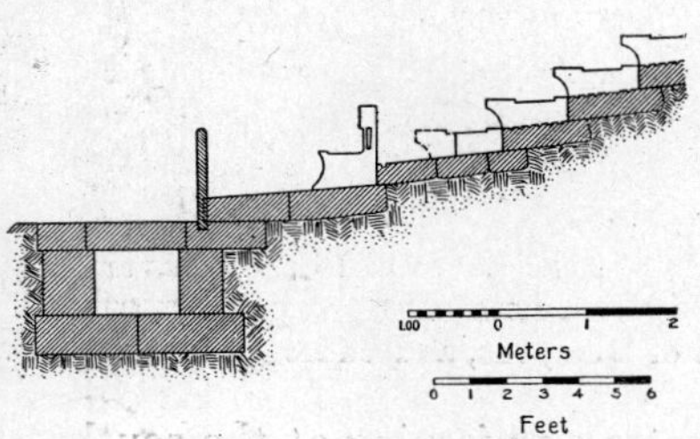


FIG. 109. — Section through canal, corridor, and staircase of the theater.

The seats of the front row, sixty-seven in all, were of Pentelic marble and had curved backs (Fig. 110). These were the seats of honor for local and foreign dignitaries who had been granted right of proedria, or front-sittings. In later times the titles of priests and officers who had a claim to seats were inscribed below the front edge, earlier titles sometimes being erased; whether carved or painted inscriptions were used in the time of Lycurgus, we cannot tell. The central throne (Fig. 111)

FIG. 110. — Dionysiac theater, from the east.

In the background, at the left, is the Hill of the Muses, surmounted by the monument of Philopappus.

bears the inscription "Of the priest of Dionysus Eleuthereus." This seat is larger than the rest and has arms and carved legs which end in lion's paws. Its back is adorned with the figures of two Satyrs in low relief; on the outside of each arm is a winged youth setting down a gamecock; and the band below the seat has an heraldic design of Orientals fighting with winged lions. Sockets in the floor indicate that this seat was covered by an awning.

FIG. 111. — Seat of honor for the priest of Dionysus Eleuthereus.

At either side are portions of other seats of honor. Behind these are seats inserted in later times, after having been removed from their regular places in the front row. The inscribed block at the left of the seats last mentioned is the base of a statue of Hadrian.

If we allow about sixteen inches for each spectator, the entire capacity of the auditorium may be estimated at 14,000. Certain marks on the edges of the seats (about 13.5 inches apart) have led some scholars, however, to estimate the total capacity at 17,000; and Plato tells us (*Sympos.* 4, 175E) that the skill of Agathon was admired by "more than 30,000 witnesses," apparently referring to the crowd that listened to one of Agathon's plays. The occupant of any seat might, of course, supply a cushion, if he wished.

On the side of the orchestra opposite the auditorium was the scene-building (skené) separated from the theatron by parodoi, or side passages (Fig. 103). Little more of the scene-building than the foundations, mostly of breccia and poros, survive, and their restoration involves a score of problems for which as yet no solution has been generally accepted. This is not the place even to summarize the discussion which has raged for a generation between the adherents of the old theory, who maintain that the plays of the best period were acted on a stage 10 or 12 feet in height, and those who think that the actors performed in front of a proscenium and on a level with the chorus in the orchestra. Suffice it here to express agreement with the view that in this period the theater of Dionysus had no stage; no one doubts that there was a stage in some Greek theaters in Asia Minor, and in all Roman theaters.

The façade of the scene-building seems to have been a wall some 12 or 13 feet high, either closely fronted by a row of columns, or with this colonnade a few feet in advance of the wall. This was the proscenium; though perhaps the proscenium proper was constructed of wood, in front of the colonnade, in different forms to meet the demands of the individual plays. Flanking the proscenium were the projecting parascenia, or wings. These were similarly supplied with columns, a few of which remain in situ in a later reconstruction (p. 198). The length of the proscenium was about 66 feet; the parascenia were about 23 feet wide. The intercolumniations of the columns might, upon occasion, be closed with wooden panels. The façade was pierced by three doors, which led into the large room, or rooms, of the scene-building (152.5 by 21 feet), the successor, in stone, of the original wooden booth. The flat roof of this building, flush with the cornice over the front columns, served as a place for the appearance of gods (theologeion), if the play demanded the representation of gods. A heavy base of stone at the back of the central room is unexplained; it may have supported certain machinery, or possibly only a flight of steps.

Behind the scene-building, and forming a part of it, was a stoa nearly 200 feet long, fronted by a Doric colonnade. Its west end, where it abutted on the old temple, was probably made into a closed room (Fig. 103). This stoa is referred to by Vitruvius as one of the shelters for spectators in time of storm (p. 213)

In Hellenistic times only slight changes seem to have been made in the theater; and these few were mainly in the scene-building. One view is that the first stone proscenium was made in this period, the former one being of wood. At any rate, the projection of the parascenia was reduced, and possibly the central colonnade between the parascenia was advanced toward the orchestra.

The history of the theater for several centuries after this is almost a blank. Apparently in the time of Nero considerable reconstruction was undertaken. The orchestra, which was no longer needed for the evolutions of a chorus, was reduced to a nearly semicircular form by building a regular Roman stage between the inner corners of the parodoi (Fig. 107). The new stage was probably about five feet high and was accessible from the parodoi and from the orchestra by steps. The scene-building was also rebuilt to form a high background, which was adorned with engaged columns, arches, and statuary, and the interior was rearranged to meet the new conditions.

About this time, too, the marble paving of the orchestra was laid, and a barrier was erected about it to protect the spectators when gladiatorial combats were presented. Indeed, before the barrier was made, wounded gladiators — Shade of Aeschylus! — are said to have stained with their blood the robes of the priest of Dionysus, sitting on his throne of honor.

The reign of Hadrian marks another period of lesser alterations, mainly in the auditorium. An imperial box was built blocking the lower end of the sixth stairway from the east, and near the bottom of each of the lower wedges a statue of the emperor was erected; the inscribed bases of several of these still exist (one is visible in Fig. 111). The front edge of the lowest row of regular seats was hewn off and a row of wooden seats of honor built behind the marble chairs (*cf.* Fig. 109). Of the latter, those that were removed to make room for the emperor's box, and, then or later, several other marble chairs of different design, were set up in various places throughout the lower wedges.

FIG. 112. — Portion of the front of the stage of Phaedrus.

At the end of the third or beginning of the fourth century of the Christian era (the exact date is not known) a final reconstruction was given to the stage by a certain Phaedrus (Fig. 112), whose dedicatory inscription is cut on the top step of the portion remaining. The limping elegiac couplet reads: "For thee, Delighter in the orgy, Phaedrus son of Zoïlus, ruler of life-giving Attica, wrought this beautiful platform of the theater." The tasteless patchwork is only interesting from the misfit Sileni, which Phaedrus added from some other building, and the reliefs, which may have belonged to the stage of Nero. The first relief to the left has been thought to portray the birth of Dionysus; the second, a rural sacrifice to the god; the third and fourth his welcome to the Athenian theater, whose situation is suggested by the columns of the Parthenon which peep over the edge of the Acropolis (p. 58, Fig. 25). The reliefs have been cut down several inches at the top to fit the "beautiful platform" of Phaedrus.

The theater was adorned from time to time with statues of famous men. "The Athenians," says Pausanias, "have in the theater images of poets of tragedy and of comedy, the majority being of poets of minor importance; for of comic poets who came to prominence none was there except Menander. Of the famous poets of tragedy, there are statues of Euripides and Sophocles. . . . The image of Aeschylus was made, I think, long after his death and long after the painting of the Battle at Marathon" (p. 127). The inscribed bases of the statues of Menander and Aeschylus have been found. From other sources we learn of several other statues, such as those of Philemon and Astydamas; a part of the base of the statue of the latter is in situ at the corner of the west parodos. In the parodoi were statues of Miltiades and Themistocles, each with a captured Persian.

As we entered the precinct of Dionysus from the street of Tripods, we passed a building of which Pausanias writes: "Near the sanctuary of Dionysus and the theater is a building said to have been made in imitation of the tent of Xerxes; this is the second building, for the first was burned by the Roman general Sulla, when he captured Athens" (p. 43). This is the Odeum of Pericles, which, we are told, was originally constructed for the musical contests of the great Panathenaic festival; it is often mentioned as the Odeum of Pericles. Vitruvius tells us that it was roofed by Themistocles, but probably he is wrong. Appian affirms that it was burned by Aristion, not Sulla; it was rebuilt by Ariobarzanes. Plutarch describes it (*Pericles* 13) as "many seated and many pillared" and says that Cratinus, the comic poet, gibed Pericles for having a head shaped like the Odeum. Whether or not it was meant to imitate the tent of Xerxes, the Odeum was clearly a round building, of considerable size, with a conical roof.

Vitruvius helps us to the more precise identification of the site of the Odeum by saying (5, 9, 1) that it was "on the left as one goes out from the theater," evidently as one goes out toward the east. It was higher than the orchestra of the theater, for the conspirators planning the mutilation of the herms, before the Sicilian Expedition, were seen to descend from it to the orchestra. This area east of the theater has not been excavated, and our only information regarding the Odeum is from literary sources.

"Upon the South Wall, as it is called, of the Acropolis, facing the theater, is a gilded head of the Gorgon Medusa, with an aegis about it." This head was the gift of Antiochus Epiphanes. Just below where the head was fastened stand two isolated Corinthian columns of late date (Fig. 113). These once bore tripods and were doubtless set up in honor of choregic victories.

Below these columns, "At the summit of the theater is a cave in the rocks beneath the Acropolis; upon this is also a tripod. In [On?] it are Apollo and Artemis slaying the children of Niobe." This cave is about 30 feet deep. It is now dedicated to the Virgin of the Golden Cave (Panagia Chrysospiliotissa), and is furnished with an icon and a light, whose glimmer is conspicuous from below by night (Fig. 113). The façade which adorned the front when Pausanias saw it was intact in the time of the English travelers

FIG. 113. — Choregic columns and the cave of Thrasyllus as one looks up from the theater.

Stuart and Revett (p. 4); it was destroyed during the Greek revolution. On Stuart and Revett's drawings and studies we are chiefly dependent for our knowledge of its construction (Fig. 114); only a few broken stones now remain. The façade was about 25 feet wide and 22.3 feet high. Above two steps rose three Doric pilasters, which supported an architrave, a frieze adorned with garlands, and a cornice, all of white marble. On these rested an attic of bluish marble, consisting of two bases with a flight of three steps between; the top step was once surmounted by a marble statue of Dionysus which is now in the British Museum.

Fragments of the dedicatory inscriptions have been found. On the architrave was inscribed: "Thrasyllus,

FIG. 114.—Monument of Thrasyllus at the middle of the eighteenth century. From a drawing by Stuart and Revett.

the Decelean, dedicated this, having won as choregus with the men of the tribe Hippothoöntis; Evius the Chalcidian played the flute; Neaechmus was archon; Carcidamus the Sotian trained the chorus." On the western base of the attic was inscribed: "The people gave the chorus; Pytharatus was archon; Thrasycles son of Thrasyllus the Decelean was referee of the contest; the tribe Hippothoöntis won the victory of boys; Theon the Theban played the flute; Pronomus the Theban trained the chorus." On the eastern base was an inscription of which the first half was identical with the last, and the remainder read: "The tribe Pandionis won the victory of men; Nicocles the Ambraciote played the flute; Lysippus the Arcadian trained the chorus." The names of the archons show that the first inscription was cut in 320/319 B.C.; the others, in 271/270 B.C., or forty-nine years later. Evidently Thrasyllus's thrifty son used his father's choregic monument to record his own victories. The heavy attic, not quite centered over the substructure, must have been added by Thrasycles; in an original construction Hymettian marble was rarely placed over Pentelic. Each of the bases may have borne one of his tripods. Thrasycles may have substituted the statue for the tripod, or placed it under the tripod, of his father. Pausanias's language leaves it uncertain whether the slaying of the Niobids was a group of statues within the cave, or a relief on a tripod. On the scarping was the silvered tripod of Aeschraeus, and somewhere near was a tripod of the orator Andocides.

Above the cave on the brink of the rock still lies a sun-dial, which is probably the same as one mentioned by an anonymous writer of the Middle Ages.

A hundred paces or so west of the cave are slight remains which may mark the position of the tomb of Calos, or Talos; of this Pausanias says: "As you go from the theater to the Acropolis at Athens, Calos is buried." Calos, the story ran, was the nephew of Daedalus, who threw him from the Acropolis in jealousy over the inventions of Calos, the saw, compasses, and the potter's wheel. Since Pausanias next mentions the Asclepieum, the tomb of Calos must have been between that precinct and the theater, of course

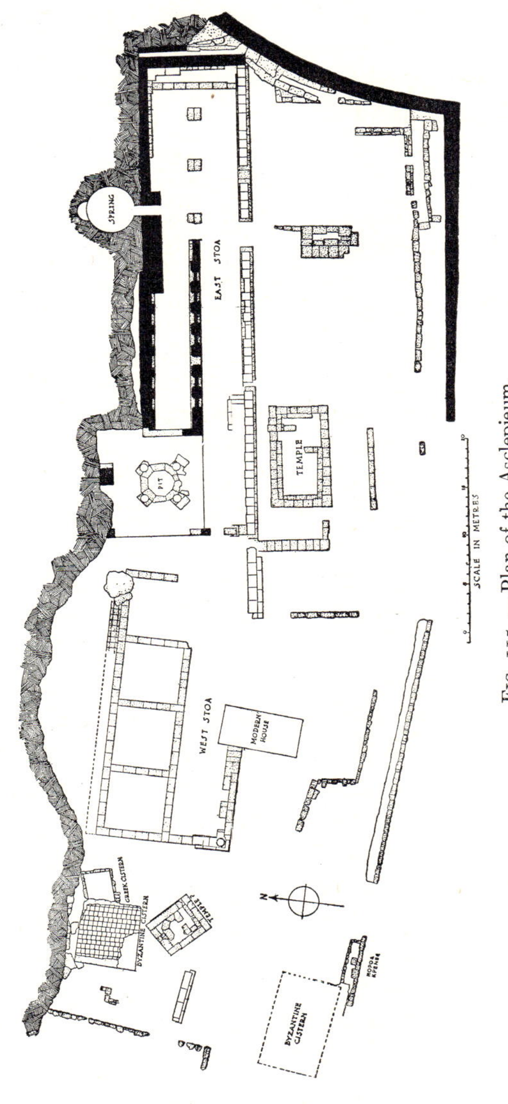


FIG. 115.—Plan of the Asclepieum.

close to the foot of the hill. A sanctuary of Perdix, Calos's mother, was near the grave.

We leave the theater by the ramp leading down between walls of breccia from the upper aisle of the auditorium. Pausanias merely says: "The sanctuary of Asclepius is worth seeing for the statues which have been made of the god and his sons, and for its paintings. A spring also is in it. . . . And here among other things a Sauromatian cuirass is dedicated; one who sees it will say that the Barbarians are no less clever at the arts than the Greeks." This would guide us correctly to the Asclepieum, even without the reference of Marinus (*Vita Procli* 29) to the proximity of the house of Proclus both "to the Asclepieum and to the theater of Dionysus." This was the Asclepieum "in the city," as distinguished from the one "in Peiraeus" (p. 401). The excavations, which commenced in 1876, have revealed the entire precinct (Fig. 115).

Limited by the rock of the Acropolis and the theater on the north and east respectively, the boundaries of the precinct on the south and west were marked by polygonal walls, though the original extent to the west is not now certain. An inscription of the second half of the fifth century B.C. is still in situ toward the end of the south wall, reading: "boundary of the spring." This seems to indicate an older occupation of the site, for we know from other inscriptions that the worship of Asclepius and Health was established here in 420 B.C., having been brought from Epidaurus. If one of these inscriptions is interpreted rightly, the new cult made its way at first against opposition and was maintained at the private expense of the founder, a certain Telemachus. The earliest literary reference to the precinct is in the *Plutus* of Aristophanes, which was first brought out in 408 B.C.

FIG. 116. — East end of the Asclepieum.

At the left are the remains of the east stoa; in the foreground the foundation of the temple. In the rear is the wall of the theater.

The most conspicuous building of the Asclepieum is the east stoa (Figs. 116, 117, 118), which evidently served as a "dormitory" for patients of the god of healing. This building was about 162 feet long by 32 feet deep, and

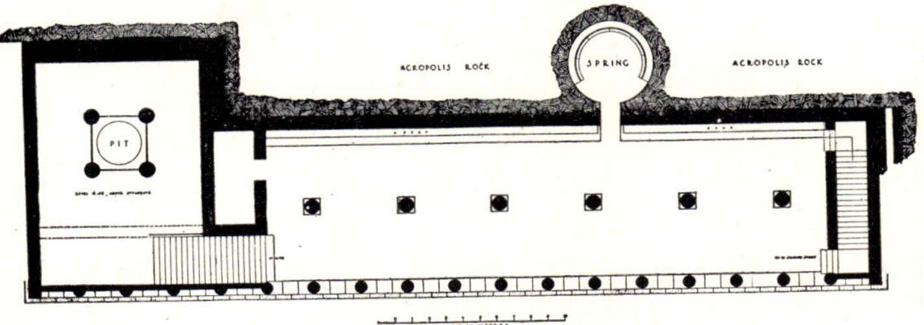


FIG. 117. — Plan of the east stoa of the Asclepieum, restored.

two stories high. It had a pent roof, with a hip at each end; the cuttings for the upper edge of the roof are visible in the rock at the back.

The foundation for the lower colonnade in front (Fig. 116) is of poros and breccia, and on this rests the stylobate, of Hymettian marble like the columns. The columns were of the Doric order, fluted, and seventeen in number between

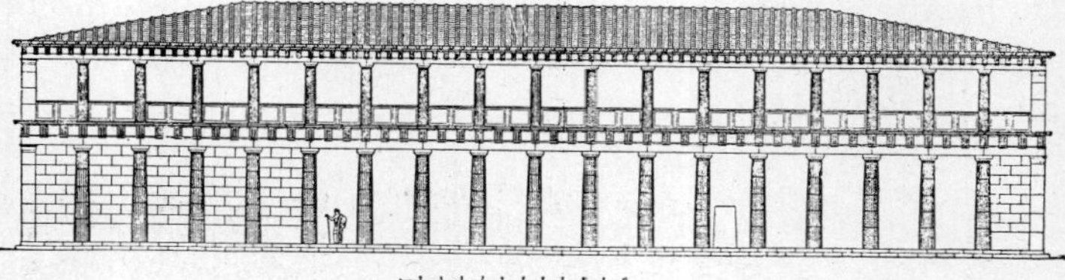

FIG. 118.—South elevation of the east stoa of the Asclepieum, restored.

antae; the first five intercolumniations to the west and the first one to the east were closed. The cornice was of Pentelic marble. Through the center of the stoa ran a row of six columns, probably Ionic. The back wall, built against the rock, was of poros, with a sort of wainscoting of Hymettian marble. At the west end the back wall comes forward a little beyond the line of the central columns, and then continues to the end of the stoa. In the space left at the southwest corner, behind the closed columns, rose the stairway to a square room about fifteen feet higher than the stylobate. In the center of this room was a pit, perhaps for the sacred serpents of the god. The pit is lined with a good polygonal wall, and about its octagonal mouth are the bases of four columns (Fig. 119).

FIG. 119.—Pit in the east stoa.

The front colonnade of the second story was of smaller Doric columns of Hymettian marble; the cornice was of Pentelic. Between the columns probably was a balustrade. This story was divided by partitions or by a row of columns. Its floor was higher than that of the square room.

The east end of the lower story was cut off by a wall directly behind the first column; in the little room so formed

FIG. 120. — East stoa of the Asclepieum, from the east.

The columns at the left belong to a reconstruction. At the right is the door into the spring-house.

was probably a stairway to the second floor; a small store-room, or possibly another stairway, was at the other end of the stoa. In the back wall a doorway opens into the rock-vaulted chamber of the spring (Fig. 120). This spring still affords a scanty stream of clear but brackish water rising at the middle of the west side, running about the chamber, and issuing from a drain through the doorway;

P

a parapet of slabs stands before the stream. The chamber is now used as a shrine sacred to the Virgin (Fig. 121).

The material and workmanship of the orginal stoa point to the fourth century B.C. as its date; but it has undergone extensive reconstructions. The lower colonnade was replaced in Hellenistic or Roman times by slender columns, which were more closely spaced, and unfluted for the lower third of their height (Fig. 120). In the Byzantine period the back wall was rebuilt, the entrance to the spring arched, and a long room with a barrel vault built toward the west end between the back wall and the curtained piers that replaced the central row of columns.

FIG. 121. — Modern shrine in the cave of the spring of the Asclepieum.

In front of the west end of the stoa lies the foundation (Fig. 116) of a temple of Asclepius. The temple was repeatedly rebuilt, and the present ruins seem to date from Hellenistic or Roman times. It was probably a tetrastyle Doric building, some 35 by 20 feet in dimensions. Halfway between the temple and the east wall of the precinct is a large foundation, which apparently belongs to the great altar mentioned frequently in inscriptions.

West of these buildings, and on a level about seven feet higher, is a second stoa approximately 92 feet long and 46 feet wide (*cf.* Fig. 115). The southern half of this building was a portico fronted by twelve Ionic columns. At the rear were four nearly square rooms, which had floors of pebble mosaic. This stoa seems to have been built much later than the other. It is usually thought to have been for the use of priests, but this is purely conjectural; it may have been a supplementary dormitory.

Between the second stoa and the west boundary wall are foundations of two small buildings in the form of temples but facing respectively toward the southeast and south. Their purpose and date are not yet known. At either side of these are two immense vaulted cisterns of mediaeval times; near one of them an old spring with polygonal walls.

An interesting inscription of the first century B.C. tells, with much legal repetition, how a certain priest, Diocles by name, reported to the assembly that "the doors of what was the former entrance into the sanctuary were in ruins, likewise the back roof of the propylum, and, besides, the temple of the old establishment of Asclepius and Health," and how Diocles was granted permission to repair them at his own expense. The inscription also uses for the buildings mentioned the terms, "the ancient propylum," "the temple opposite the entrance," and "the ancient temple." On this inscription the theory has been based that the precinct had two entrances; this seems logical. The further inference, that there were two temples, an older and a younger, seems less plausible. No foundation of an older temple has been found in the area, and all other literary references point rather to a single temple. As we have seen, the temple in front of the west stoa has been repeatedly rebuilt.

Pausanias mentions with special interest the Sauromatian corselet, which was dedicated in the Asclepieum. This was but one of countless votive gifts made by grateful patients. The usual type was a plastic counterpart, in metal or stone, of the member healed, hand, foot, ear, or eye, as in some Christian shrines to-day. Many of these votive offerings have been discovered (Fig. 122), and others are mentioned in the inscriptions. Some worshipers dedicated marble reliefs in the precinct (Fig. 123); still others dedicated hymns of praise or prayer.

*A*

*B*

FIG. 122. — Votive offerings dedicated in the precinct of Asclepius (National Museum, Athens).

The most conspicuous ruins on the south side of the Acropolis are those of the Stoa of Eumenes and the Odeum of Herodes Atticus. The Stoa Pausanias passes without notice, as he did the Stoa of Attalus in the Agora (pp. 130 ff.); the Odeum was not yet built when he wrote his description of Athens, but he mentions it in a later book (7, 20, 6).

Beginning some thirty feet from the theater, the Stoa of Eumenes extends about 534 feet west to the Odeum and is 58 feet deep (Fig. 124). The extant portions are mainly the foundation walls of the front and medial colonnades, and the strong rear wall which served also to support the terrace behind it. This rear wall is really composed of three walls: one at the back, built of blocks of breccia; a row of forty-two arches of the same material; and a facing of poros, with a wainscoting of Hymettian marble. The arches, which are now so conspicuous, were merely structural and were originally concealed. Few other remains of the structure survive. The building was two stories in height, with front colonnades of Doric and probably inner rows of Ionic columns. The west end of the building shows signs of having been cut off when the Odeum was erected, but probably only a small portion was then destroyed. At the southwest corner are the square foundations of a stairway which led to the second story (Fig. 126).

FIG. 123. — Relief representing Asclepius, his daughter, Hygieia, and several adorants (National Museum, Athens).

Our evidence for the name of the builder and for the date of this imposing structure is meager. In his chapter on the theater Vitruvius advises (5, 9, 1) that behind the stage colonnades be built for refuge in case of sudden showers, "as at Athens the Eumenian porticoes, the fane of father Bacchus, and the Odeum," apparently thus naming the Stoa of Eumenes, the Stoa of Dionysus behind the scene-building of the theater, and the Odeum of Pericles, in their order from west to east. We note further the fact that materials common to Hellenistic buildings are used in the Stoa, and that the building closely resembles the Stoa of Eumenes at Pergamum. The Stoa seems, then, to have been erected by Eumenes II, king of Pergamum from 197 to 159 B.C. An inscription of the archonship of Xenocles (between 168 and 159 B.C.), found near the Propylaea records the people's thanks to a certain Diodorus, the "friend of King Eumenes and his brothers," thus adding its mite of corroborative evidence.

Just southeast of the Stoa of Eumenes lies a small foundation of breccia and Acropolis limestone (Fig. 125),

FIG. 124. — Stoa of Eumenes, and other buildings.

In the immediate foreground is the foundation of the later temple of Dionysus. The long row of arches belongs to the Stoa of Eumenes;

about 55 feet long and 39 feet wide, but nearly five feet wider beyond the cross-wall toward the western end. This foundation has recently been excavated and identified with the choregic monument of the younger Nicias, which formerly was supposed to have been located

FIG. 125. — Foundation of the choregic Monument of Nicias.

near the Odeum of Herodes Atticus. It was temple-like in form, but faced the west (Fig. 126). It had six columns across the front and a wide porch; upon its summit must have stood the tripod of the dedicator. What makes the building of greatest interest is the fact that a large number of its architectural members are built into the Beulé Gate (p. 237) at the entrance to the Acropolis (Fig. 127). These members, including portions of the cornice, metopes, triglyphs, and architrave are nearly all of Pentelic marble. The stones have long been assigned to the choregic monument, but the correct foundation has only recently been discovered. Across the architrave, as it is set up over the

Beulé Gate, can still be read the inscription: "Nicias son of Nicodemus of Xypete dedicated this; having won with a chorus of boys for the tribe Cecropis; Pantaleon the Sicyonian played the flute; the Elpenor of Timotheus was the song; Neaechmus was archon." The name of the

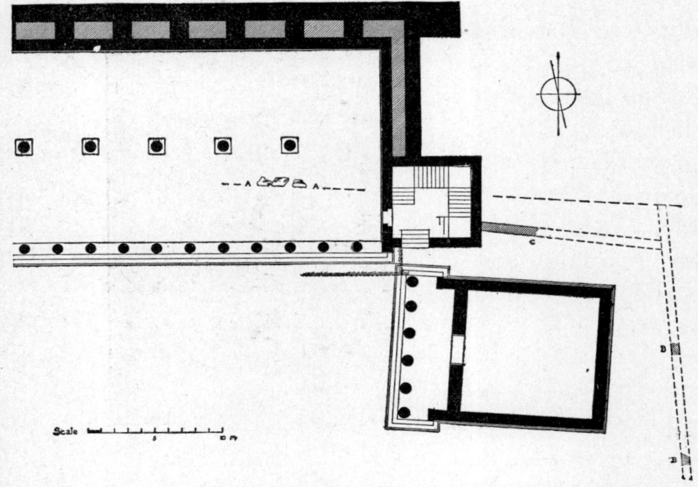


FIG. 126. — Plan of the east end of the Stoa of Eumenes and of the choregic Monument of Nicias.

archon shows that Nicias's victory was won in the same year (320/319 B.C.) as that of Thrasyllus (p. 204), which doubtless gives us the date of the temple. It is thus seen to be earlier than the Stoa of Eumenes, and it doubtless determined the eastern limits of that building. The monument was torn down, and its parts built into the Beulé Gate, in late Roman or early mediaeval times.

Cutting off the end of the Stoa of Eumenes on the west, and connected with it by a small door, is the Odeum of Herodes Atticus, or of Regilla (Figs. 128 and 129), built in honor of the benefactor's wife Regilla, who died about 161 A.D. The building is in the form of a Roman theater, and had, as Philostratus tells us, a roof of cedar. It is constructed mostly of poros, with filling of brick, concrete, and small stones; on the inside it was originally faced with slabs of marble. The massive walls of the front, to a height of three and four stories, and a considerable part of the auditorium, survive. The building seated some 5000 or 6000 spectators.

FIG. 127. — Beulé Gate, at the entrance to the Acropolis, including remains of the Monument of Nicias.

The hollow of the cavea (Fig. 130), measuring about 250 feet across, was hewn from the rock, and at its top was a heavy circuit wall strengthened by buttresses. Above it ran a wide corridor flanked by an outside terrace wall and probably fronted by a colonnade. The seats were of white marble, and in two zones, with an aisle between them; many of the lower seats remain, but in a ruined condition. The lower zone is divided by six stairways into five wedges. The benches for dignitaries, in the lowest row, had backs and arms. The upper zone had eleven stairways and ten wedges. As ordinarily in Roman theaters, spectators who had seats in the lower zone reached their places through vaulted passages opening on the orchestra, or conistra; those for the upper zone, from the aisle between the zones, to which access was

FIG. 128. — Odeum, or Music Hall, of Herodes Atticus, from the southwest.

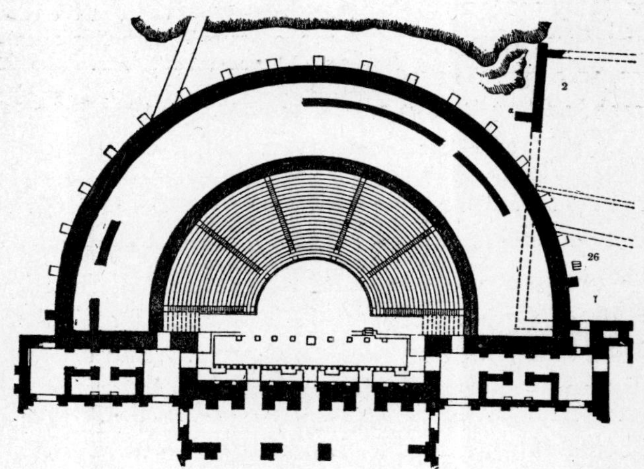

FIG. 129. — Plan of the Odeum of Herodes Atticus.

gained from stairs in the stage-building or from the corridor above.

The semicircular orchestra, about 62 feet wide by 39 feet deep, is paved with alternate slabs of white and bluish marble, and is surrounded by a covered drain. It had no parodoi (p. 196) but was entered through the

FIG. 130. — Interior of the Odeum of Herodes Atticus.

vaulted corridors at the corners. From the orchestra three short flights of steps led to the stage.

The stage-building, including its auxiliary rooms and stairways, is about 300 feet in length. Its original height has not been determined, but the side wings seem to have been higher than the central part of the structure. How this was laid out and ornamented on the exterior is largely a matter of conjecture; the building needs a careful re-examination and study, as the reconstructions hitherto made are deficient in many details.

The stage proper, about 115 feet long by 26 feet deep, and rising nearly five feet above the orchestra, had a wooden floor, with foundations and a façade of stone. At each end is a large door, and at the back are three doors opening into a sort of narthex, of which only the foundations remain. In front of the rear wall stood grouped columns forming a colonnade, which supported a balcony. Above this were two or three rows of windows with vaulted tops which sloped upwards toward the outside; between the windows of each story were pilasters. Niches for statues are about the stage and in other parts of the building, which was richly decorated with sculpture.

The area between the Odeum and the Asclepieum and behind the Stoa of Eumenes seems to have been occupied by no important buildings. Broken walls found in this region are variously explained. Some scholars have connected certain polygonal walls situated here with the Pelargicum (pp. 51 f.), resting their argument partly on the Delphic oracle of the first years of the Peloponnesian War to the effect that it were "better for the Pelargicum to be idle," that is, without buildings; but this is a doubtful forcing of the oracle. At any rate the walls in question seem too frail to have formed a part of the Pelargicum. The auditorium of the Odeum cuts across a heavy foundation of breccia, which until recently was supposed to belong to the Nicias monument (p. 215); data are lacking for its correct identification.

We now return to Pausanias. Somewhere between the Asclepieum and the entrance to the Acropolis must have been the sites which he next mentions. "After the sanctuary of Asclepius, as you go this way to the Acropolis, is a temple of Themis. A memorial to Hippolytus has been heaped up before it — they say that he met his end as a result of the curses; and to every one, even a Barbarian who has learned the language of the Greeks, the love of Phaedra and the nurse's bold act of service are well known. . . . When Theseus brought together the Athenians from the demes into one city, he established the worship of Aphrodite of All the People (Pandemus) and Persuasion (Peitho). The old statues no longer existed in my time, but those of my time were the work of no mean artists. There is also a sanctuary of Earth the Youth-nourisher (Curotrophus), and of Verdant Demeter (Chloë)."

No general agreement has been reached as to the precise situation of these several sites. For the temple of Themis the older of the two small temple-like structures at the western end of the precinct of Asclepius has been claimed; but we have no good evidence. The memorial to Hippolytus seems to have been in the form of a barrow. Near it may have been the temple of "Aphrodite in honor of Hippolytus" founded by the love-sick Phaedra "by the rock of Pallas," the Acropolis. Perhaps we may assume that modern "Barbarians," too, know Euripides's *Hippolytus*—or Racine's *Phèdre*—and omit the tale. Euripides, and after him Diodorus, says that from the shrine of Aphrodite "in honor of Hippolytus" the land of Troezen was visible. If this is to be taken literally, it limits the site to the region near the end of the sanctuary of Asclepius, for farther west the Hill of the Muses cuts off the view.

We have previously noticed that the sanctuary of Aphrodite Pandemus was at the western foot of the Acropolis "near the Ancient Agora" (p. 83). A portion of an architrave adorned with doves holding a knotted fillet in their beaks and engraved with a late dedicatory inscription to Aphrodite Pandemus was found in a Turkish wall in this vicinity, and now lies beside the steps leading up to the

Acropolis (Fig. 131). This was probably taken from a small temple in antis, either a later restoration of an earlier building attributed to Theseus or a new building in a precinct which previously had no temple. An inscription of 283 B.C. provides for the care of the worship in this shrine, for supplying a dove for its purification, and for cleaning the altars, covering the roof with pitch, and washing the statues.

FIG. 131. — Architrave of the temple of Aphrodite Pandemus.

The architrave lies along the wall beside the modern steps leading up to the Acropolis.

The shrines of Earth the Youth-nourisher and Demeter Chloë evidently were in close proximity, as the divinities were allied by nature. In Aristophanes's *Lysistrata* (v. 835) the women guarding the Acropolis spy a man approaching them "past the sanctuary of Chloë;" this locates the site near the entrance to the Acropolis. A boundary stone of the precinct of the Youth-nourisher and an inscription mentioning the entrance to the inclosure of Blaute and the Youth-nourisher were also found near here. Perhaps neither sanctuary had a temple originally, but a mutilated inscription seems to mention a temple of Demeter. A fragment of the comic poet Eupolis says: "But I am going straight to the Acropolis, for I must sacrifice a ram to Demeter Chloë."

Fig. 132. — Acropolis, from Museum Hill.

# CHAPTER VIII

## THE ACROPOLIS

### THE ENTRANCE AND ITS BUILDINGS

THE natural conformation and the various fortifications of the citadel of Athens (Figs. 132 and 133) have already been considered (Chapters I and III). Substantially correct is the statement of Pausanias: "There is one entrance to the Acropolis; it affords no other, being all precipitous and having a strong wall." In his time the prehistoric postern (p. 51) at the northeast corner had long been closed; the stairway descending through a cleft in the rock near the center of the north side is mediaeval. Possibly the steps leading up from the ledge near the caves of Pan and Apollo were still accessible, but so rarely used as to be passed without mention. The ordinary approach must always have been at the gently sloping west end of the hill, "in front of the Acropolis," as Antigonus rightly puts it (*Hist. mirab.* 12).

This approach varied somewhat in different periods. A series of depressions and a roadway hewn and worn in the rock at the foot of the bastion occupied by the little temple of Athena Victory (Fig. 134) mark the earliest regular approach. During the Periclean Age, this pathway was covered with earth, and in the mediaeval period, as the excavators report, by a rough pavement, which they broke up. Rounding the bastion, the cuttings disappear under the

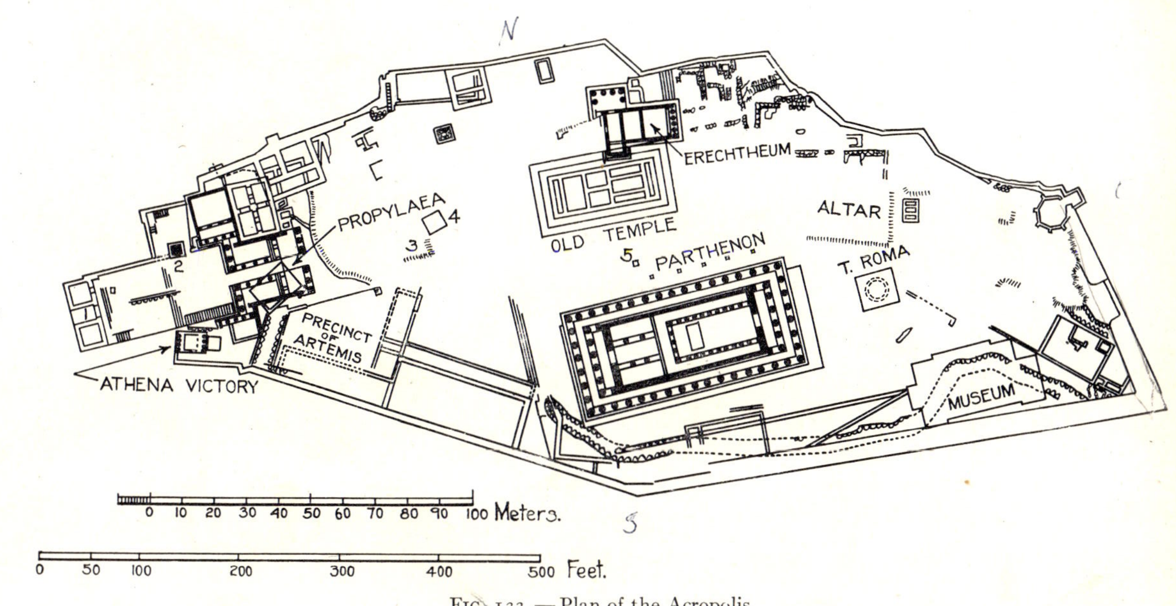


Fig. 133. — Plan of the Acropolis.

modern steps. The way must have led up past the bit of Cyclopean wall now hid in the bastion to the upper gate of the Enneapylum (p. 51).

Here at some time before the Persian Wars an ornate gateway was constructed. Fortunately the builders of its

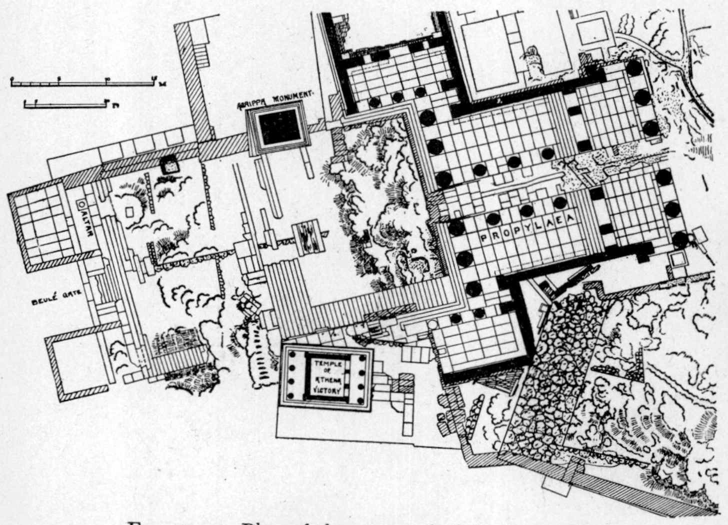


FIG. 134. — Plan of the west end of the Acropolis.

more elaborate successor did not entirely obliterate the earlier structure. Cuttings in the rock in the broad central doorway of the later building mark the location of one corner of the early Propylum, while behind the southwest wing of the Propylaea are considerable remains of the corner diagonally opposite, built against the end of the old Pelasgic wall (Fig. 135). Resting on three marble steps is a wall of poros blocks faced by a marble anta; a corresponding wall and anta are to be restored at the opposite corner of the façade, and between were two Doric columns (Figs.

136 and 137). Behind the surviving anta is a piece of the marble side-wall of the building, about 15.5 feet long, with a bench at its lower edge. One block of the marble floor is also in situ, and various cuttings for the placing of statues

FIG. 135.— Extant corner of the early Propylum of the Acropolis.

remain. The east end of the building must have been constructed in a similar manner, but at the top of a flight of steps by which the higher level was reached. Whether or not the building had an interior cross-wall with doors cannot be determined. Thus the Propylum, which was about 46 feet long by 36 feet wide, faced the southwest, its axis bisecting the angle between the old Pelasgic wall and a later polygonal wall (Fig. 3) which runs nearly east and west

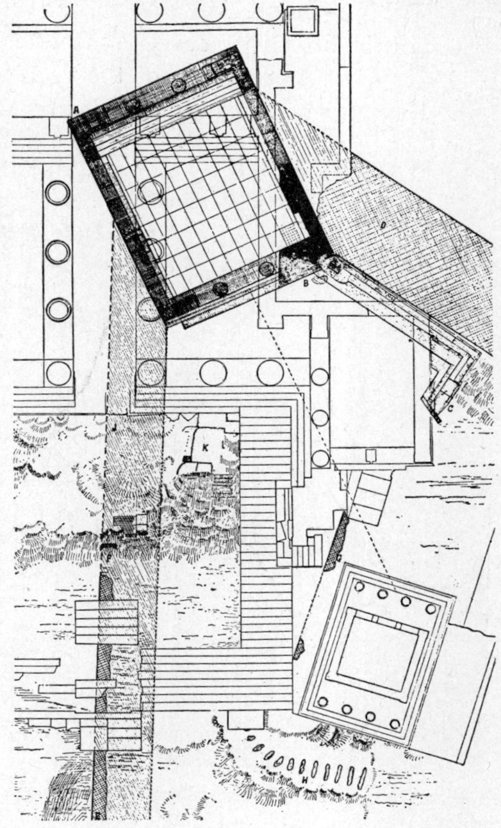

FIG. 136. — Plan of the early Propylum.

along the middle of the present ascent, and probably once stretched up to the Propylum.

Outside of the existing anta and before the Pelasgic wall is a square base, apparently for a tripod of bronze, and beyond it begins a long marble seat which reappears on the other side of the corner of the southwest wing of the Propylaea, here abutting on the Pelasgic wall. Below the opposite corner of the façade are cuttings (K in Fig. 136) which may mark the site of the bronze Chalcidian chariot (p. 345); Herodotus says (5, 77) that this was, in his day, "on the left hand as you enter the Propylaea on the Acropolis." The Propylum probably was burned by the Persians, but it was rebuilt and so continued well into the age of Pericles.

In 437 B.C., the year after the gold and ivory statue of Athena was installed in the nearly completed Parthenon,

FIG. 137. — Elevation of the early Propylum, restored.

new Propylaea were begun under the direction of the architect Mnesicles (Fig. 138). This building was constructed of white Pentelic marble, and the work was ended in the almost incredibly brief time of five years, at a cost, we are told, of 2012 talents, or above \$2,000,000. The building was justly admired. Demosthenes, speaking on the Pnyx, points with pride to "yonder Propylaea;" "Propylaea nobilia," writes Cicero; and Pausanias says appreciatively: "The Propylaea have a ceiling of white marble, and in their ornamentation and the size of the stones are supreme up to my time."

FIG. 138. — Propylaea and temple of Athena Victory, from the west.

... polygonal wall illustrated in Figure 2. The steps ascending beside the bastion are modern. The temporary

For the new gateway the orientation was changed, so that the façade faced the west, and the building was designed to stretch across the entire end of the hill. The problem was rendered the more exacting for the architect because of the sloping nature of the rock on which he was to build. This difficulty Mnesicles met by providing a flight of steps at the center of the building, and in front by constructing a

FIG. 139. — Pinacotheca and front of the Propylaea, from the southwest.

high foundation, which was to be concealed with earth, as its rough structure indicates (Fig. 139). Through the middle of the building from west to east runs an inclined roadway; this in late times was paved with grooved slabs, a few of which are left.

The original plan of the Propylaea (Fig. 140) comprised a cross-wall pierced by doorways; in front of this a large megaron combined with a west portico, behind it an east portico; northwest and southwest wings; and larger northeast and southeast wings. The east wings were never

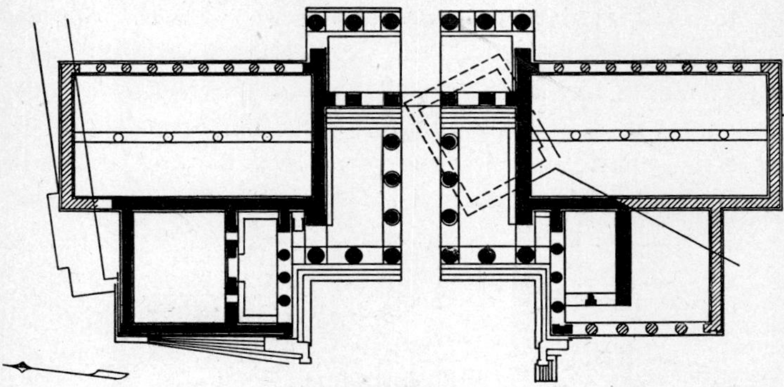

FIG. 140. — Plan of the Propylaea.

The portions indicated by hatched lines were projected but never completed.

constructed, and the dimensions of the southwest wing were contracted. As designed the total width of the building would have been 223 feet; its actual width is 156 feet, its depth about 112 feet. The five doorways in the cross-wall (Fig. 141) form the entrance proper. Of these the central doorway is 13.7 feet in lower width and 24 feet high; its lintel is a huge block nearly 19 feet in length. On either

FIG. 141. — Propylaea, from the east.

The scaffolding about the building is being used by the Greek Archaeological Society for reconstruction.

side is a doorway 11.3 feet wide and 17.7 feet high; and at either end of the cross-wall is a small doorway 4.8 feet wide and 9.6 feet high. The doorways narrow slightly toward the top. The ancient bronze-sheathed casings and doors of wood have perished; the marble casings now partly preserved are of a late date. In front of the cross-wall is the

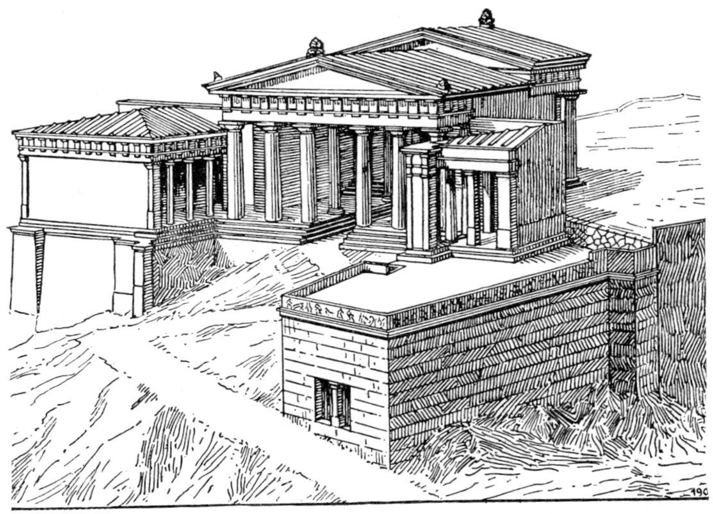

FIG. 142. — Propylaea from the southwest, restored.

The temple of Athena Victory is omitted in order to make visible the middle portion of the Propylaea.

flight of five steps, interrupted by the middle doorway. The top step is of black Eleusinian stone, which is also used for the orthostatae, or wide lower course of the wall, rising behind the benches which ran along the sides of the megaron.

One of the charming features of the Propylaea is the happy combination of the Doric and Ionic orders (*cf.* Figs. 139 and 142). Resting on the marble floor on either side of the roadway are three slender Ionic columns 33.8 feet high and 3.4 feet in lower diameter. The western megaron and portico are 50 feet deep. In front are six heavier Doric columns 29.9 feet high and 5 feet in lower diameter. The central intercolumniation is wider than those at the sides, three metopes and two triglyphs being over the central space instead of two metopes and one triglyph, as at the sides and as is usual in most buildings of the best period. When circumstances demanded, the Greek architect did not hesitate to vary from norm. The east portico is 24 feet deep, and is also fronted by six Doric columns, almost three feet shorter than those at the west. The floor of this portico is nearly level with the surface of the rock on the east, being separated from it only by the stylobate and a low step. Both rooms of the central portion of the building had coffered ceilings of marble, of exceptional beauty. The roof of this portion ended in an unsculptured pediment over each façade; over the cross-wall the roof was interrupted and continued at a different level (Fig. 142); the roof-tiling was of marble. At the west the columns rest above four marble steps; these extend at right angles westward in front of the wings, where, however, the lowest step is of black, or dark gray, Eleusinian stone. The steps terminate in antae, which later supported statues of horsemen. To these we shall return (pp. 238 f.).

The north wing of the building is the Pinacotheca (Figs. 139, 140, 142), or picture gallery, of which Pausanias presently speaks. It is a nearly square room, about 35 by 29 feet; apparently it was never floored. The deep portico is fronted by three Doric columns about 19 feet in height; the triglyph frieze above the columns also runs around the west and north sides of the building. The partition wall behind the portico has a doorway 7.6 feet wide and 14.9 feet high, with a sill of black Eleusinian stone, and on either side of the doorway a narrow window. Beneath the windows and around the inner room at the same level is a narrow band of the black stone, probably indicating the lower edge of the pictures which the room contained. The doorway and the windows are not centered but apparently arranged proportionally with reference to points of view near the opposite wing of the building. A hip roof covered the wing. West of the Pinacotheca the rock drops off suddenly, and the wall on this side is supported by a fanlike foundation nearly twenty feet in height.

The architect obviously intended that the southwest wing should be of the same size as the northwest wing, but planned that it should have a colonnade instead of a blank wall on the west side. But, probably in consequence of effectual opposition on the part of the priests of the precinct of Athena Victory, he was compelled to curtail his plan, though he still built in such a way that the original design might be carried out when circumstances permitted. The north colonnade was constructed according to specifications, so as to counterbalance that of the Pinacotheca, but the south wall was brought up to about 20.5 feet behind the colonnade and shortened to 29.4 feet; then a pier was placed between the anta at the end of this wall and the colonnade. An irregular hip roof covered the wing, with a smaller hip roof over the projecting anta west of the columns; this anta with the adjacent column has now disappeared. Above the entire wing a high "Frankish tower" was built in the Middle Ages and stood until 1874 (Fig. 231). Along the closed sides of the wing ran a long base, or series of bases, the purpose of which is unknown.

Mnesicles's plan also included large northeast and southeast wings extending to the edge of the Acropolis on either side (Fig. 140); various clews remain to tell us of it. These are partly finished antae just back and outside of the ends of the side-walls of the east portico; slanting cuttings above these antae, to accommodate the roofs of the wings; and an interior cornice and holes for the beams of the ceiling and roof in the east wall of the Pinacotheca and the north wall of the central building. But, seemingly, again the protests of the priests, this time of the sanctuary of Brauronian Artemis on the south, together, perhaps, with the troubles preceding the outbreak of the Peloponnesian War, availed to check the execution of the plan, and the wings were never finished. They were each to have been about 76 by 42 feet in size and fronted by a colonnade, probably of eight columns. Whether they were to have an inner row of columns is uncertain.

Various other details, such as the unremoved bosses on the walls (Fig. 135), give added evidence that the building was not fully completed. But even thus, it formed a magnificent portal to the precinct. Though the building was not adorned with sculpture, it was designed and constructed with great skill. The architectural members had the usual painted decorations, the design of which is still discernible on some fragments which lie about the building.

The problems relative to the approach to the Acropolis are not fully solved. The front foundations of the Propylaea were clearly not meant to be seen (p. 231), and we may be sure that the space between the wings was filled with a sloping terrace, or terraces, of earth up to the bottom of the front steps, thus permitting ascent at any point. That the approach was always difficult we may conclude from a passage of the *Lysistrata* of Aristophanes (v. 286 f.) in which the chorus of old men is represented as toilsomely climbing the steep slope. That the animals for sacrifice were dragged along a zigzag path to the middle doorway through the Propylaea is quite likely; but we have no reason to believe, as some have done, that a regular zigzag footpath was laid out, which would render practically useless the steps in front of the building, and all the doorways except the middle one.

Toward the middle of the first century of our era, perhaps in the reign of the Roman emperor Caligula (37–41 A.D.), a broad flight of marble steps was made between the wings. Considerable portions of these stairs remain; the present narrow stairway at the right, however, though of ancient materials, was built in the last century.

In late Roman or even Byzantine times, the two towers were built which flank the "Beulé Gate" (Fig. 127), as it is called from the name of its discoverer. These towers are nearly square and are made of poros blocks, taken, at least in part, from some earlier structure. Between them was some sort of a gate, which was later replaced by the existing gateway, constructed largely of architectural members of the choregic monument of Nicias (p. 215). A vaulted corridor once existed behind the towers and gate; while behind the north tower and at a lower level an archaic altar has been found in situ (*cf.* Fig 134).

In this connection mention should be made of the guards and gatekeepers of the Acropolis whose names are preserved in inscriptions; they probably belong to the period when the staircase was built up the ascent to the Propylaea.

Before we leave this region we may notice a structure not mentioned in any ancient author, the lofty monument of Agrippa, which stands west of the Pinacotheca (Fig. 143). The monument is about 44 feet in height and consists of a foundation, built of Hymettian marble and limestone, and a tapering pier of alternate wide and narrow courses of Hymettian marble resting on three steps, of which the uppermost is of Pentelic marble; the structure is capped by a cornice and blocks which have incisions for the mounting of a quadriga. The quadriga probably bore a statue of Agrippa. The basis is turned somewhat from the axis of the Propylaea, a fact often explained by a supposed orientation on a zigzag path, which we have seen reason to reject; but the monument is nearly parallel with the bottom of the fanlike foundation of the Pinacotheca, probably a sufficient explanation of its peculiar position. On its west side a little below the cornice is an inscription in large letters: "The people [dedicated this statue of] Marcus Agrippa, son of Marcus, thrice consul, their benefactor." The mention of Agrippa's third consulate establishes the date of the basis as 27 B.C.; but we do not know what Augustus's able minister had done for Athens to merit the distinction.

FIG. 143. — Basis of the Monument of Agrippa, from the temple of Athena Victory.

We have already seen (p. 234) that the antae at the western ends of the steps of the Propylaea bore bronze statues of horsemen. Pausanias must have looked at these only casually, for he says: "I cannot state definitely whether the images of the horsemen are the sons of Xenophon or are merely decorative." Parts of the bases on which the horsemen stood have been found, and one base has been restored on the southern anta (Fig. 144). This block bears an inscription (now inverted )which reads: "The horsemen from the spoils of the enemy; the hipparchs, Lacedaemonius, Xenophon, Pronapes; made by Lycius of Eleutherae, son of Myron." From the forms of the letters the date may be determined as near the middle of the fifth century B.C., before the historian Xenophon was born! The Xenophon of the inscription is apparently the son of Euripides of Melite, who was general at Samos in 440 B.C. and died at Potidaea eleven years later. Lacedaemonius is probably the son of the Cimon who was general at Corcyra in 433 B.C. Of Pronapes we have no further knowledge. On the front of the restored block the same inscription is repeated in later letters, and there are incisions in both the upper and the lower surfaces to receive the equestrian statue. The second inscription was no doubt cut when the statues were set up after the construction of the Propylaea; where they stood before that time we do not know. In 17 or 18 A.D., the southern statue was rededicated to the Roman Germanicus, and on the block of the anta beneath the base of the statue was carved: "The people [dedicated this statue of] Germanicus Caesar, descendant of the divine Augustus."

After mentioning the statues of the horsemen Pausanias continues: "On the right of the Propylaea is a temple of Wingless Victory. Thence the sea is visible, and there Aegeus cast himself off, as they say, and was killed," that is, when his son Theseus returned from Crete under black sails. "And in his honor the Athenians have the heroum called the Heroum of Aegeus."

The temple of Wingless Victory (Fig. 144), properly called Athena Victory, as inscriptions tell us, stands on the high bastion that juts out to the west of the Propylaea. From Pausanias's statement, "thence the sea is visible," the inference has justly been drawn that the Cimonian

FIG. 144. — Temple of Athena Victory, from the top of the Pinacotheca.
The hill in the background is the Hill of the Muses.

Wall shut out the view from the interior of the Acropolis (pp. 57 f.). A leveled area immediately below and south of the bastion (Fig. 20) has been plausibly conjectured to be the site of the Heroum of Aegeus, though Pausanias does not state directly that the Heroum was situated where Aegeus fell.

In the early days, when the Acropolis was essentially a fortified castle, the bastion on which the temple of Athena

Victory was afterwards built was an effective outwork against approaching enemies, who, as at Tiryns and other primitive citadels, could be attacked from above on their unshielded right side. The wall of the bastion has been repeatedly rebuilt, but the evidence is too scanty to permit as yet a final interpretation of its history, and opinions are still diverse. A piece of the early Cyclopean north wall is buried in the bastion and has a different orientation from the present north face (G in Fig. 136). The Cimonian Wall probably continued about the bastion; but on the south it has been replaced by a mediaeval and modern wall. The north and west faces are nearly intact; in the opinion of some these are the work of the period when the temple was built. The extant portions are built of well-fitted blocks of poros laid in even courses, and on the west the bastion reaches the height of 28 feet. The greater part of the wall is made of alternate headers and stretchers (p. 9); but along part of the north and west faces — perhaps where the old Cyclopean wall behind interfered — false joints were grooved in the alternate layers of stretchers, so as to give the appearance of headers. This makes it evident that the face of the wall was intended to be seen; but at the time when the broad staircase of approach was built in Roman days (p. 237) the north and west walls seem to have been covered with a veneering of marble. The holes for the cramps by which the marble was fastened are plainly visible. The wall is capped on these faces with a coping of marble partly built into, and so contemporaneous with, the temple. In the lower part of the western face of the bastion are two contiguous niches whose purpose is unknown.

At the end of the north wall, where it abuts on the anta of the Propylaea (Fig. 144), is a small flight of steps, 4.3

feet wide, leading up to the temple platform from a ramp whose foundations are below and to the east of the steps. At present five steps are left; formerly one or two more were added at the bottom of the flight and two and a half at the top. To these steps and their foundations, with a few other bits of evidence, a considerable literature has been devoted in the effort to determine which is of earlier date, the Propylaea or the temple and the wall of the bastion. It seems probable that the steps were formerly longer and perhaps bedded in a wall at the east, as they now are at the west, and that they were cut off when the anta of the Propylaea was built, though it is fair to add that quite opposite opinions are based by others on the same evidence. The rough ends of the steps and the condition of the foundation below them seem to confirm the view stated. We may assume that the half step at the top was originally of full height, and that it was lowered, with the platform, when the temple was constructed. If this is correct, the chief objection to the opinion that the temple was earlier than the Propylaea is obviated, for this objection is founded on the theory that the direction of the north wall of the bastion was determined by the orientation of the Propylaea. The other important objection, that the sculpture of the temple is of too late a style to have been wrought at the middle of the fifth century B.C., before the date of the Propylaea, is too subjective to be allowed to transcend the other evidence.

A new stage in the discussion respecting the age of the temple was reached upon the discovery in 1896 of an inscription (Fig. 145 A) recording a decree which provides for the appointment, and the mode of payment, of a priestess of Athena Victory, the supplying of the sanctuary of the divinity with a door, or doors, the building of a stone altar, and the erection of a temple under the direction of Callicrates, one of the architects of the Parthenon. From the forms of its letters the inscription may be dated about the

*A*

*B*

Fig. 145.—Inscriptions relating to the construction of the temple of Athena Victory.

middle of the fifth century B.C. On the back of the marble slab bearing the inscription is another decree (Fig. 145 B) of a later date, perhaps the beginning of the Peloponnesian War, and apparently the work of two stonecutters. This sets forth provisions for the payment to the priestess of Athena Victory of the sum defined in the earlier decree. The presumption, then, is decidedly in favor of the view that the temple was built when provided for by the earlier decree, or about the time when the Parthenon, the masterpiece of Callicrates, was also building.

The temple of Athena Victory is of the Ionic order and is built entirely of white Pentelic marble. It rests on three steps and measures about 18.5 by 27 feet on the stylobate; the cella is about 12 by 14 feet. In front it has two square pillars between the antae; between these is the doorway, while the side spaces were filled originally with bronze gratings. The temple is amphiprostyle tetrastyle, having four columns at each end. The columns are exceedingly graceful, and their shafts are monolithic. The corner columns in front were joined to the cella by marble barriers; and the corner capitals are canted, as usual in Ionic buildings, so as to present volutes on both front and side. A molding corresponding in outline to the bases of the columns runs about the lower edge of the cella, the top course of which is also profiled. The temple was crowned by the customary roof of wood over the entablature, which included a sculptured frieze about 18 inches high (Fig. 146). Parts of the frieze were removed by Lord Elgin and are now in the British Museum; these portions were later replaced by copies in terra cotta, which are now blackened by the weather.

The frieze on the east end represents an assemblage of the Olympian gods, that on the west end, a combat of Greeks with Greeks; on the north and south sides a contest of Greeks with Persians is portrayed. The subject of the east section is therefore mythological, of the others historical; yet identification of the scenes of battle is impossible. The frieze is badly mutilated, but the grace and vivacity of style are worthy of the best period of Greek art. The pediments were unsculptured.

In front of the temple, on a foundation still extant, was a large altar, doubtless the one for which the decree

FIG. 146. — Southeast corner of the frieze of the temple of Athena Victory.

provides. The cella was occupied by the ancient cult statue of Athena Victory, a wooden figure holding in the right hand a pomegranate, in the left a helmet; no replica of the statue has been identified.

At some unknown date near the end of the fifth century B.C., the north, west, and south sides, and the ends of the east side of the platform were surrounded by a marble balustrade, about 3.5 feet high, of which considerable portions are now preserved in the Acropolis Museum; the cornice of the bastion retains the marks of the fastenings. The inside of the balustrade was smooth, the outside was covered with a series of reliefs representing winged Victories occupied in sacrifice or triumph. These graceful figures with the flowing draperies that envelop them are among the most beautiful works of Greek sculpture (Figs. 147 and 148).

The group of buildings at the entrance to the Acropolis has undergone severe vicissitudes. Just before 1687, while expecting the attack of the Venetians, the Turks tore down the temple of Victory, which had been in use for the

FIG. 147. — Victory adjusting her sandal; slab from the balustrade about the temple of Athena Victory.

FIG. 148. — Victory adjusting her sandal, restored; from a modern copy in marble.

storage of powder, and used its members to strengthen the fortification wall, which extended from the bastion nearly to the monument of Agrippa, and rose ten or twelve feet higher than the bastion; here they planted their cannon. About 1835 the fortification wall was destroyed, and the temple was rebuilt and restored with new stones in place of the blocks which were lost; a few of the old blocks have recently been identified in different parts of the Acropolis.

At least as early as the fourteenth century the Propylaea began to be used as a palace. Somewhat later the spaces between the columns were closed by a rough wall, a lofty parapet was built above the Pinacotheca, and a high tower above the southwest wing (p. 235). In the middle of the seventeenth century the building was struck by lightning and much injured by the explosion of powder stored in it. As late as 1794 one of the columns was converted into lime, and during the Greek Revolution the building suffered severe injuries. At present it is being carefully and scientifically restored.

To return to Pausanias; "On the left of the Propylaea," he continues, "is a room having pictures." This, we have seen (pp. 234f.), is really the northwest wing of the Propylaea itself. The name Pinacotheca is commonly applied to it, but without ancient authority. "Of the pictures which time has not effaced are Diomedes and Odysseus, the latter carrying off the bow of Philoctetes in Lemnos, the former the image of Athena from Ilium; here too is Orestes killing Aegisthus, and Pylades killing the sons of Nauplius who came to Aegisthus's aid; Polyxena is about to be slain near the tomb of Achilles. . . . These were painted by Polygnotus. He also painted Odysseus standing by the girls washing with Nausicaä at the river, in the manner described by Homer. Among other paintings is that of Alcibiades, and tokens of his victory with horses at Nemea are in the picture. Perseus is being brought to Seriphos, carrying the head of Medusa to Polydecte. . . . Passing by the picture of the boy bearing the water-jars, and the wrestler which Timaenetus painted, here is Musaeus." Whether these pictures were frescoes, or free pictures hanging on the walls, or easel pictures, is a moot point. They are several times referred to as tablets (pinaces), and Polemo is said to have written a book *On the Tablets in the Propylaea.* Furthermore, Polygnotus seems to have visited Athens a generation or so before the Propylaea were built, and if the pictures attributed to him were really his, they must have been brought from some other place. This evidence would incline us to the opinion that the pictures were free paintings hung on the walls. No holes for hooks of suspension, however, are discoverable, and this fact taken into consideration, along with the strip of black stone (p. 235), which apparently marks the lower edge of paintings, as at Pergamum and elsewhere, points rather to frescoes; so the problem remains open. Of the individual pictures we know little more than the names. We are told that the figure of Alcibiades was painted by Aristophon, or Aglaophon, and that he was represented as seated in the lap of the personified Nemea, and "more beautiful than the faces of women." Plutarch adds (*Alcibiades* 16) that the older men disapproved of the picture, as "smacking of tyranny and unlawful."

"Close by the entrance to the Acropolis is a Hermes whom they call Propylaeus; and the Graces, they say, Socrates son of Sophroniscus made." And with these must be associated a statue which Pausanias mentions in another place (2, 30, 2): "Alcamenes was, I think, the first to make three statues of Hecate together, which the Athenians call On the Tower (Epipyrgidia). It stands by the temple of Wingless Victory." The threefold statue of Artemis Hecate was a type often repeated in later times. Since the work made by Alcamenes stood "on the tower," we are perhaps safe in assigning it to the open space south of the temple of Victory (Fig. 149).

Pausanias does not give us the name of the sculptor of the Hermes Propylaeus, but happily we can now supply it. In 1903 a herm in excellent preservation was found in the excavations at Pergamum (Fig. 150). The epigram engraved upon it says: "You shall see Alcamenes's beautiful statue, the Hermes before the gates; set up by Pergamius

FIG. 149. — Temple of Athena Victory and surroundings, restored.

(or a Pergamene?)." The herm seems to be a copy of the statue of Alcamenes, and from it have already been identified a number of other replicas in European museums. The discovery is important, for it has restored to us the first authenticated copy of a work by the well-known pupil of Pheidias, whose style it not a little resembles. The bearded head has a strain of archaism about it which permits us to guess that it may have been an early work of Alcamenes; possibly it was set up first in the old Propylum.

Pausanias's belief, reiterated in another passage (9, 35, 7), that the Graces were the work of the famous Socrates, is expressed also by several other ancient writers, and apparently reflects a popular tradition. These divinities, whose names at Athens were Auxo, Thallo, and Carpo, are represented in a number of ancient reliefs (Fig. 151) which seem to go back to a common original, an original, however, of a style which antedates the period of the philosopher. For this reason the tradition is now generally believed to be based upon a confusion of names arising perhaps from the fact that the great Socrates was a statuary in his youth. This explanation, however, rests on the assumption that the extant reliefs are copies of the work ascribed to Socrates, and of this we are at present by no means certain.

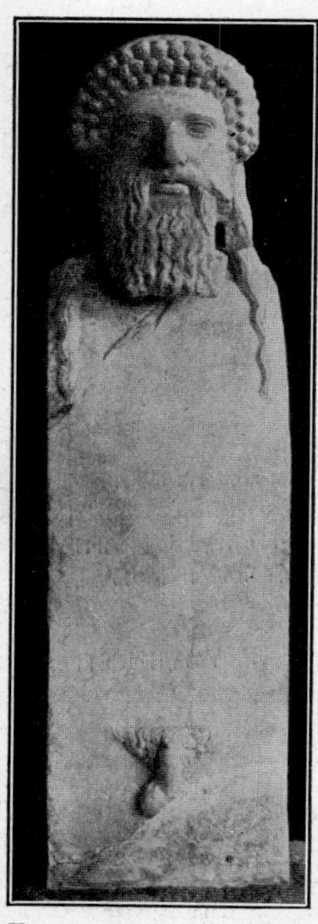

FIG. 150. — Replica of the Hermes of Propylaeus, by Alcamenes; from Pergamum (Constantinople Museum).

The three works of art, the Hermes, the Graces, and the Hecate, are more or less closely associated in our literary references; they cannot have stood far apart. Pausanias says, in the second passage referred to, that the Graces were "before the entrance into the Acropolis," and that a mystic ceremony was enacted before them. Pliny (*Nat. hist.* 36, 32) asserts that they stood "in the Propylum," while a scholiast on Aristophanes (Tzetzes, schol. on *Clouds* 773) states that they were "carved on the wall behind the Athena," which must be a piece of misinformation, or an incorrect reading. The suggestion has been made that the Hermes stood in the niche between the anta of the Pinacotheca and the adjacent anta of the Propylaea,

FIG. 151. — Relief representing the Graces (Vatican Museum, Rome).

while the Graces were in the corresponding niche by the southwest wing. Cuttings in the floor show that both of these places were once occupied by statues, but no evidence is at hand regarding their character. Possibly the more plausible conjecture is that the Graces stood in the corner south of the southwest wing of the Propylaea; this would be a secluded place for mystic rites. The Hermes may be identical with one named the Uninitiated (Amyetus); but this does not help us to find its situation, for the Hermes Uninitiated is merely known to have been "at Athens on the Acropolis" (Hesychius, *s.v.*).

### FROM THE PROPYLAEA TO THE PARTHENON

The mention of Socrates leads Pausanias to speak of the "seven wise men." In this connection he names Hippias, who after the assassination of his brother Hipparchus spent his fury on many, conspicuously on a woman named Leaena (Lioness), the mistress of Aristogeiton, who refused to betray her friends, even under torture. "And for this reason, after the tyranny of the Peisistratids ended, the Athenians erected a bronze lioness in memory of the woman. Near this is a statue of Aphrodite, which is said to be a votive offering of Callias and the work of Calamis. Near by is a bronze statue of Dieitrephes pierced with arrows. . . . Near Dieitrephes (for I do not wish to write of less important images) are statues of the goddess Hygieia, who is said to be the daughter of Asclepius, and of Athena, whose by-name is also Hygieia. And there is a stone, not a large one, but big enough for a small man to sit on, where they say the Silenus rested when Dionysus came to the land. . . . I know, from having seen them, the other things on the Acropolis of the Athenians, including the bronze boy, holding the lustral basin, by Lycius son of Myron, and Myron's Perseus, who has performed his task against Medusa. There is also a sanctuary of Brauronian Artemis."

Where were these various objects? The base of the statue of Athena Hygieia rests in situ in front of the southeast column of the Propylaea; the entrance into the precinct of Artemis Brauronia is some forty feet to the east

(Fig. 152). These are fixed points. If Pausanias is following a strictly topographical order, the bronze lioness, Aphrodite, Dieitrephes, the "less important images," and Hygieia should lie within the Propylaea or immediately before the east portico. Except for the words of Pausanias we have no clew to the situation of any of the group save

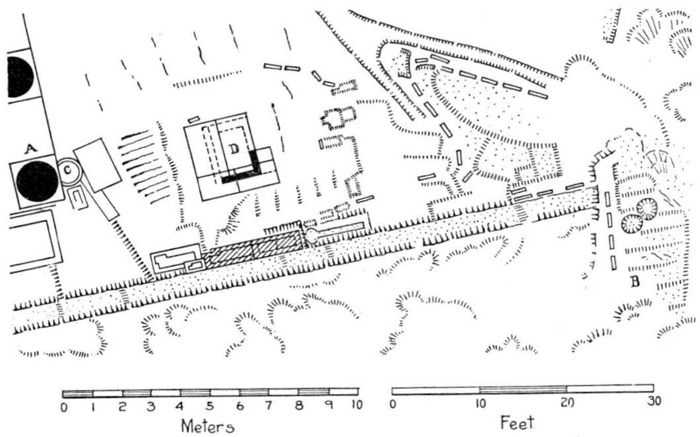


FIG. 152. — Plan of the precinct of Hygieia.

*A* — corner of Propylaea; *B* — steps at entrance of precinct of Brauronian Artemis; *C* — base of statue of Athena Hygieia; *D* — altar of Hygieia.

for the statement of Plutarch (*De garrul.* 8) that in honor of Leaena the Athenians set up a tongueless lioness — symbolizing Leaena's silence — "in the gates of the Acropolis," and a passage, which may be an interpolation, in Polyaenus (8, 45) stating that it was "in the Propylaeum;" but these passages are late and not necessarily to be interpreted with absolute literalness in the light of other conditions. Neither the floor nor the stylobate of the east portico of the Propylaea, nor the rock in front of it, shows the customary incisions for the placing of bases of statues. Furthermore, in either of these places the statues would seriously have impeded progress through the doors of the building. Now in front of the base of Athena Hygieia are the remains of a large altar (Figs. 152 and 153), probably the one beside which Plutarch says (*Pericles* 13) the statue of Athena was set up, and which, he adds, "existed before, as they say." The construction of the altar, with its broader platform on the west, shows that the officiating priest must have stood with his back to the statue of Athena Hygieia, but undoubtedly facing the cult statue, that is, of Hygieia, to the east. And here, east of the altar and around it, are abundant cuttings for bases of statues. Here accordingly we may with greater reason look for the location of the various statues, and they would be in a group, which would account for Pausanias's deviation from a precise topographical order of treatment.

FIG. 153. — Altar of Hygieia.

The statue of Aphrodite probably stood on a base of Pentelic marble which formerly lay in front of the Propylaea but now seems to have disappeared.[1] It bore in old Attic letters of about 475 to 450 B.C. the inscription: "Callias son of Hipponicus dedicated it." This Aphrodite has been identified conjecturally with Calamis's famous Sosandra, which is praised by Lucian. His ideal statue, he says (*Imag.* 6), "Sosandra and Calamis shall adorn with modesty, and its grave and furtive smile will be like hers; the trim

[1] At any rate I have been unable to find it.

and orderly garb will also come from Sosandra, save that the head will be uncovered."

Another base found west of the Parthenon, near where it now lies (Fig. 154; so surrounded by other bases as to be difficult of access), bears the inscription: "Hermolycus son of Dieitrephes [dedicated this as a] primal-offering; Cresilas made it." The incisions on the top of this base are very shallow, and the statue which it bore must have been small, or so crouched as to bring the center of gravity low. Pliny speaks of a statue by Cresilas representing a man "wounded and fainting, in whom one can see how little life remains." Pausanias's "old-world Sebastian" may be the same statue and may have occupied the base in question, but the Dieitrephes supposed by Pausanias to have been represented was alive in 411 B.C., while the inscription seems to be a generation older. The discrepancy cannot now be explained.

FIG. 154.—Base of a statue by Cresilas, perhaps that of the statue of Dieitrephes.
The inscription on the base has been retouched.

Among the "less important images" which Pausanias saw must have been the one of the mother of Isocrates, which, we are told, stood "beside Hygieia." Hygieia herself was probably represented as a maiden accompanied by the sacred serpent of the Asclepiad cult. The base of a statue dedicated to Augusta Hygieia, that is, to Livia, the wife of Augustus, was found in the east portico of the Propylaea.

The base of the statue of Hygieia still occupies its old

position, slightly overlapping the stylobate of the Propylaea at its southeast corner and covering the drainage channel at the foot of the column before which it stands (Fig. 155). It is a trifle more than semicircular in form, about 3 feet in diameter and 1.3 feet high, and has a molding at top and bottom. On its northeast face is the inscription: "The Athenians to Athena Hygieia; Pyrrhus the Athenian made it." The deep markings for the feet show that the statue was of bronze, of about life-size, and that it stood with the weight on the advanced right foot. According to Plutarch (*Pericles* 13) the statue was set up by Pericles in gratitude for the miraculous healing of a favorite workman who fell from the Propylaea. Pliny relates (*Nat. hist.* 22, 44) the same story but brings it into connection with "a temple," presumably the Parthenon, and mentions a statue of the workman rather than that of Athena. On these and certain structural grounds the ascription to Pericles has been questioned by some, but for reasons which seem inadequate. Plutarch's story is clear and circumstantial.

FIG. 155. — Base of statue of Athena Hygieia, in front of the southeast column of the Propylaea.

The inscription reads: Ἀθηναῖοι τῇ Ἀθηναίᾳ τῇ Ὑγιείᾳ· Πύρρος ἐποίησεν Ἀθηναῖος.

South of this base is another, apparently for a stele, and before it is part of a marble barrier designed to divert the rain-water. A large base, whose use is unknown, lies west of the barrier. In front of the base of Athena Hygieia and partly resting on earth, therefore of a later date, is a large, flat block of marble with holes for the erection of a sacrificial table.

The stone on which the Silenus sat is otherwise unknown. The bronze boy holding the lustral basin may have stood at the entrance to the Brauronium, whose steps are still visible. Lycius has already been mentioned as the sculptor of the bronze horsemen (p. 239). Pliny also speaks of a Perseus of Myron, possibly the one named by Pausanias; it may be represented in existing replicas (Fig. 156).

Fig. 156. — Head supposed to be a copy of the Perseus of Myron (British Museum, London).

The precinct of Artemis Brauronia is the westerly sloping trapezoidal area southeast of the Propylaea (Figs. 152 and 157). The old Pelasgic wall bounds it on the west, the Cimonian circuit wall on the south, while on the east the rock is hewn down at the edge of the terrace beyond. On the north the precinct was originally larger, but when the Propylaea were built, the rock was cut down vertically in a line parallel with the new building and a precinct wall constructed, the west end of which remains to a considerable height. The sides of the area measure about 130 feet on the east and south and 140 and 60 feet on the north and west respectively. The entrance is formed by eight broad and low steps hewn in the rock at the northeast corner.

Along the south and east sides of the area are parts of the foundations of two colonnades, meeting at the southeast corner and extending thence to the boundaries of the precinct. The east stoa seems to have had ten columns on its front, the more southerly being half columns before a closed wall. In the little room thus formed are cuttings for bases; here the statues of Artemis may have stood, for

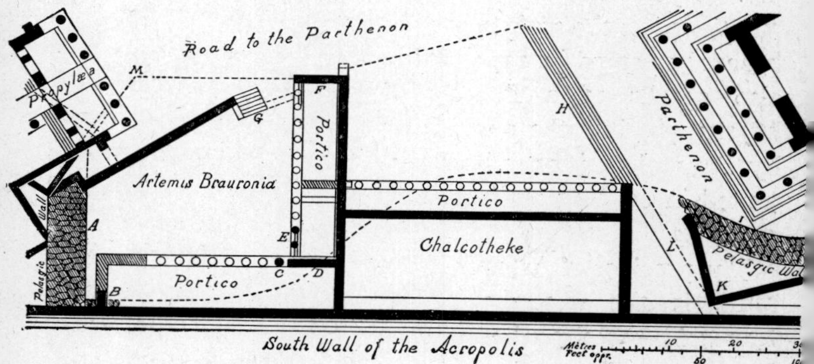


FIG. 157. — Plan of the precincts between the Propylaea and the Parthenon, restored.

the precinct seems to have had no temple. The columniation of the other stoa is uncertain.

Pausanias informs us: "The statue is the work of Praxiteles, and the goddess has her name from the deme of Brauron; the ancient xoanon is in Brauron, the Taurian Artemis, as they call it." From inscriptions, however, we learn that the precinct contained two cult statues, an ancient "hedos" of stone and a standing image. If the old xoanon brought from the land of the Taurians was at Brauron, or at Sparta, as Pausanias elsewhere holds (3, 16, 9), the Acropolis precinct had one also. We have no clew as to its type unless by inference from the name hedos and by contrast with the other, which is explicitly called "standing" or "erect," we infer that it was a seated figure. The type of the later statue by Praxiteles is also doubtful; we possess no description of it. The conjecture that it was the original of the statue in the Louvre, called Diana of Gabii (Fig. 158), is interesting but unproved.

FIG. 158. — "Diana of Gabii," supposed to be a copy of Brauronian Artemis by Praxiteles (Louvre Museum, Paris).

A remarkable series of inscriptions datable about the middle of the fourth century B.C. records a quantity of votive offerings stored in the precinct and the names of their donors, who, of course, were women, since the goddess was Artemis. The places where the objects were stored are given as "next to the wall," or "in the prostomium," or "in the chest," or "next to the pilaster," or "next to the column where is the doe," or "next to the doe," and the like. The inventory is made up mostly of cast-off raiment dedicated to Artemis. Some of the entries are: "a white cloak edged with purple, which clothes the stone hedos;" "a wrap inscribed 'Sanctuary of Artemis,' about the standing statue — dedicated by Theano;" "a white circular, uninscribed, about the standing statue, in rags;" "a mirror with an ivory handle, next to the wall — dedicated by Aristodamea;" "a new embroidered cape with a design of Dionysus making a libation and a woman pouring wine." A marble bear in the Acropolis Museum was probably one of the offerings.

On and about the steps at the entrance, and elsewhere in the precinct, are cuttings for the placing of inscriptional stelae, which have now disappeared.

Adjoining the Brauronium on the east, and somewhat higher, is a larger trapezoidal area (Figs. 133 and 157). On its eastern side is a flight of eight or nine steps communicating with the area, formerly paved, behind the Parthenon. The steps that remain are mostly hewn in the rock, but originally they extended to the south wall of the Acropolis, the addition being constructed in part of stones from the Old Temple (p. 316). Cuttings in the steps show that numerous inscriptional stelae were set up here.

The north half of the area is roughly hewn to a level, but its purpose is not known. Along the south side extended a large building, 134.5 feet in length and 49 feet wide, fronted by a colonnade 11.5 feet deep; the main building is so deep that a middle row of columns may be assumed. At present only the rock-cut bedding for the walls and a few stones of the foundation are left; these are of poros, Acropolis limestone, and débris from pre-Persian buildings, suggesting a date before the time of Pericles. The front colonnade cuts into the steps along the east side of the area, apparently indicating that the colonnade was either destroyed when the steps were made, or not built until after they had fallen into disuse.

The purpose of this building is still in dispute. The most plausible suggestion is that it was the Chalcotheca, which is mentioned in inscriptions of the latter half of the fourth century B.C. as a storehouse for numerous treasures of Athena, as well as an armamentarium for the preservation of shields, war-engines, and, upon occasion, the equipment of a hundred war-galleys. This attribution is based on the size of the structure in question, which seems to be the only unidentified building on the Acropolis large enough to meet the demands of the Chalcotheca; the inconsistency of dates may be obviated on the theory that the building was first constructed, with or without the colonnade, for some other purpose.

After leaving the precinct of Artemis Brauronia Pausanias mentions a series of interesting statues which cannot be located with certainty until we come to the statue of Earth, situated north of the west end of the Parthenon (pp. 267 ff.). We can be sure only that they must have stood between the Brauronium and the statue of Earth, or in the Brauronium.

"The Wooden Horse, as it is called, is set up in bronze. That the creation of Epeius was a contrivance for the destruction of the wall every one knows who does not attribute folly to the Trojans. This horse is said to have contained the bravest of the Greeks and so with the figure of the bronze horse, out of which are peeping Menestheus and Teucer besides the sons of Theseus." A scholiast on the *Birds* of Aristophanes adds (v. 1128) the information that the horse bore the inscription: "Chaeredemus of Coele son of Evangelus dedicated it." But the scholiast neglected to speak of the additional inscription below the other: "Strongylion made it." The entire inscription is now to be read on the end of the base, which lies near the west

FIG. 159. — Base of the "Wooden Horse" of bronze made by Strongylion.

The inscription reads: Χαιρέδημος Εὐαγγέλου ἐκ Κοίλης ἀνέθηκεν· Στρογγυλίων ἐποίησεν.

end of the Brauronium. Four of the original six marble blocks are left (Fig. 159); the base was about 11.5 feet in length. Where the horse was located we do not know. Two of the extant blocks were found in the precinct where the base now lies, and here it may have stood.

Pausanias's next words, "Of the statues that stand after the horse," seem to be followed by a lacuna, and then he continues: "Critias made the image of Epicharinus, who practiced running in heavy armor." The base of this statue also has been found, and now lies to the northwest of the Parthenon along the main way to the east (Fig. 160). The mutilated inscription reads: "Epicharinus the —— dedicated it; Critius and Nesiotes made it." The missing word cannot be deciphered, and we find that Pausanias has mentioned only one of the two artists, that too with a wrong spelling of the name, according to all the manuscripts. Critius and Nesiotes we have met as the sculptors of the famous group of the Tyrannicides (pp. 105 ff.), and their names are found on other bases on the Acropolis. The sockets on the top of the base show that the figure of Epicharinus was of bronze and rested on one foot and faced the left, as one looks at the inscription.

FIG. 160. — Base of the statue of Epicharinus by Critios and Nesiotes.

Along the upper edge is the inscription: Ἐπι[χ]αρῖνος [ἀνέ]θηκεν ὁ . . .· Κριτίος καὶ Νεσ[ι]ώτης ἐπο[ιησ]άτην.

"The efforts of Oenobius were useful to Thucydides son of Olorus, for Oenobius was successful in getting passed the decree for Thucydides to return to Athens. . . . The facts relating to Hermolycus the pancratiast and Phormio son of Asopichus I pass by, since others have narrated them;" but then Pausanias adds the story of Phormio's debts, which were paid by the Athenians, in order that he might become their admiral. Evidently the presence of statues of these three men was the reason for Pausanias's mention of their names, but this is all we know about them.

FIG. 161.—Athena and Marsyas; Athenian coin.

In regard to the next statue we are more fortunate. "Here has been made an Athena striking the Silenus Marsyas, because he picked up the flutes when she wished them to be thrown away." Pliny in speaking of the sculptor Myron refers to the same statues when he says (*Nat. hist.* 34, 57): "He made also a Satyr wondering at the flutes and a Minerva," which gives us the name of the artist. The motif of the group is indicated in various reproductions, such as coins (Fig. 161), vase-paintings (Fig. 162), and a large marble urn (Fig. 163). While differing in details these agree in their general features. Athena and Marsyas stand opposite each other and apparently are looking at the flutes which lie on the ground between them. None of the copies seems to depict Athena as striking Marsyas, nor is Marsyas in the act of picking up the flutes, but springing back with his hands uplifted in wonder. Pausanias may have misunderstood the artist's conception, or the copies may be inexact.

FIG. 162.—Athena and Marsyas; vase painting.

Upon this and similar evidence two excellent figures of

Marsyas have been identified, a life-sized marble statue in the Lateran Museum at Rome, the hands of which have been wrongly restored with castanets, and a bronze statuette, of the same type but of later period, in the British Museum. The technique of the marble as well as of the statuette shows that the statue of Myron was of bronze. Quite recently several good copies of the Athena belonging to the group have also been identified. These include headless statues of marble in Frankfort, Madrid, Toulouse, Paris, and Rome, and a helmeted head in Dresden. With the aid of the coins and other reproductions these have now been brought, in plaster casts, into a group (Fig. 164) which can differ from the original only in minor details — a striking illustration of what the application of scientific method is accomplishing in the restoration of lost works of ancient art.

Fig. 163. — Athena and Marsyas, on the "Finlay vase" (National Museum, Athens).

"Beyond those that I have mentioned is what is termed the fight of Theseus with the bull called the Bull of Minos, whether this was a man or, as the tradition has it, a beast." This cautious description may be a partial apology for applying the name to a man with a bull's head; at any rate such is the type of Minotaur which appears oftenest on coins (Fig. 165), vases, and other works of art. Whether or not these representations were influenced by the statue in question is doubtful.

"Here too is Phrixus son of Athamas, brought to Colchis by the ram; he has sacrificed it to some god — perhaps to

Fig. 164. — Athena and Marsyas, by Myron, restored (Brunswick Museum).

Laphystian Zeus, as he is called by the Orchomenians — and having cut out the thigh-pieces, according to the usage of the Greeks, is watching them as they burn." If this is the same as a statue of Naucydes described by Pliny (*Nat. hist.* 34, 80) as "a man sacrificing a ram," it may have stood on an extant base bearing the inscription, in letters of the fourth century: "[N]aucydes the Argive made it;" unhappily the first letter is not sure.

Fig. 165. — Theseus and Minotaur; Athenian coin.

"After these, among other statues, is one of Heracles, who, as the story has it, is strangling the serpents. There is an Athena rising from the head of Zeus (Fig. 166); also a bull, a votive offering of the Senate of the Areopagus — whatever the reason may be why the Senate dedicated it;

any one who wishes may make many guesses." From other sources we learn that this last statue was of bronze and that "the bull on the Acropolis" became proverbial for a thing strange and marvelous; but as to the occasion of its dedication, "any one who wishes may make many guesses,"

FIG. 166. — Birth of Athena from the head of Zeus; vase painting. The vase painting may follow a group made by Alcamenes in competition for the decoration of the east pediment of the Parthenon.

and modern scholars have not been backward in accepting the challenge.

"I have said before that the Athenians are more zealous than others in matters divine [p. 127]; so they were the first to name Athena the Worker (Ergane), the first [to dedicate?] the limbless herms —— and at the same time they have in the temple a divinity called Earnestness (Spoudaeon)." Without much doubt the text of Pausanias is mutilated here, and we are left in perplexity as to the identity of "the temple." The most commonly accepted hypothesis is that a temple of Worker Athena, containing also the image of Earnestness, stood on the terrace east of the Brauronium and in front of the large building which we have called the Chalcotheca (pp. 260 f.). No traces of such a temple have been found, but the space for one is ample and its bedding may have been hewn away. Various inscriptions mentioning Worker Athena have been discovered, at least three of them in or near the area in question. On the other hand Pausanias may be referring to the temple of some other divinity; owing to the lacuna the statement is not clear.

"Any one who sets greater store by works that have been cleverly made than by those that go back into antiquity will be interested in seeing a man wearing a helmet, the work of Cleoetas; the finger-nails Cleoetas inlaid with silver." Later on in his description of Olympia Pausanias adds (6, 20) that Cleoetas invented the starting-place in the hippodrome there, and that he was so proud of his deed that he inscribed on this statue at Athens: "The man who invented the starting-place of the horses at Olympia, Cleoetas son of Aristocles, wrought me." Cleoetas seems to have lived in the fifth century B.C.

FIG. 167.—Inscription and bedding for statue of Fruit-bearing Earth.

The inscription, slightly retouched in the illustration, reads: Γῆς Καρποφόρου κατὰ μαντείαν.

After this long list of uncertain locations we come again to a fixed point. "There is also a statue of Earth praying Zeus for rain, whether begging for a shower on behalf of the Athenians alone, or on occasion of a general drought over all Greece." About ten yards north of the Parthenon and in front of the seventh column from the west a quadrangular depression is cut in the rock, which is unquestionably the site of the statue of Earth; for just

FIG. 168. — Gê rising from the ground, contest of Poseidon and Polybotes; vase of Erginus and Aristophanes.

behind it, on a space smoothed for the purpose, is cut the inscription: "Of Earth the fruit-bearer (Carpophorus) according to the oracle" (Fig. 167). The statue may have had no base; it was, perhaps, in the form of a matronly woman, the personification of Earth, arising from the ground with arms uplifted, as in various ancient representations (Fig. 168).[1] The inscription and the bedding for the statue have now been surrounded with an iron fence.

Behind the inscription of Earth lie three blocks of marble belonging to a slightly curved base (Fig. 169) and bearing an inscription which read when complete: "Conon son of Timotheus; Timotheus son of Conon." The blocks were found near the spot where they now lie and belong to the statues of which Pausanias says: "Here also are placed Timotheus son of Conon, and Conon himself." The foundation seems to have been composed of four blocks; the one at the left end is lost. The cramp-marks upon the upper surface show that upon these blocks the base which bore the statues rested. Other statues of these men were placed in the Agora (p. 91).

FIG. 169. — Lower part of base of statues of Conon and Timotheus.

Between this spot and the front of the Parthenon must have stood the statues which Pausanias next mentions: "Procne planning the death of her son, both herself and Itys, were dedicated by Alcamenes. Athena displaying the olive-plant and Poseidon showing the wave have also been made." The group of Athena and Poseidon probably differed little from the contest represented in the west pediment of the Parthenon (pp. 288 f.). The type is portrayed, with differences in detail, in numerous works of art (Fig. 170).

[1] A suggestion has recently been made that the figure was seated upon, or rested its feet upon, an omphalos. The site is precisely at the middle of the Acropolis.

"There is also a statue of Zeus by Leochares, and another named Guardian of the city (Polieus)." Probably these were in or near the precinct of Zeus, otherwise known as the "seats and lot of Zeus" or the "ballot of Zeus," situated near the northeast corner of the Parthenon. In this precinct Zeus is said to have decided the contest of Athena and Poseidon. The sanctuary had a bronze table for

FIG. 170. — Contest of Athena and Poseidon; vase painting.

bloodless sacrifices and perhaps an altar; here were performed the extraordinary rites of the ancient festival of Diipolia.

## THE PARTHENON

We are now at the east end, the front, of the Parthenon, the temple of the Parthenos, the Virgin Goddess, — perhaps the most perfect work of architecture that the genius of man has created. Pericles was, in general, the sponsor of the building; Ictinus and Callicrates were the architects. The general oversight of the work is said by Plutarch to have been in the hands of Pheidias, but the truth of this statement has been doubted. At all events Pheidias made the splendid gold and ivory cult statue of Athena which stood in the cella; whether or not he made other parts of the sculptural ornaments we do not know. The building probably was begun in the year 447 B.C., though some scholars would set the initial date from three to seven years earlier. Pheidias's great statue of the goddess was ready and was installed in 438 B.C., and the temple must have been nearly finished at that time, but work of some kind was still in progress five or six years later. Practically the entire structure above the foundation was built of white Pentelic marble; this the oxidization of the centuries has covered with the golden-brown patina which adds so much to the charm of the imposing ruins to-day.

The present Parthenon was not the first building on the site. Two earlier temples, or, more accurately, two earlier

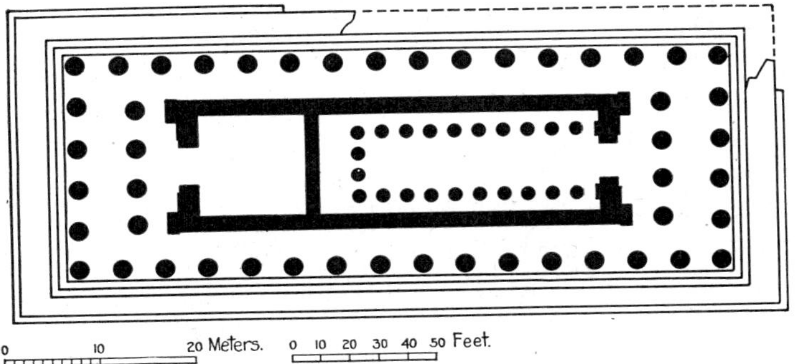


FIG. 171.—Plan of Pre-Persian Parthenon.

stages of the same temple, preceded it, but were never brought to completion. Substantially the same foundation served for the three buildings, but the earlier structures were longer and narrower than the last (Fig. 171). The extension of the foundation to the east, about fourteen feet beyond the present structure, is clearly visible. The original northwest corner can be detected by the difference of construction in the foundation at the northwest corner of the Parthenon (Fig. 172).

Fig. 172. — Northwest corner of Parthenon.

The extension of the foundation begins just below the man.

Along its north side the foundation of the first temple rose little above the level of the rock; on the south side, near the southeast corner, it goes down to a depth of about forty feet. As recent investigations have shown, this podium seems to be a solid mass of poros blocks laid in courses. On the south side can be seen the lower two of the poros steps which led up to the temple. The superstructure also was probably designed to be of poros. Estimating from the extant steps, the temple must have measured about 246 by 97 feet on the stylobate or basis of the columns. It was to be hexastyle, with great Doric columns of poros, like those of the earlier temple of Olympian Zeus (p. 162). The plan of the cella cannot be determined.

When the construction of this first temple was commenced we can only conjecture. Perhaps the most likely period is that of Cleisthenes, after the expulsion of the Peisistratids at the end of the sixth century B.C. At all events this was an epoch of great building activity. But some unknown circumstance, possibly the first invasion of the Persians, brought the work to a standstill, apparently soon after the foundation was completed.

Who was responsible for the resumption of work on the

temple, we can only guess. Possibly the builder was Aristeides the Just, who was "overseer of public revenues" in 489/8 B.C., shortly after the Battle of Marathon. The plan of the building was now considerably altered. Its size was contracted, the dimensions being about 222 feet by 77 feet on the stylobate, thus leaving a border of the podium from seven to ten feet wide around the temple. The lowest step, of Kará limestone profiled in three fasciae, is still in situ along most of the south side, behind the lowest step of the Parthenon. Its southwest corner can be seen about ten feet from the west end of the Parthenon, where a piece of the step of the Parthenon is broken away, and its continuation is visible near the southeast corner of the Parthenon, where a block of the lowest step of the present building has been pushed forward (Fig. 178). The profiled edge is also to be traced on the east edge of the old foundation and in a pit in the north corridor; the latter furnished a datum for estimating the width of the building. The step above this one of Kará stone, and the third step, or stylobate, were of Pentelic marble, which was also to be the material of the superstructure. This temple, like the first, was to be hexastyle, with six Doric columns across the ends and sixteen columns along each side. A considerable number of unfinished drums of the columns lie about the Acropolis, and twenty-six are built into its north wall northeast of the Erechtheum (Fig. 24). Many of the drums are fluted at the bottom; this was done to guide the stonecutters in completing the flutings after the columns were all in place. Other drums have no flutings, therefore were not lower drums; a study of the series makes it seem probable that the columns were erected to the height of only two drums when the work ceased.

The cella was to be tetrastyle, with four columns across the ends. Its walls had a molded base resting on two steps. One block (Fig. 173), which originally formed the base of either the southeast or the northwest anta, has recently been found beneath a broken portion of the floor of the Parthenon; similar blocks, whose moulded face can be felt by thrusting the arm into the interstices of the wall, are built into the Parthenon at the entrance to the Turkish minaret at the southwest corner of the building. Besides these, other blocks, some of them having double-T-shaped cramps smaller than those of the Parthenon, are built into the present temple. The plan of the cella is conjectural; apparently it was similar to that of the Periclean temple.

FIG. 173. — Base of anta of earlier Parthenon.

The foundation and the columns of the second temple bear manifest signs of calcination; this fact, and evidence derived from a study of the walls south of the Parthenon, seem to justify the conclusion that the temple was burned in scaffold at the time of the capture of the Acropolis by the Persians in 480 B.C. If so, it must have been left in ruins for an entire generation.

Something has been said about the walls (Fig. 174) which the excavators of the Acropolis uncovered just south of the Parthenon. These include a part of the foundations of a large rectangular building, which seems to have been a workshop for the builders of the Parthenon, and a series of terrace walls; the position of these and the strata about them bear an important relation to the study of the various stages of the temple. The matter is too extended for our present consideration.

A faint tradition has been preserved of an oath alleged to have been taken by the Greek states after the Persian Wars not to rebuild the temples which the invader had destroyed, but to leave them as perpetual memorials of Persian impiety. This may account for the long inactivity. About the middle of the fifth century Pericles is said to have proposed an interstate congress, to consider the rebuilding of the ruined temples. The scheme fell through, but Athens now had an abundance of funds derived from the treasury of the Confederacy of Delos, and Pericles may have resolved to carry out his project alone. At any

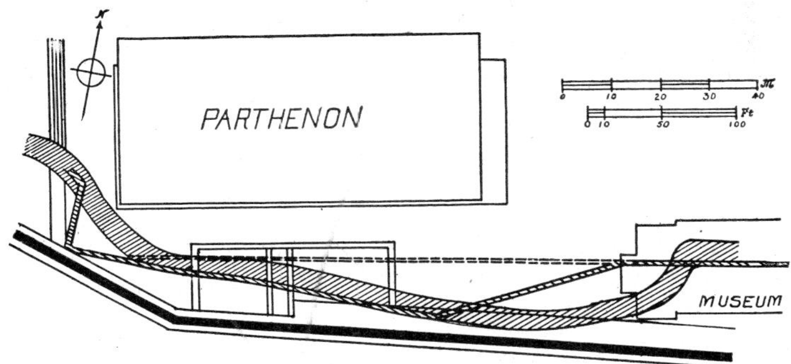


FIG. 174. — Complex of walls south of the Parthenon.

rate the building of the Parthenon was again undertaken, and this time the temple was brought to completion (Fig. 175).

The plan once more was materially altered. The old podium was utilized, though it was widened toward the north, now measuring 250 by 105 feet, the length of the building being diminished (Fig. 176). On the stylobate the temple measures about 228 by 101 feet. It rises on three steps, of which the lower two are each 1.7 feet high, the uppermost, or stylobate, a trifle higher. Marks of weather-

Fig. 175. — Parthenon, from the northeast.

ing at the middle of either end show that half-steps were here introduced, so as to afford easier access.

The temple structure (Fig. 175) is octastyle and peripteral; it has a surrounding colonnade, with eight columns at the ends and seventeen on each side, counting corner columns twice. The columns in most instances have twelve drums; their lower diameter is 6.25 feet, their height about 34.2 feet; they have twenty flutings. Above the colon-

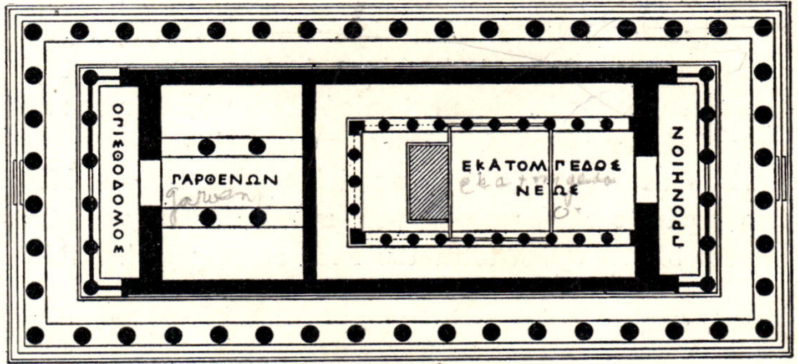


Fig. 176. — Plan of the Parthenon.

nade is the usual Doric entablature, consisting of architrave, triglyph frieze, and cornice. The building was originally covered with a roof framed of wood, upon which were laid marble tiles. Antefixes in the form of palmettes crowned the ridge and ran along the eaves, except at the corners, which were terminated by lions' heads. On the summits and corners of the gables were colossal acroteria in the form of scrolls and palmettes.

The pteron, or corridor inside the peristyle, is about sixteen feet wide on the ends and fourteen feet on the sides. Like the rest of the building, it is floored with marble; originally it was covered with a richly coffered marble ceiling.

The temple proper is elevated, by two steps, about 2.3

feet above the corridor, and is 193.6 feet in length by 71.3 feet wide. The side walls and the cross-wall are 3.8 feet thick; the end walls are somewhat heavier. At each end is a portico formed by six Doric columns, a little smaller than those of the peristyle. The corner columns stand in front of the antae, which terminate the side walls. Between the antae and the columns an iron grating, holes for fastening which can still be seen, extended up to the architrave, transforming the porticoes into closed rooms. Above the columns was the usual architrave marked off by regulae and guttae, but instead of a frieze of triglyphs and metopes a continuous Ionic frieze extended above the columns and around the entire cella.

The sanctuary (Fig. 177) was divided by a cross-wall into two separate rooms; this wall is now destroyed. The marble blocks which form the floor are 9.5 inches thick,

FIG. 177.—Interior of the Parthenon, from the east.

the thickness being increased to 15 inches where they carried columns or walls.

The larger chamber, or cella, to the east was ninety-eight feet long and about sixty-three feet wide. It was divided lengthwise into a nave and side aisles by two rows of small Doric columns. The columns also continued across the back of the chamber, forming an aisle there similar to those on the sides. The small columns supported an architrave, but no gallery, and above them similar columns supported the coffered ceiling. So great is the span that we may assume that the ceiling was of wood. The nave has a floor about an inch lower than that of the aisles. It was divided further into three nearly equal sections by a balustrade, traces of which can be detected on the floor. The balustrade also linked together the central columns and closed to the public the space before the statue, which stood in the rear third of the nave. The greater part of the area covered by the base of the statue is floored with poros instead of marble, and in the center of the area is a rectangular hole in which the central timber of the inner framework of the statue was probably fixed.

The rear, or west, chamber was about forty-four feet deep; its width was the same as that of the east chamber. Its coffered ceiling was supported by four lofty columns, possibly Ionic, whose location is indicated by square blocks in the floor. The columns divided the room into three nearly equal aisles.

From inscriptions and literary references we learn the names of the different chambers of the temple. The east portico was the Pronaos, or Proneïon. In it were stored numerous articles of value, mentioned in the treasure lists of the goddess. The great east room, the cella, in which, besides the cult statue, there were other works of art and treasures, was the Hekatompedos neôs, or Hundred-foot temple. This name it carried over from the Old Temple (p. 313) because of its length. Careful measurements have shown that the length of the room on the inside is exactly 100 Aeginetan, or early Attic, feet, the foot being reckoned at 11.65 inches by English standard; including the front and cross-walls, the length is 100 Solonian, or later Attic, feet, the Solonian foot being equivalent to 12.91 English inches. The Aeginetan foot is in general the standard in the construction of the Parthenon and other Periclean buildings. For the earlier buildings on the site of the Parthenon the Solonian foot was used.

The other large room was the Parthenon, or chamber of the Parthenos; later the designation was extended to the whole temple. This room may have been intended originally as a second sanctuary, but it came to be the most important repository for treasures of all sorts. The Thirty used it as an arsenal; and the servile Athenians of the end of the fourth century B.C. gave it over as the place of residence of Demetrius Poliorcetes, who desecrated it with his immorality.

Thus far the nomenclature is secure; but whether the name Opisthodomos belongs to the rear portico or to a separate building, it is not possible now to determine. All four names, Pronaos, Hekatompedos neôs, Parthenon, and Opisthodomos, are found in the same inscriptions, and Opisthodomos is the usual name for the rear room or portico of a temple. If this be not the correct designation here, the rear portico of the Parthenon is left unnamed in the inscriptions. On the other hand this portico, closed only by gratings, has seemed to some to be unsuitable as a storehouse of such treasures as are said to have been preserved in the Opisthodomos; and several of the literary references may be interpreted as referring to an independent building. For these and other reasons some scholars would give the name to the rear portion of the Old Temple (pp. 312 ff.); others, to the building which we have called the Chalcotheca, or to another building. Although the evidence does not warrant a positive decision, we shall probably be safe if we call the rear portico of the Parthenon the Opisthodomos, and leave undetermined the question whether all the treasures referred to were stored here.

Until recent years the method by which the cella of the Parthenon was lighted was the subject of much debate. Some scholars held that the Parthenon was hypaethral, having a skylight or other opening in the roof. But it is now reasonably certain that not many Greek temples were hypaethral (p. 165). When the great doors of the cella of the Parthenon were opened, there was an aperture of about 540 square feet; in the bright, clear air of Athens this was large enough to light the front of the chamber with considerable brilliancy, while at the rear the wonderful statue of the Maid against a dimly lighted background seemed to stand forth as a shining apparition.

The workmanship of all parts of the Parthenon, whether visible or concealed, is of an extraordinary degree of excellence. Architects, sculptors, and laborers were men of sincerity as well as skill, wherein is a lesson for men of other times and other lands. To assert that the technical execution is in every way so precise as can be secured with modern instruments would be an overstatement; but the painstaking of the builders has seldom left anything to be desired. Of this the accurate fitting of every block to its place, the exact joinings, the anchoring with cramps and dowels, the finish of the surfaces, and many other details, bear abundant witness.

But most admirable of all are the delicate deviations from rigid mathematical lines that mark the difference between the frigidity and hardness of mere architectural precision and the warmth and elasticity of a masterpiece of art. Art transcends mere constructive skill, and so subtle are these refinements in the Parthenon that they were unsuspected until seventy-five years ago. The true explanation of the effect on the eye of these slight compromises is psychological, and the final explanation in all cases cannot yet be given. Only a few examples of the refinements can be mentioned. Some of them the Parthenon shares with other temples, but in none other are the effects wrought out

FIG. 178. — South steps of the Parthenon, showing horizontal curvature.

with so great care. The most notable is perhaps the convex curvature of the horizontal lines. The steps and stylobate are not strictly horizontal, as they seem to be, but rise in a gentle curve from the corners to the middle; on the south side (Fig. 178), for example, the middle is about nine inches higher than the corners; the podium has the same curvature (so, we infer, the earlier buildings), and the entablature nearly the same. The walls of the cella have an imperceptible batter, or in-slope, so as not to seem top-heavy. The columns incline inwards, the corner columns being slightly more massive than the rest and more closely spaced, both for optical effect and for the adjustment of their position in relation to the triglyphs above them. The shafts of the columns have entasis, or swelling, which in modern architecture is so often misunderstood and exaggerated; the maximum deviation from a straight line in a column of the Parthenon 34.2 feet high is about 2.25 inches. The list might be extended to a considerable length, without taking into account the sculpture, the delicate moldings with their studied effects of light and shade, and the bright colors with which the building was decorated (p. 302).

The sculptures of the Parthenon constitute its supreme glory. They are of four kinds: the pedimental groups, the metopes, the frieze about the cella, and the cult statue of the goddess.

For an understanding of the pedimental sculptures we should be well-nigh lost without the statement of Pausanias, exasperatingly meager as it is: "As you enter into the temple which they name the Parthenon, all that is in the eagles, as they are called [the pediments, from their fancied resemblance to eagles], has to do with the birth of Athena; that in the rear is the contest of Poseidon with Athena for the land." Of the marvelous statues that made up these two groups a considerable number has been preserved. A few fragments are on the building, or in the Acropolis Museum; some portions are in the Louvre and other con-

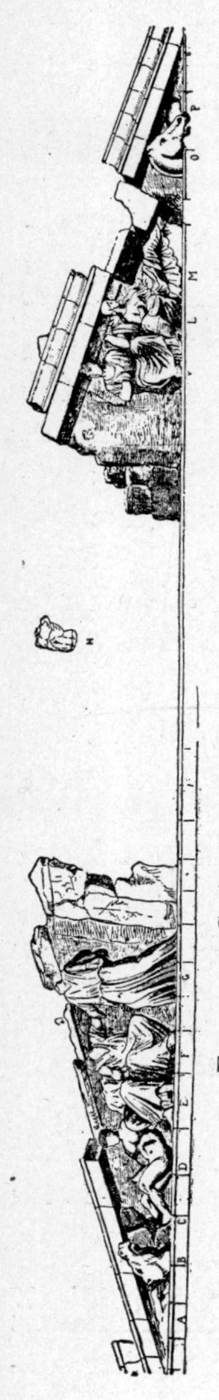

FIG. 179.—Carrey drawing of the east pediment of the Parthenon.

tinental collections; but the majority are in the British Museum. Besides these remains several other pieces of evidence are available for the restoration of the groups. First in importance are the drawings made in 1674, while the Parthenon was still almost intact, by a draughtsman in the service of the Marquis de Nointel (p. 4); though the designation may be incorrect, we may for the sake of convenience speak of these as the Carrey drawings. A careful examination of the cuttings and cramp-marks in the back wall and the floor of the pediments and in the extant statues has also proved of great value. Representations or imitations on vases, reliefs, and other works of art are useful as auxiliary testimony.

The central portion of the east pediment had already been destroyed when the Carrey drawing was made (Fig. 179). Two types of representation of the birth of Athena, the theme of this pediment, are found in ancient art. One is that of certain vase paintings (Fig. 166) and engraved mirrors, on which Athena is depicted as a doll-like figure issuing from the head of Zeus. This motif seems hardly consistent with the dignity of the group which occupied the front pediment of the Parthenon; furthermore the cuttings in the extant cornice show that a pair rather than a single figure stood in the middle. A sculptured puteal, or well-head, in Madrid (Fig. 180) probably gives a correct clew to the arrangement of the figures. In this relief the majestic king of the gods is seated at the left, facing Athena, who has already issued, full armed, from his head and is springing away.

FIG. 180. — Birth of Athena; relief about a marble puteal at Madrid.

A Victory hovers between them and is about to crown Athena with a wreath. Hephaestus, or Prometheus, is stepping back after having cloven the head of Zeus. To the right are the three Fates, with their usual attributes. Naturally the puteal cannot be trusted for the accessories, but the attitude of the principal figures probably reflects the design of the pediment (Fig. 181). The suggestion has recently been made that the rendering of the vase-paintings may have followed an unsuccessful model of Alcamenes submitted in competition as a design for the pediment (Fig. 166).

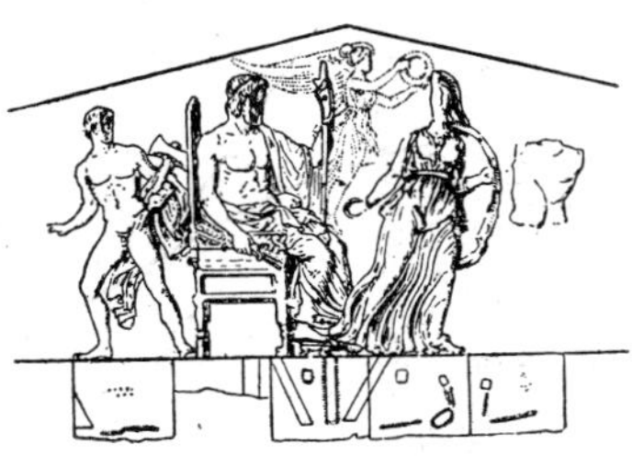

FIG. 181. — Central group of the east pediment of the Parthenon, restored.

All the figures represented in the Carrey drawing are extant, most of them being in the British Museum; fragments of the figures at the ex-

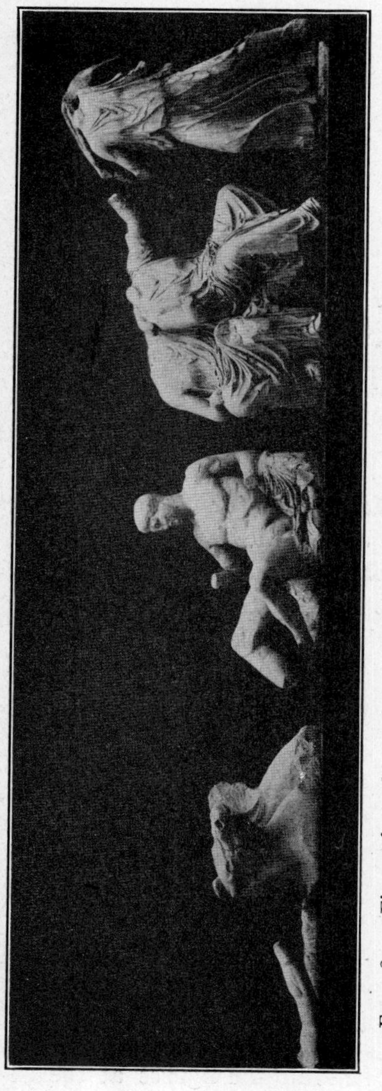

FIG. 182. — Figures from the south side of the east pediment of the Parthenon (British Museum, London).

treme ends are still on the Parthenon. At the left end Helius, the Sun, is driving his four-horse chariot up from the rippling sea; at the right end Selene, the Moon, is descending with her steeds below the horizon. The interpretation of the remaining figures is more problematical. Opinions are divided chiefly between two groups of critics. Some believe that the figures represent divinities on Olympus, or in part Attic heroes; others think that they are personifications, or, at all events some of them, of mountains, rivers, and other natural phenomena. For instance, the heroic figure (Fig. 182) next to Helius on the right has been variously interpreted as Heracles, Dionysus, Olympus, Theseus, and Cephalus, and the interpretations of the others have been quite as diverse. The Theseus, as he is traditionally named, is one of the most beautiful figures of the entire series, the only one whose head is preserved undetached. His youthful form rests easily upon a rock over which he has thrown his mantle and panther's or lion's skin. Back of him are two female figures seated on what seem to be mystic chests, which suggest their identification as Demeter and her daughter Persephone,

FIG. 183. — The "Fates," from the east pediment of the Parthenon (British Museum, London).

though by some they are called Hours. Rushing toward these, with garments floating back in the breeze, is a figure usually known as Iris, the messenger of Zeus; but the identification is doubtful. Next to Selene, at the other end of the pediment, are three seated female figures, which may be the Fates (Fig. 183); they have also been called Clouds, while the two at the right have been interpreted as the Sea reclining in the lap of Earth. About eleven figures from the center of the pediment are lost; no doubt these were the most splendid, as they were the largest, in the group. A Victory which has long been placed next to the

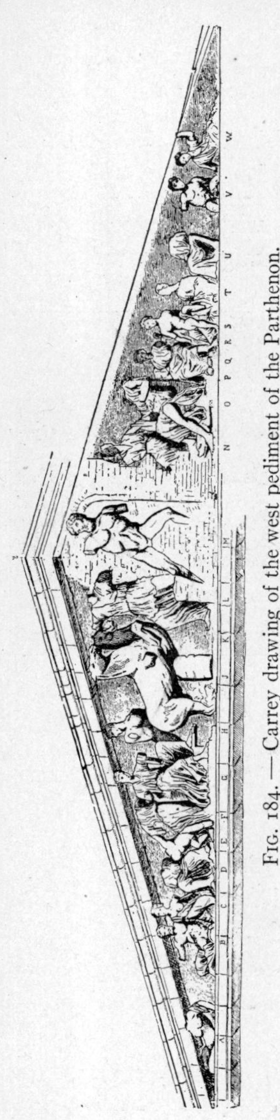

FIG. 184. — Carrey drawing of the west pediment of the Parthenon.

Fates is now to be assigned to the other pediment. All the extant figures are mutilated, but the noble living forms, full of simple dignity whether in action or in repose, the rich and graceful draperies, and the exquisite carving are beyond the highest praise. Nothing in sculpture excels them.

Of the statues of the west pediment, which depicted the contest of Athena and Poseidon for the land, fewer have been preserved, but fortunately the group was in better condition when the Carrey drawing (Fig. 184) was made. Several figures then existing were ruined in 1687 by Morosini (p. 304), and the majority of the remainder had disappeared before Lord Elgin came to rescue them (p. 306). From the drawing we can understand the general design. At the middle stood Athena and Poseidon, springing apart; between them were the olive tree brought forth by Athena and the salt spring produced by Poseidon (*cf.* Fig. 170). On either side of the chief actors stood their chariots and bounding steeds. Athena's car is probably driven by Victory, Poseidon's by Amphitrite. Behind the one chariot is a figure which seems to be Hermes, behind the other was probably Iris. At the

FIG. 185. — Parthenon from the northwest.

ends of the pediment were on the left the river god Ilissus, or Cephissus, on the right the nymph Callirrhoë (p. 108).

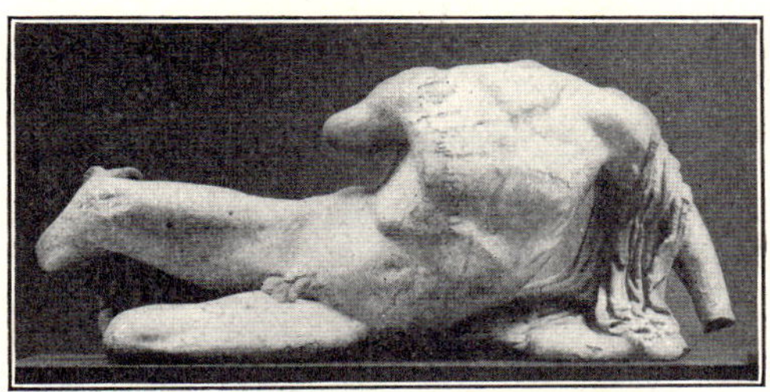

FIG. 186. — "Ilissus," from the west pediment of the Parthenon (British Museum).

The remaining figures may be of gods and heroes, or Attic divinities and heroes, or personifications. Two figures, perhaps Cecrops and his daughter Pandrosus, are still on the Parthenon (Fig. 185); the torso of a recumbent figure is at the right end of the pediment, and a portion of a crouching youth, which was placed next to Cecrops, has recently been identified in the Acropolis Museum. The figure of Ilissus (Fig. 186) is the best preserved from this pediment, but the torsos of the principal figures, Athena and Poseidon, have also been found.

Fig. 187. — Lapith and Centaur; metope from the Parthenon (British Museum).

All of the ninety-two metopes of the temple were sculptured in relief so high as almost to be in the round. The metopes are about four feet square, and were heavily framed in by the triglyphs, cornice, and architrave. The fourteen metopes of the east end, the fourteen of the west end, one of the south side, and eleven of the north side are still on the building. Fifteen are in the British Museum, three and the greater part of a fourth in the Acropolis Museum, and one in the Louvre. The fifteen in the British Museum, all from the south side, are the best preserved. Scores of fragments are in the museums mentioned, some in Copenhagen, and other pieces are being found from time to time. Besides the remains we have also the Carrey drawings of thirty-two of the series.

The metopes at the east end represented scenes from the battle of the gods and giants. Those at the west probably portrayed the conflict of Athenians and Amazons. The metopes of the south side seem to be divided into three groups, of which the principal subject is the battle of Lapiths and Centaurs (Figs. 187 and 188), but the interpretation of the nine central metopes is doubtful; possibly they represent scenes in the life of Erichthonius, and possibly the metopes usually assigned to this part of the frieze belong to the north side. More than half of the metopes of the north side are lost, and the subject is uncertain; those toward the west may relate to the siege of Troy.

Fig. 188. — Lapith and Centaur; metope from the Parthenon (British Museum).

The extant metopes vary greatly in style and technique and must have been carved by sculptors of widely divergent training and skill. Some are so archaic that they have even been thought to have been made originally for the earlier building. Others are developed in style and very beautiful.

The Ionic frieze, 524.1 feet in length and 3.25 feet in height, ran entirely about the sanctuary, some forty feet above the floor of the corridor. Nearly all of the west section (Fig. 189), about 70 feet long, is still on the temple. Approximately 247 feet are in the British Museum; about 58 feet are known only from the drawings of Carrey and Stuart. Only 45 feet are lost without record or remains.

The frieze is carved in relief, averaging about one and

one half inches in projection at the top, in places as much as two and one fourth inches, and about one and one fourth inches at the bottom; thus seeming slightly to tilt forward to meet the vision of the spectator on the ground below. The frieze contained some six hundred figures. It was carved with such consummate skill that as many as seven

FIG. 189.—West frieze of the Parthenon, in situ.

horsemen riding abreast are portrayed without the slightest confusion of planes. A nice appreciation of the delicacy of treatment is found in Ruskin's comment on a portion of a chariot group.[1]

"The projection of the heads of the four horses, one behind the other, is certainly not more, altogether, than three quarters of an inch from the flat ground, and the one in front does not in reality project more than the one behind it, yet, by mere drawing, you see the sculptor has got them to appear to recede in due order, and by the soft rounding

[1] *Aratra Pentelici*, Section 179.

of the flesh surfaces, and modulation of the veins, he has taken away all look of flatness from the necks. He has drawn the eyes and nostrils with dark incision, careful as the finest touches of a painter's pencil: and then, at last, when he comes to the manes, he has let fly hand and chisel with their full force; and where a base workman (above all, if he had modeled the thing in the clay first) would have

FIG. 190. — Section of the north frieze of the Parthenon (British Museum).

lost himself in laborious imitation of hair, the Greek has struck the tresses out with angular incisions, deep driven, every one in appointed place and deliberate curve, yet flowing so free under his noble hand, that you cannot alter, without harm, the bending of any single ridge, nor contract, nor extend, a part of them."

The scene depicted on the frieze is the great Panathenaic procession, which every four years conveyed from the Outer Cerameicus to the Acropolis the peplos, or robe, of Athena, woven by chosen maidens of the city. The procession of the frieze begins at the southwest corner of the building. From this point it advances along both sides toward the center of the east end. Across the west end (Fig. 189) are youths preparing for the procession; in front of them, along the sides of the temple, are trains of cavalry (Fig. 190), riders and horses in every position of pulsating activity. Next advances a series of chariots, sometimes a full-armed apobates leaping off or on the car while the driver urges on his steeds. Before these march a number of old men, and then the musicians, preceded by men carrying trays and water-jars. Last on the sides of the temple are youths leading the cows and sheep for sacrifice. After the corners

FIG. 191. — Athena, Hephaestus, Poseidon, Apollo, and Artemis, from the east frieze of the Parthenon (British Museum, London, and Acropolis Museum, Athens).

of the east front are turned, matrons and maidens advance with sacrificial implements; these lead the procession, and approach groups of magistrates, or the tribal heroes, who lean on their staffs and watch the coming of the parade. The middle portion of this end of the frieze is occupied by the groups of seated gods and goddesses (Fig. 191) calmly gazing at the approaching cavalcade. All the Olympian divinities save Hestia are here, and Dionysus and Eros are added. Between the two groups of divinities and over the great door (Fig. 192) stands a woman receiving two girls, who carry stools on their heads, and beside her a bearded man and a boy holding between them a folded cloth. This cloth has been variously interpreted but it probably represents the sacred peplos borne in the procession, borne, indeed, as the sail of the Panathenaic ship (pp. 362 ff.), but the artist has refrained from portraying on the frieze the ship, which did not enter the Acropolis with the procession — if a ship was used at all in the fifth century.

FIG. 192. — Central episode of the procession, from the east frieze of the Parthenon (British Museum).

The scene probably represents the delivery of the *peplos* of Athena.

The frieze betrays some differences of style and workmanship, but the general design is manifestly the conception of one master mind. For truth and vividness of life and motion the reliefs are unsurpassed. The colors with which the frieze was adorned and the bronze accessories will be mentioned later.

The center of interest in the temple was, of course, the chryselephantine statue of Athena, which, with its base, towered upwards of forty feet above the floor of the cella. As in all such statues the inner framework was of baser materials. However fair the exterior, as Lucian says of this class of images (*Somn.* 24), "if you stoop down and look inside, you will see bars, bolts, nails running through and

FIG. 193. — Varvakeion statuette of Athena Parthenos (National Museum, Athens).

through, logs, wedges, pitch, clay, and all sorts of shapeless things." Over this core were incrusted the plates of gold for the drapery and of ivory for the exposed parts of the flesh. The weight of gold used for the Athena is given by Thucydides as forty talents, perhaps equal in value to about $50,000. Both the gold and the ivory could be removed for weighing, as the court was reminded by Pericles when Pheidias was charged with peculation.

Since the statue has perished, we must judge of its style from descriptions and from the copies and imitations, which are fairly numerous. Once more Pausanias is our guide. "The statue itself," he says, "is made of ivory and gold. In the middle of the helmet is the image of a Sphinx . . . and on either side are Griffins in relief. . . . The statue of Athena is erect, in a tunic reaching to the feet, and on her breast is the head of Medusa inlaid of ivory. She holds a Victory about four cubits high, and in the other hand a spear. At her feet is set her shield and near the spear is a serpent, which may be Erichthonius. In relief on the base of the statue is the birth of Pandora; for Hesiod and other poets have it that this Pandora was the first woman, and that before Pandora was born the female sex did not exist." Plato adds the information (*Hipp. maj.* 12) that the pupils of the statue's eyes were "of stone" — crystal, doubtless — and Pausanias tells us in another place (5, 11, 10) that the ivory was kept from splitting by the use of water and not, as in the case of the Zeus at Olympia, by the use of oil; the reservoir for the water cannot be located. Further details are added by other writers; thus we are informed that the relief on the base contained the figures of twenty gods, and that on the interior of the shield was painted the battle of the gods and giants.

The most servile extant copy of the statue is the Varvakeion statuette (Fig. 193), so named from the school in Athens near which it was found. This is about three feet four inches in height, a mechanical reproduction by an uninspired stonecutter, probably of the time of Hadrian. It cannot be depended upon for details, least of all for the soul of Pheidias's matchless work. As one critic remarks, "It bears the same relation to Phidias's statue as the coarsest German oleograph after the Sistine Madonna bears to the picture which it affects to reproduce."[1] More spirited, but sketchy and incomplete, is the Lenormant statuette (Fig. 194), which is about a foot and four inches high, also in the museum at Athens. An imitation of heroic size has been found at Pergamum (Fig. 195), and a marble statuette at Patras. Besides these, numerous other replicas are preserved in various European museums, but few of them are at all faithful, and they add little to our knowledge of the original. For individual features we possess

FIG. 194. — Lenormant statuette of Athena Parthenos (National Museum, Athens).

[1] Gardner, *A Handbook of Greek Sculpture*, p. 255.

other reproductions. To mention only a few, the head of the goddess is admirably depicted on two gold pendants found in the Crimea (Fig. 196); on a superb gem signed by Aspasius (Fig. 197); and in a terra cotta mold recently discovered at Corinth. Of the shield several more or less fragmentary replicas exist, the best and most complete being the "Strangford shield" now in the British Museum (Fig. 198).

Fig. 195. — Colossal figure adapted after the Parthenos of Pheidias; from Pergamum (König. Museum, Berlin).

From such various sources we are enabled to obtain a reasonably complete conception of the statue. The goddess was represented as standing in an easy attitude on a high basis; her weight is thrown on the right foot, the left leg being slightly bent. Her right hand supports a winged Victory; her left rests lightly on the rim of her shield; her spear leans against her shoulder and may have been grasped also by her hand; inside the shield is coiled the sacred serpent. The simple tunic, folded down and girt at the waist, leaves both arms bare. Over her shoulders is the aegis; on her head is a crested helmet.

FIG. 196. — Gold pendant with a representation of the head of the Parthenos (Hermitage, St. Petersburg).

The pillar which in the Varvakeion statuette supports the right hand is not Greek in style, and its Pheidian origin has justly been questioned. The brittle marble of the statuette demanded it, but in a chryselephantine statue surely a little cleverness might have obviated the necessity of so clumsy an expedient; artistically it seems impossible. The pillar does not appear in Athenian coins that show the statue, although it is seen, in one form or another, in a few other representations. Possibly the support was added at a later time, when the framework, burdened by the weight of the Victory, had developed signs of yielding to the strain.

FIG. 197. — Gem signed by Aspasius with representation of the head of Athena (Vienna Museum).

The sculptor took advantage of almost every available space for ornamentation; to this fact the elaborate helmet, the aegis, the borders of the robe, the edges of the sandals, the painted inner and sculptured outer surfaces of the shield, and the reliefs on the base, bear witness. Among the figures in the battle of the Greeks and Amazons on the exterior of the shield Pheidias is said to have introduced himself as a bald old man raising a stone in both hands, and Pericles poising his spear in such a way that his arm partially concealed his face. These figures are represented in a free manner on the Strangford shield, but we have no means of testing the story repeated by a number of writers that the figures were so cleverly connected with the framework of the statue that their removal would have imperiled the entire statue; the tale sounds improbable.

FIG. 198. — Strangford shield (British Museum).

The serenity, grace, and beauty of the perfect statue can only be imagined. Ancient writers abound in its praise, some of them even including it among the "seven wonders." As Cicero puts it (*Brutus* 257), "The Athenians were more concerned about having sound roofs to their houses than about the most beautiful statue of Minerva; but I should rather be Pheidias than even the best of carpenters."

The Parthenos still existed in the fourth century of the Christian era, when Nestorius placed a small statue of Achilles "at the foot of the statue of Athena set up in the Parthenon" (Zosimus 4, 18). Indeed, it probably endured a century longer, for the philosopher Proclus, who died in 485 A.D., apparently saw its removal "by those who move even things immovable" (Marinus, *Vita Procli* 30).

A very inadequate conception of the Parthenon and its sculptures, as, indeed, of any Greek temple, will be gained without consideration of the use of polychromy in enhancing the general effect. Whether the shafts of the columns and the broad surfaces generally were toned down by the application of some neutral stain is not certain. But we know that the upper plastic members were richly adorned with color, dark blue, red, and less often green, yellow, and gilt. Thus the triglyphs, mutules, and regulae were painted blue; the remainder of the soffit of the cornice and the taenia of the architrave were red; other moldings combined these colors alternately. Maeanders and similar patterns still survive on fragments which have been less exposed. Backgrounds of sculpture were painted red or blue; of the statues themselves the draperies, or at least their borders, the hair, the lips, and the eyes were colored in more or less natural tints. The flesh was probably stained with a tempering medium. Accessories, such as the bridles and reins of horses of the frieze, were added in bronze, the removal of which accounts for the absence of these details to-day.

The Parthenon remained practically unaltered throughout the Hellenistic and Roman periods. On the east architrave can be seen the traces where shields were once affixed, some of them perhaps a part of the "three hundred Persian panoplies" presented by Alexander the Great after the battle of Granicus. Between the marks of the shields are groups of small holes in which were fastened the bronze letters of a long inscription, which, by a clever study of the position of the holes, has been deciphered and found to be a decree in honor of Nero, dating from 61 A.D. A few years later Plutarch names the Parthenon first among the works of Pericles, which, he declares (*Pericles* 13), were "made in a brief time, for long duration. For in beauty each was ancient from the very moment of its creation, while in vigor they are fresh and new until now." About half a century later Pausanias seems also to have found the Parthenon intact.

In the fifth century of our era the Parthenon became a Christian church. At first, apparently, it was sacred to

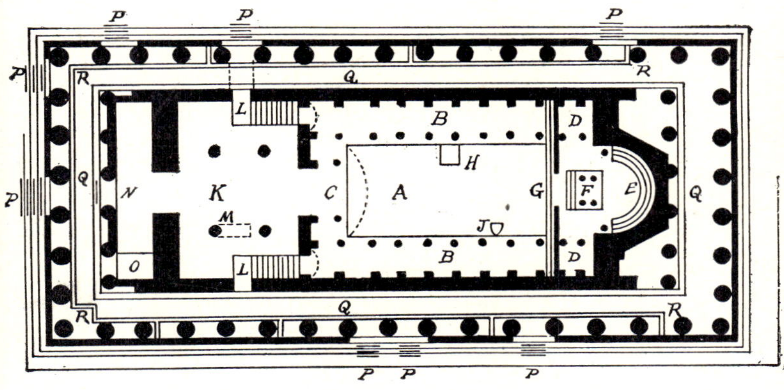


FIG. 199. — Plan of the Parthenon as it was in early Christian times.

*A*, nave; *BBC*, aisles and galleries; *DD*, sacred bema; *E*, apse; *F*, high altar; *G*, beautiful gate; *H*, ambon; *J*, bishop's throne; *K*, narthex; *LL*, side entrances to galleries; *M*, basin; *N*, door; *O*, chapel (later, spiral staircase of minaret); *PP*, steps in stereobate; *QQ*, corridor (pteron); *RR*, water channel.

"Holy Wisdom" (Hagia Sophia), but at least as early as the tenth century it was consecrated to the "Mother of God" (Theotokos). To the Christian period belongs the beginning of extensive alterations in the building (Fig. 199). The chief entrance was transferred to the west end; a large doorway was cut through the cross-wall, while at the east end an apse closed the door and filled the largest part of the pronaos. A new series of inner columns supported a gallery for the women, who could enter from the outer corridor by stairways accessible through doors let into the side walls. Windows were made to lighten the interior, and the walls were covered with paintings, abundant traces of which are still visible. Only the cella was now roofed; the intercolumniations of the peristyle were filled with rude walls (Fig. 231) and the corridor was open to the sky. Shortly after the occupation of Athens by the Turks, about 1456 A.D., the church was made over into a mosque, and at the southwest corner was erected a lofty minaret (*cf.* Fig. 231), the lower part of which still remains and by its spiral staircase gives access to the western summit of the building. There are few literary references to these changes, only the scanty reports of early travelers; in the main the pathetic story must be deciphered from the battered ruins.

After all its vicissitudes the Parthenon remained almost complete until a little more than two centuries ago. In 1687 the Turks were being besieged in the Acropolis by the Venetians under Morosini. On the twenty-sixth of September of that year a German gunner succeeded in dropping a shell on the roof of the building. A quantity of powder stored in the cella exploded, destroying some three hundred lives and hurling into ruins the entire middle part of the structure. Morosini, who soon took the Acropolis, attempted to lower the horses of Poseidon from the west pediment, but his ropes broke and the sculptures were dashed in pieces on the rock beneath. After the Venetians retired, the Turks again took possession of the citadel, and a little later built a small mosque, turned toward Mecca, on the floor of the ruined temple (Fig. 200). Many portions of the sculptures and other remains were carried off

FIG. 200.—Parthenon, with Turkish mosque and houses, from the east. From a drawing by Stuart and Revett.

or demolished from time to time, and in 1801, and several years following, the Earl of Elgin, under the authority of a firman from the Sublime Porte permitting him "to take away any pieces of stone with old inscriptions or figures thereon," appropriated and later shipped to England nearly all the remaining statues of the pediments, much of the frieze, and numerous metopes, and other fragments. Unfortunately his emissaries were not always scrupulous, and no little damage was done to the building itself, considerable portions of the cornice and other blocks being torn away in order to free the sculptures. But the removal served a good purpose, the withering censure of Byron and others notwithstanding. The few sculptures which remain on the building have suffered far more than those in the British Museum; and the marks of cannon balls on the columns show what the rescued statues must have undergone had they been left in place. After the revolution (1821–1829) a few columns of the building were restored with an ugly patchwork of brick, an experiment happily soon discontinued. A stupid project for building a royal palace on the Acropolis with the Parthenon in its court was fortunately abandoned.

Of the precious objects once preserved in the Parthenon we have long inventories in the inscriptions which have been mentioned. These treasures were of many different kinds; among them were bullion, gold and silver vessels, armor and weapons, articles of furniture, and musical instruments. The marble slabs engraved with the treasure lists were set up every four years, and a large number of them have been recovered; we have an almost complete series from 434 to 404 B.C. The Parthenon proper, or rear room of the temple, among other things contained the silver-footed throne on which Xerxes is said to have sat during the battle of Salamis, and a bronze pillar bearing a description of the great statue. Somewhere in the temple were painted portraits of Themistocles and Heliodorus Halis. "The only statue that I saw there," says Pausanias, "was that of king Hadrian; and by the entrance one of Iphicrates, who performed many marvelous deeds." Hadrian's statue may have stood on the inscribed base found on the Acropolis. "Ask them," cries Aeschines (3, 243), "why the people gave them presents and set up statues; they will all answer you in a breath . . . and to Iphicrates [a statue was set up] because he slew a brigade of Lacedaemonians," in 392 B.C. The statue, as Demosthenes tells us, was of bronze; it was set up twenty years after the distinguished service of Iphicrates.

## EAST END OF THE ACROPOLIS

"Beyond the temple," but whether Pausanias means east or south we cannot tell, "is a bronze Apollo; they say that Pheidias made the statue. It is called Locust (Parnopius), because once when locusts were injuring the land the god said that he would avert them from the country. That he did avert them, they know, but they do not say how. I know of my own knowledge that three times locusts vanished from Mt. Sipylus in different ways: once a violent wind fell upon them and swept them out; again, the god brought a rain storm and then intense heat killed them; and again they were caught and destroyed by sudden cold. These things I have seen happen.

"On the Acropolis of the Athenians are statues of Pericles son of Xanthippus and of Xanthippus himself, who took part in the sea-fight at Mycale against the Medes; but the statue of Pericles is set up in another place (p. 346).

"Near Xanthippus stands Anacreon the Teian, who was

the first after Sappho the Lesbian to make the majority of his compositions love-songs. His attitude is that of a man singing while tipsy.

"The statues near by of Io daughter of Inachus and Callisto daughter of Lycaon were made by Deinomenes. The stories of both these women are in every way alike, the love of Zeus and the anger of Hera, and the transformation of Io into a heifer and of Callisto into a bear.

"By the south wall are groups of statues portraying the war called the War of the Giants, who once dwelt around Thrace and the Isthmus of Pallene, the Battle of the Amazons and Athenians, the action against the Medes at Marathon, and the destruction of the Gauls in Mysia. These were set up by Attalus, and each is of about two cubits in stature."

No trace of the statues now remains, but the truth of Pausanias's statement as to their situation is confirmed by the remark of Plutarch (*Anton.* 60) that "just prior to the battle of Actium the Dionysus from the Gigantomachy was hurled down into the theater by a hurricane," which also overturned the colossi of Eumenes and Attalus (p. 43). Pausanias's estimate of the size of the figures — which may originally have numbered upwards of sixty — has led to their identification with a series of ten or more prone statues, about three feet long, which are in various European museums. As each statue has its separate base, it seems probable that they are copies rather than parts of the original groups. Indeed, the statues of the Acropolis were apparently of bronze. The extant figures are all of the defeated foes, none of the victors having been preserved. When discovered the figure of an Amazon now in Naples is said to have had an infant clinging to her breast (Fig. 201). Pliny informs us that such a group as this was made by the sculptor Epigonus, who is known to have made other statues for Attalus I (p. 41) at Pergamum. The inference seems plausible that Epigonus may have been the sculptor of some or all of the figures of Attalus's offering on the Acropolis. The extant copies are said to be of Asiatic marble.

Fig. 201. — Copies in marble of Giant and Amazon from the offering of Attalus (Naples Museum).

"There is also a statue of Olympiodorus," says Pausanias, following the remark with a long digression on this man's success in opposing the Macedonians, probably in 288 B.C. "And near the image of Olympiodorus is a bronze statue of Artemis surnamed Leucophryene. This was erected by the sons of Themistocles; for the Magnesians whom the king gave to Themistocles to rule hold Leucophryenian Artemis in honor." Artemis's surname Leucophryene was taken from the town of Leucophrys on the Maeander River. The figure of what may be the statue dedicated by the sons of Themistocles is found on certain Athenian coins.

In a "sudden access of haste" Pausanias now passes over we know not how many objects of interest with the words: "But I must press forward with my narrative, if I am to go through all Greece in a similar manner. Endoeus was an Athenian by birth but a disciple of Daedalus, and he accompanied Daedalus to Crete, when Daedalus fled on account of the murder of Calos (pp. 204 f.). Endoeus's work is a seated statue of Athena bearing an inscription to the effect that Callias dedicated it and Endoeus made it." As a matter of fact Endoeus was probably an Ionian of the sixth century B.C.; the archaic style of his Athena would seem to have given rise to the story of his connection with the mythical Daedalus. The statue of Endoeus has been identified conjecturally with a mutilated Athena of island marble which was found at the foot of the Acropolis (Fig. 202). The goddess is seated, and wears a long tunic, over which is her aegis adorned with the Gorgon's head.

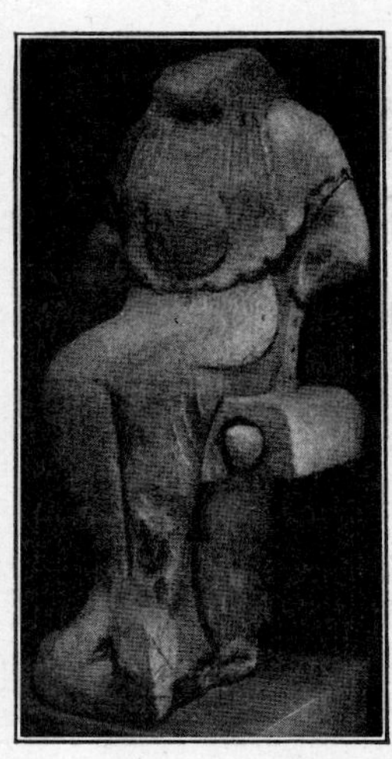

FIG. 202. — Seated Athena, ascribed to Endoeus (Acropolis Museum, Athens).

A little northeast of the Parthenon, on the highest point of the Acropolis, are the remains of what the inscriptions style "the great altar of Athena." At present only the rock-hewn core is left, together with a few stones of the encircling wall and cuttings for votive offerings and stelae.

In ancient literature no mention is made of a small circular temple standing some twenty-five yards east of the center of the Parthenon (*cf.* Fig. 133). Here still remains a square foundation of poros, with a few architectural fragments (Fig. 203). The temple was of white marble and a little more than twenty-five feet in diameter. Its peristyle was of nine Ionic columns, made in imitation of those of the Erechtheum, and it had a conical roof. Whether or not it had a cella and cult statues we do not know. A beautifully carved inscription on one of the blocks of the architrave (see figure) shows us that it was dedicated to "the goddess Rome and to Augustus Caesar," and that it was built "in the archonship of Areus the Paeanian, son of Dorion." Unfortunately the date of

FIG. 203. — Remains of the temple of Rome and Augustus.

this archon is not known, but the fact that Octavius bears the title Augustus indicates a date after 27 B.C.

In the southeast corner of the Acropolis, partially covering remains of Cyclopean house-walls, is a foundation of poros blocks belonging to a large structure, probably of the sixth century. This building was upwards of 130 feet long and 50 feet wide. Upon a part of the foundation is now built the annex to the Acropolis Museum. What the building was is uncertain. The abundance of marble chips strewn about has suggested the theory that it was a workshop for the builders of the second temple on the site of the Parthenon.

## THE ERECHTHEUM AND ADJACENT MONUMENTS

With the words, "There is also a building called the Erechtheum," Pausanias brings us back to the middle of the north side of the Acropolis. In this region were the earliest buildings of Athens, and some of her most sacred tokens. Numerous ruins of Cyclopean house-walls of Acropolis limestone occupy the area, and at the northeast corner are the remains of an early stairway (Fig. 20), which led down to a postern gate. Immediately south of the Erechtheum are the scanty remains of what seems to have been the palace of the prince of the primitive city. The most that can be seen to-day are two bases of stone (one is visible at the left in Fig. 214), which probably supported the wooden columns before the royal vestibule, as at Tiryns and other Mycenaean strongholds. We may guess, therefore, that here was the "strong house of Erechtheus" of which Homer speaks and with which were associated the names of the other heroes, Cecrops and Pandion. In the present state of our knowledge, to advance beyond these conjectures is to tread on quicksand.

The excavations also uncovered here the foundations of a large temple (Figs. 204 and 205), which has become the object of a voluminous literature. For the want of a surer name on which all can agree, this building is usually known as the Old Temple. The foundation of the cella is of Acropolis limestone; that of the peristyle, of Kará limestone. On the south the foundation consists of only a single course of stone; on the north the rock slopes away so that the wall rises some ten feet above it (Fig. 212).

FIG. 204. — Foundation of the "Old Temple."

In the background is the Erechtheum.

The material of the foundation of the cella argues an earlier date than that of the peristyle (p. 314), and this inference is borne out by extant fragments of the superstructure. The form of the foundation shows that it was unadorned by columns except at the front and rear. Its total length was 113.8 feet, its total width, forty-four feet.

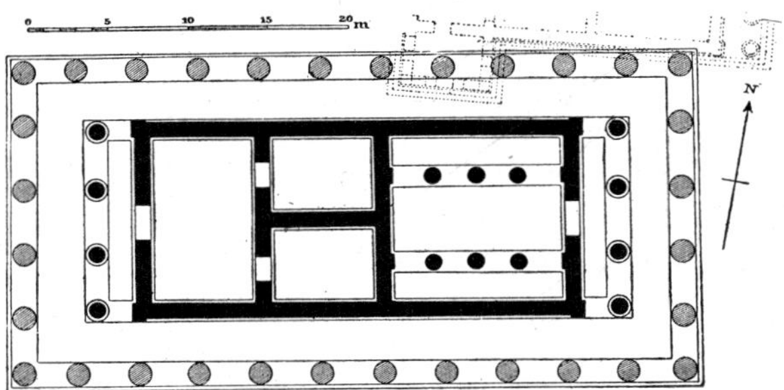


FIG. 205. — Plan of the "Old Temple."

On its platform, however, it measured precisely one hundred old Attic feet (p. 280), whence its official name, the Hecatompedum. Whether it was a temple in antis and had two columns between the pilasters on the ends of the prolonged sides, or was amphiprostyle, with four columns across each end, is uncertain. Its interior was divided by a closed cross-wall into nearly equal parts. The east chamber was divided by rows of columns into a nave and side aisles; the west section was set off by partitions into a large west chamber with two small rooms behind it. Above the foundation the temple was constructed of poros. It must have been erected not later than the end of the seventh or the beginning of the sixth century B.C.

The excavations yielded also a large part of the pedimental sculptures, which gradually have been pieced together. These too are of poros. As to their arrange-

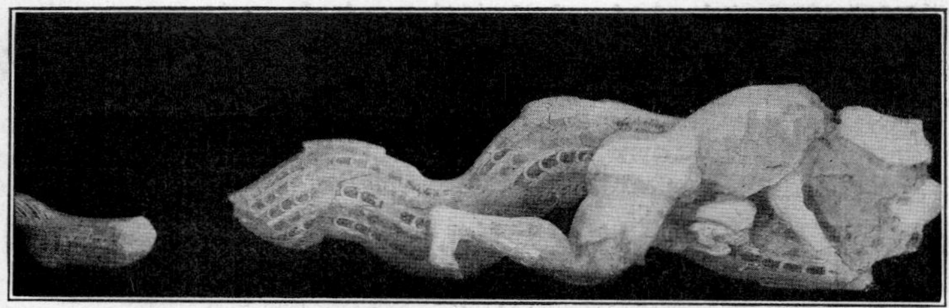

FIG. 206. — Heracles and Triton, from pediment of the Hecatompedum (Acropolis Museum, Athens).

ment in the pediments various theories have been proposed. One plausible scheme would place on the south side of the east pediment the figures of Heracles wrestling with the Triton (Fig. 206) and on the other side the three-headed monster known as the Typhon (Fig. 207). The west pediment probably bore two immense coiled and rearing serpents, with a group of gods between them. These figures are wrought in quaint archaic style and, as the remains abundantly show, were brightly adorned with colors. For example, the Typhon's flesh was red; the hair and beard, blue; the irises of the eyes, green; and the eyebrows, eyelashes, and the pupils of the eyes, black.

At a later time, probably the period of the Peisistratids, the temple was remodeled. A Doric peristyle was thrown about it, and at the same time the columns at the ends of the cella may have been changed to Ionic. The restored temple had but one step, a single block of which remains in situ on the north side. The columns and walls of the building were of poros, but a part, if not all, of the metopes and perhaps the cornice, the roof tiling, and some other members were of marble, as were the sculptures.

Portions of the new pedimental groups are preserved, and their advanced style is manifest. The group of the

FIG. 207. — Typhon, from pediment of the Hecatompedum (Acropolis Museum, Athens).

east pediment now represented the battle of the gods and giants. In the center was Athena transfixing a giant with her spear (Fig. 208). The recumbent giants from the corners of the pediment and a few other fragments are extant. The theme of the west pediment is unknown. Traces of color have been distinguished on the extant

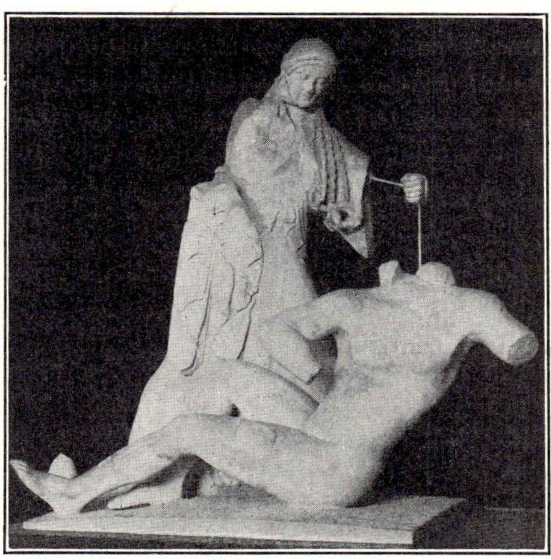

FIG. 208. — Athena and the giant Enceladus, from the pediment of the "Old Temple" (Acropolis Museum, Athens).

figures, and doubtless they also were picked out in color, as were the earlier statues. Some fragments of a frieze have been found, which may have run about the cella, though this view has been disputed.

That the Old Temple was destroyed by the Persians is generally agreed. After their return, following the battle of Salamis, the Athenians built into the wall of the Acropolis a considerable portion of the architrave, metopes, triglyphs, cornice, some of the drums of the columns, and other members (p. 56). Some of the marble metopes were used to face the Pelasgian wall south of the old Propylon, and other architectural members were utilized in the steps west of the Parthenon (p. 260), and elsewhere on two of the metopes had been carved now famous inscriptions of 485/4 B.C., known as the Hecatompedum inscriptions.

The subsequent fate of the building has been the subject of endless discussion. That the peristyle was never rebuilt is fairly certain. As to the temple chamber the adherents of one view believe that it too was not rebuilt; a second group of scholars maintain that all, or the rear half of it, was reconstructed to serve as a temporary treasury, and that it was destroyed by a fire in 406 B.C. by which, as Xenophon tells us (*Hellen.* 1, 6, 1) "the old temple of Athena was burned;" a third view is that, after this fire, it was again rebuilt, that it was seen by Pausanias and mentioned by him either in a lacuna already considered (p. 266) or after his description of the Erechtheum, and that it stood even down into the Middle Ages. The discussion is involved and we must be content with the expression of the opinion that the second view is correct.[1]

Quite as difficult a problem is the determination of the

[1] An excellent summary of the argument is given in D'Ooge's *The Acropolis of Athens*, Appendix III.

divinity, or divinities, to whom the Old Temple was sacred. Without much doubt the east chamber of the temple was dedicated to Athena. Whether the rear rooms were used as a treasury or were devoted to certain gods and heroes is hard to say. According to the second of these possibilities Erechtheus, Poseidon, and Butes have been suggested, since they were associated with Athena in the Erechtheum. Not less plausible would be the conjecture that the worship of the hero Cecrops was prominent here, as was that of Erechtheus in the Erechtheum; in that case the Old Temple must have been the Cecropium. From literary sources we know that the Acropolis bore a Cecropium, or sanctuary of Cecrops, containing a grave of that hero; in one of the building inscriptions (p. 320) the Caryatid Porch and the southwest corner of the Erechtheum are designated as "towards the Cecropium" and "by the sanctuary of Cecrops;" and a plausible restoration of one of the Hecatompedum inscriptions makes the text provide a prohibition of the priests from removing anything "from the temple or the pronaos or the altar or from the south of the temple inside of the Cecropium or throughout all the Hecatompedum." If this hypothesis is correct, much else becomes clear.

Pausanias's description of the Erechtheum (Fig. 209) is more extended than that of any other building in Athens. "There is also a building," he says, "called the Erechtheum. In front of the entrance is an altar of Most High Zeus where they sacrifice nothing having life, but after laying on cakes are accustomed to make no more use of wine. When you have entered there are altars, one of Poseidon, on which they also sacrifice to Erechtheus according to the oracle; one of the hero Butes; and a third, of Hephaestus. Upon the walls are paintings of the family of the Butads.

FIG. 209. — Erechtheum, from the southwest.

In the immediate foreground are blocks from the Parthenon; the foundation beyond is of the "Old Temple."

And (for the building is double) there is also sea-water in a well. This is no great marvel, for other people who dwell inland, for example, the Aphrodisian Carians, have the same; but this well is worthy of note, since it echoes the sound of waves when the south wind has been blowing. There is also the mark of a trident in the rock. This is said to have appeared as a witness for Poseidon in his contest for the land.

"The rest of the city and likewise the whole country are sacred to Athena, for whatever other gods they are accustomed to revere in the villages, they honor Athena none the less; but the holiest thing in the commonwealth, supposed to have existed many years before they came together from the villages, is a statue of Athena on the present Acropolis, then named the Polis [City]. The story about it is that it fell from heaven; but I shall not enter into the discussion of the question as to whether this is true or not. A golden lamp for the goddess was made by Callimachus. They fill the lamp with oil and then wait until the same day of the following year; and that oil suffices in the meantime for the lamp, which shines day and night. Its wick is of Carpasian flax, the only kind not consumed by fire. Stretching above the lamp to the roof is a bronze palm tree, which carries off the smoke. Callimachus, who made the lamp, while inferior to the foremost sculptors in real artistic ability, was so much the best of them all in cleverness that he was the first to use the drill on stone, and he gave himself the title of the 'Refiner of Art,' or rather accepted the title when others gave it to him.

"In the temple of the Polias a wooden Hermes is set up. This is said to be a votive offering of Cecrops, but it cannot be seen for the myrtle branches which cover it. Votive offerings worthy of note are the following: of archaic things, a folding chair, the work of Daedalus; of the spoils from the Medes, the cuirass of Masistius, the commander of the cavalry at Plataea, and a scimitar, said to be that of Mardonius."

The beautiful temple thus described is called the Erechtheum only by Pausanias, Plutarch, and Heliodorus, whence we may judge that the name came into use only in

FIG. 210. — Erechtheum, from the southeast.

late times. One of the extant building inscriptions calls it "the temple in which [is] the ancient statue," but this unwieldy nomenclature was probably temporary. Since the temple took the place of an earlier temple on the same spot, the name Ancient Temple seems later to have become official, and the building generally in literature and inscriptions is thus designated, unless, as some scholars think, this name was applied to the Old Temple, and no earlier temple existed (p. 337).

The temple may have been begun a short time before the Peloponnesian War; more probably, during the Peace of Nicias, about 421 B.C. We learn from the inscriptions that it was nearly finished in 409 B.C. and practically complete two years later. A dozen years later some work yet remained to be done, unless an inscription which records the details is wrongly dated.

The Erechtheum is unique in several respects. Owing to the uneven surface of the rock and the necessity of preserving the sacred tokens, the east and south sides are

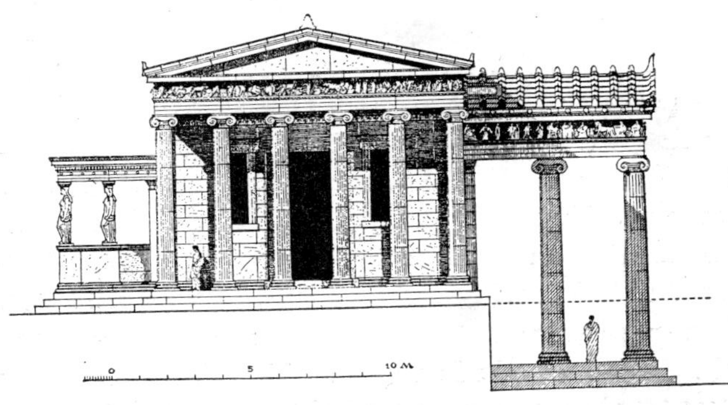


FIG. 211. — Erechtheum, from the east, restored.

built about nine feet higher than the west and north sides. Vitruvius says, with some exaggeration (4, 8, 4): "All things which are usually in front have been transferred to the sides." He doubtless refers to the north entrance and the porch of the Maidens, but other peculiarities not a few have made the interpretation of the building puzzling.

The width of the temple, measured on the topmost of its three steps, is about thirty-seven feet; its length about seventy-four feet. The foundation is of poros, the superstructure of white Pentelic marble, save the background of the frieze, which is of dark-gray Eleusinian stone. The temple was fronted by six ornate Ionic columns, twenty-two feet high. Five of these are still in place; the one to the north was carried off by Lord Elgin. Behind the columns was a narrow porch, with a coffered ceiling of marble. From the porch the cella was entered through a central door, on

FIG. 212 — Erechtheum, from the west.

either side of which was a small window, a feature already noticed in the Pinacotheca of the Propylaea, but not common in Greek temples. At the west end of the temple four half-columns stand on a high wall (Fig. 212). As recently restored these columns with the windows and marble screen between them have the characteristics of Roman construction. The intercolumniations of the original columns were probably closed by wooden grilles (Fig. 219), except the one to the south, which was left open (p. 335). The temple was crowned with the usual Ionic entablature and wooden roof, with marble tiles. The pediments contained no sculptures.

At the northwest corner of the temple is the beautiful north porch. This is about thirty-five feet wide by twenty-two feet deep. It is raised on three steps and paved with marble slabs resting apparently on a solid foundation of poros. Six Ionic columns, about four feet higher than those of the east porch, support the entablature. The ceiling is constructed of marble beams twenty feet long, bearing coffered slabs between them. The deep-set coffers are adorned with delicate moldings; originally they were painted and in the center of each was a gilded rosette.

From the porch a broad doorway, fifteen feet high, leads into the west cella (Fig. 213). Its lintel was reconstructed in later times, yet not without taste, and the portal is still the most superb in Greek architecture. The inner linings of lintel and jambs are Byzantine. The porch extends toward the west beyond the end of the cella, and here is a small doorway that leads from the porch into the area behind the temple.

FIG. 213. — North door of Erechtheum.

On the south side of the building, directly opposite the north porch, is the Caryatid porch (Fig. 214), or porch of the Maidens; for so the statues which support the roof are called in the inscriptions. This porch measures about 10 by 15 feet, and rises above three steps. The six figures, a half larger than life, stand on a parapet about six feet high. On their heads they poise cushion-like capitals on which the entablature rests. As if to lighten their burden the frieze of the entablature is omitted and a band of dentils takes its place. The ceiling of this porch also is of marble, and has coffers which formerly were colored. At the northeast corner an

FIG. 214. — Caryatid porch, or Hall of the Maidens.

opening has been left in the parapet, to give admission to the porch, but probably not for the general public, as the delicate molding beneath the threshold seems to indicate. Inside the porch a flight of steps, now mostly destroyed, led down into the west cella.

The stately figures of the Maidens are disposed with great skill. The three to the west of the middle bend the left knee slightly; those to the east, the right knee, so that an inward thrust is given to the group. In contrast with similar figures of other times, whose uplifted, straining arms emphasize their struggling effort, the Maidens seem to disregard the weight which their erect heads lightly bear. Yet the sculptor by means of the masses of hair at the neck and the columnar effect of the simple drapery has secured both real and apparent stability. What masterpieces the Greek artist could create as mere architectural accessories! All the figures are mutilated now, and for one taken away by Lord Elgin a terra cotta figure has been substituted. A modern Greek folk-song relates how the surviving Maidens mourned for their lost sister, the statue which is now in the British Museum.

Still another doorway, having a block of double thickness for its lintel, pierces the west wall a little north of the middle. Strangely enough this doorway is immediately beneath one of the columns. A possible explanation of its position is mentioned later; in the original plan of the building the unusual situation would have been less conspicuous.

The architectural details of the Erechtheum are treated with an elegance that is known in no other Greek building. The slender columns have an ornate base; their capitals, with the double roll in the volutes, the elaborate moldings, and the anthemium band about the necking, are rarely beautiful. The bases and capitals of the antae are also richly carved and their decoration in a modified form is carried around the entire temple (Fig. 215). When these various members were entire and still bore their polychrome decoration, the charm of the building must have been greatly enhanced.

The plan of the temple's interior (Fig. 216) is enigmatical. The changes which it underwent as a church, and later as a

FIG. 215. — Carved border crowning wall and anta of the Erechtheum.

The ornamentation of the anta is a little more elaborate than that of the adjacent wall on the left. The picture is from a cast.

FIG. 216. — Interior of the Erechtheum, from the east porch.

Turkish harem, have obliterated most of the traces of its internal construction. The east wall and its foundation were largely broken up when the apse of the church was built; of cross-walls and floors only the barest suggestions remain (Fig. 217.) The two walls which divide the cella

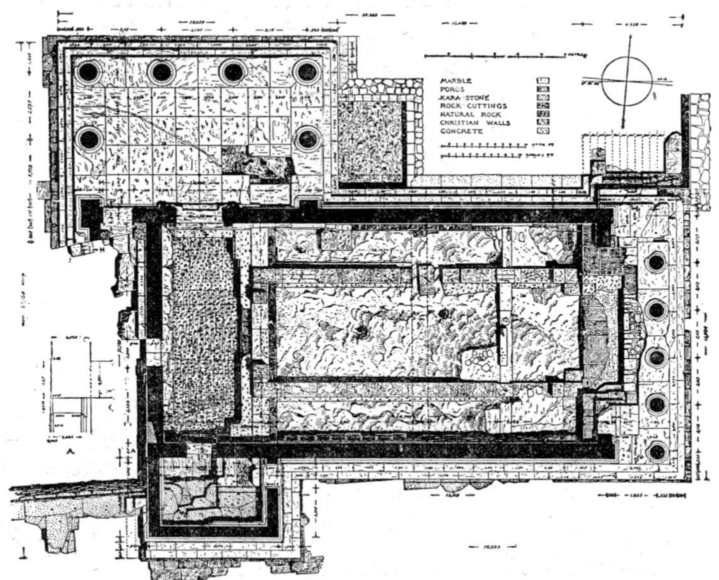


FIG. 217.—Plan of the Erechtheum, actual state.

longitudinally into nave and aisles are unmistakably Christian. Even the extant west cross-wall, at least in its present state, is probably Roman, as is shown by its lack of juncture with the foundation of the building and by the dove-tail cramps which join its marble stylobate with the walls of the cella. A little east of the center of the building are slight projections and cuttings in the side-walls which mark the position either of pilasters or of a cross-wall, but these marks run no lower than the orthostatae, or wainscoting and the rock between the sides at this point bears no traces of the usual bedding for a wall. In the side-walls above the Roman cross-wall are similar marks of pilasters or a cross-wall. In the northeast and southeast corners what have been taken for projecting fragments of a floor a

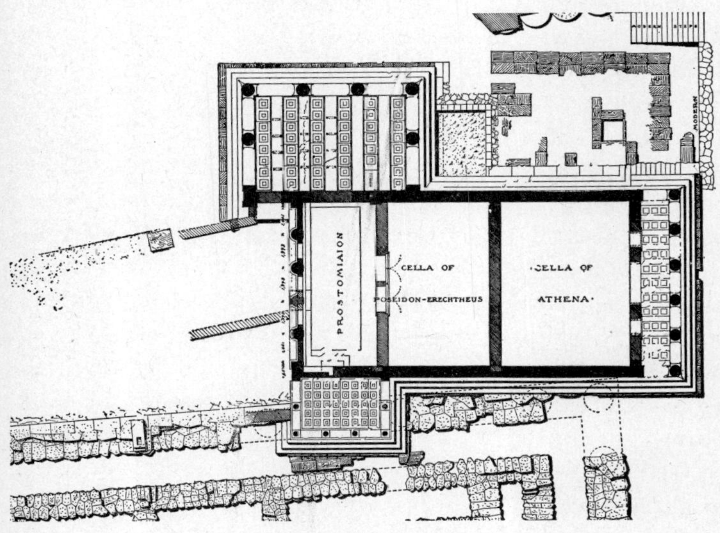


FIG. 218. — Plan of the Erechtheum, restored.

trifle higher than that of the east porch lie under the antae and upon the pavement of the porch. The inner face of the north wall is too badly broken to permit the tracing of a possible continuation of the one fragment, but the south wall is sufficiently preserved to show that the other fragment could not have extended much farther toward the west. The existence of a floor at this level, as has lately been observed, is therefore doubtful. At the rear of the building fragments of floor project from beneath the wall, but here too a variation of level between the north and south halves has not been satisfactorily explained.

Such being some of the difficulties, we must not be surprised to find that none of the plans that have been worked out are altogether satisfactory. For the present we must be content with presenting the view that is most commonly received, making the reservation that much of it is certainly incorrect. According to this view, then, the temple was divided by a cross-wall into two rooms (Fig. 218). The east room, about thirty-two feet wide and twenty-four feet deep, had its floor approximately on a level with that of the east porch, the floor of the west half of the building being about nine feet lower and on a level with that of the north porch. A second cross-wall in the position of the extant Roman wall divided the west section into two rooms, about fifteen and twenty-one feet deep, respectively. Instead of being a solid wall, this is supposed to have been a screen wall bearing the columns which supported the ceiling, but, as has recently been argued with much reason, a "bent beam" mentioned in the building inscriptions may have crossed the temple at this point, the columns, if they existed at all, being a later addition (Fig. 219). Beneath the floor of the most westerly chamber the rock has been hewn away to form a large cistern, which may have contained the "sea-water in a well," though this location is not without topographical difficulties. The central room must also have had an open space beneath its floor, possibly for the sacred serpent; for at its northwest corner is a small doorway under the wall, connecting with a hollow beneath the adjacent corner of the north porch, where certain curious depressions have been identified with almost complete unanimity as the "mark of a trident in the rock." The depressions seem to have been interesting to visitors, for an opening was left in the floor of the porch to permit inspection. In the ceiling of the porch a similar opening is seen, which, in the opinion of some, was made in order to expose the trident-mark, as a divine token, to the sky; the opening in the ceiling, however, has been observed to be

FIG. 219. — Interior of the southwest corner of the Erechtheum, restored.

farther south, and not directly over the opening in the floor. Part of the lintel over the small door under the wall is a heavy block in the back of which a vertical hole is cut in such a position that we must regard it as original. Possibly the altar of the Thyechoös, or Sacrifice-pourer (or Thyecoös, Incense-diviner), located by the inscriptions in the north porch, was here, the hole in the ceiling having some connection with the altar.

The east chamber of the temple is supposed to have been devoted to Athena Polias, Protectress of the City. In her cella must have stood the "ancient image" which "fell from heaven." For this image was made the peplos brought in the Panathenaic procession (p. 293). Whether the statue was erect or seated we do not know; we are probably safe in assuming that it was a standing figure and of crude workmanship. It seems to have been kept in a small chapel, or aedicula. Near the statue were the lamp of Callimachus and the brazen palm tree which Pausanias describes.

To Erechtheus, who is here identified with Poseidon, must be assigned the west cella. Why this chamber was divided by the screen-wall, which, of course, had a doorway in it, is not clear. Still more curious is a niche, at the side of the metopon, or pilaster (p. 335), of the inscriptions, in the corner over the doorway into the porch of the Maidens. The ceiling of both rooms of the temple was of wood, with painted coffers. The inscriptions supply many details of its construction and decoration.

The problem of the plan of the temple is closely bound up with that of the route of Pausanias. Since he comes from the east, we should expect him to enter by the front door and to notice the altar of Zeus Most High "in front of the entrance" at the east end of the temple. But he first mentions as "inside the building" the three altars of Poseidon-Erechtheus, Butes, and Hephaestus, and these we should expect to find not in the cella of Athena but in that of Erechtheus. Accordingly many have thought that he entered by the north door; but this explanation is not more free from difficulties than the other. We get little direct aid from the remainder of Pausanias's description. The paintings of the Butads he saw "on the walls." A scholiast on Aristides mentions a painting of Erechtheus, whom Butes succeeded in the kingship, as being "behind the goddess." Supposing this painting to have been a part of the painting of the Butads, these may be located on the cross-wall, but whether on its east or its west face is uncertain. Since the discovery that the east chamber was lighted by windows (Fig. 211) the view that the paintings were in this room has been strengthened. Of the well of sea-water Pausanias merely says that it was "within." Here for the first time he remarks, "for the building is double," and mentions directly the well and the mark of the trident, naming the latter in this place, perhaps, in order to connect the miraculous tokens.

The statement that follows respecting the image of Athena is troublesome, no matter by what door we assume that Pausanias entered. If the cross-wall were solid and he entered by the north door, he must now have gone back to the front entrance which he had formerly passed without remark. If he entered by the east door, he must have left at once to visit the west room before recording the presence of the image and the objects near it, and now have returned again. Either hypothesis is sufficiently unnatural. A curious "sign" recounted by Philochorus may cast light on the dilemma. He says, according to Dionysius of Halicarnassus (*De Din.* 3): "A dog entered the temple of the Polias, descended into the Pandroseum, mounted upon the altar of Zeus Herceius under the olive tree, and lay down; now it is a tradition among the Athenians not to admit a dog to the Acropolis." The Pandroseum, with the altar of Zeus and the olive tree, was west of the temple, and if we assume an inner stairway between the rooms of the temple, the incident is readily understood. The dog enters the east door, descends the stairs, and goes straight out the west door into the Pandroseum. Otherwise her course is impossibly circuitous, or else she did not enter into the cella of the Polias at all. An inner stairway of some twenty steps is found in the Ionic temple of Apollo at Didyma in Asia Minor, leading down from the front vestibule into the cella. Such an arrangement would not entirely explain the route of Pausanias, but it would make this easier to understand. His description may not be quite consecutive, or our whole conception of the plan may be erroneous. A theory recently published, that the floor of the entire temple was on one level, represented by that of the north porch, and that steps descended into the cella, as at Didyma and also at Sardes, has much in its favor.

If the opinions of some scholars be correct, the architect of the Erechtheum, like the architect of the Propylaea (p. 236), met with difficulties that caused him to curtail his plan. According to these views the original plan (Fig. 220) contemplated a building nearly twice as long as the present structure, with a portico at the west end similar to the portico at the east; the north porch and the porch of the Maidens would then stand at the middle of the sides of the building. The theory, however, cannot be said to have been fully demonstrated.

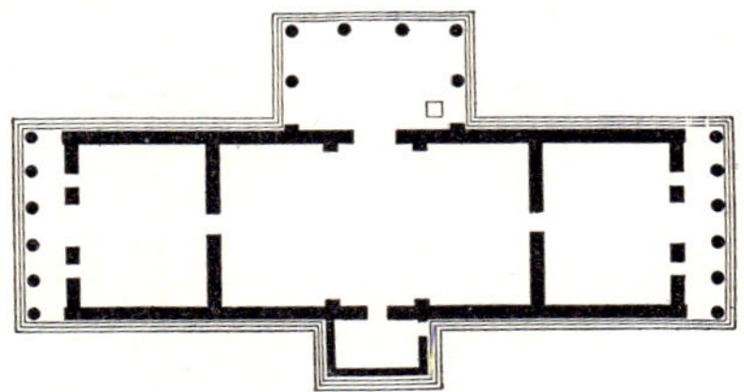

FIG. 220. — Possible original plan of the Erechtheum.

The votive offerings of which Pausanias speaks were only a few of the many that the Erechtheum contained. Herodotus informs us that the cuirass of Masistius was covered with golden scales. The sword of Mardonius and the silver-footed throne of Xerxes were once stolen by a defaulting treasurer named Glaucetas, of whom an inscription recently found on the Acropolis and Demosthenes speak. From the association of the two "spoils" in the story of the theft, the hypothesis is possible that the throne also was in the Erechtheum instead of the Parthenon (p. 306). Extant inscriptions name a number of other offerings which were stored in the temple. Among these were silver bowls, "a little silver owl on a wooden pillar," "a gilded shield dedicated by Iphicrates," and "an ivory cavalry-dagger." The placing of the objects was designated by various terms, as, "by the parastas," "behind the door on the right as you enter," and "in the manger."

The reference in the inscriptions to "the columns on the wall toward the Pandroseum" locates this precinct definitely as west of the Erechtheum. Of the sanctuary and the objects which it contained Pausanias says: "About the olive tree they have nothing to say further than that this was the goddess's token in the contest for the land. They add also that the olive tree was burned down when the Mede set fire to the city of the Athenians, and that after it burned, on the same day it grew up about two cubits. Contiguous to the temple of Athena is a temple of Pandrosus. She was the only one of the sisters innocent in the matter of the trust" (p. 155).

The west door of the Erechtheum and the side door of the north porch opened into the Pandroseum, which doubtless had another entrance to the west. A bedding in the rock shows the location of the north wall, which ran from the slanted corner of the porch obliquely toward the west, then turned southwards. Pausanias speaks of a temple of Pandrosus "contiguous to the temple of Athena." At the southeast corner of the precinct are traces of some structure which has disappeared. No bedding in the rock can be seen, but the wall of the Erechtheum south of the west door is left unfinished, the steps which extend from the north porch cease beyond this rear door, the steps and moldings of the porch of the Maidens end irregularly at the corner of the temple, under this corner is a large open space spanned by a huge block now supported by an iron post, and at the edge of this space the wall of the temple becomes thinner and tapers inward; all these are indications of the original presence of some important structure that the builders of the Erechtheum dared not destroy; in connection with this, in fact, they may have constructed the niche and metopon mentioned above (p. 331), and have left open the south intercolumniation between the west columns. Here is usually located the Cecropium (p. 317). This may, however, be the site of the temple of Pandrosus, which many have despaired of finding, some even supposing Pausanias in error as to its existence.

The sacred olive tree and the altar of Zeus Herceius in the Pandroseum have already been mentioned. Herodotus differs somewhat in his account of the miracle of the olive tree. He asserts that after its destruction by the Persians it grew about one cubit on the second day — but one must not be too exacting; either version is sufficiently marvelous.

Was there an earlier temple on the site of the Erechtheum? Some of the lower stones in the foundation, while they seem to occupy their original bedding, have been cut on their upper surface for their present use, and traces of what seems to have been an earlier entrance can be seen near the west door of the Erechtheum. These data do not yield decisive evidence. The sacred tokens, however, existed long years before the erection of the Erechtheum, and must have had some protection. Whether this protection was afforded by a temple or by a mere inclosure is

FIG. 221. — Erechtheum, at the middle of the eighteenth century. From a drawing by Stuart and Revett.

the question at issue. The strong probability is that the Erechtheum is not the first temple built over them, and the name Ancient Temple, if correctly applied to the present building, as is likely (p. 320), may imply an earlier temple of great antiquity. On its literary side especially the problem is linked with that of the Old Temple (p. 316, note)

FIG. 222.—Relief from an archaic pediment, probably representing the old Erechtheum.

Not without reason some scholars have thought that the predecessor of the Erechtheum is imitated on a small scale in a poros relief found in fragments and now preserved in the Acropolis Museum (Fig. 222). That the relief represents some building connected with the sacred olive tree is reasonably certain. In front of the little temple on the relief stands a figure, apparently of Athena, and worshipers are approaching. The relief was originally picked out in colors.

"What made me wonder most were certain matters that are not familiar to everybody, so I shall write what happens. Not far from the temple of the Polias dwell two girls, whom the Athenians call Arrhephori. For a certain period they live with the goddess, and when the festival is on, they perform at night the following ceremony: They put upon their heads what the priestess of Athena gives them to carry, neither she nor they knowing what she gives them. Now there is an inclosure in the city not far from the so-called Aphrodite in the Gardens and through it a natural descent underground. Here the girls go down and leave below what they carry; then they receive something else which is covered and take it away. Thereafter they are dismissed and other girls are brought to the Acropolis in their stead." This curious passage must be left to speak for itself; the study of it belongs to mythology rather than topography. The court of the Arrhephori had a space in which the girls could play ball, and near it was situated a bronze statue of Isocrates as a youth.

In the vicinity of the Erechtheum numerous statues of priestesses seem to have stood; the bases of several are preserved. In a passage which can now be supplemented from the inscribed base, Pausanias mentions the statue of a maidservant of one of the priestesses. "Next to the temple of Athena," he says, "is the image, about a cubit in height, of an old woman named Sye—, who is said to have been a servant of Lysimache." Unfortunately the end of the woman's name is corrupted in our manuscripts of Pausanias, and the same letters are broken away on the stone. The diminutive base, about 19 inches high and 8 by 11 inches at the top, was found near the temple, where the statue caught Pausanias's attention. At the end of the inscription is the name of the sculptor, Nicomachus, who lived in the third century B.C.

Pliny tells us (*Nat. hist.* 34, 76) that Demetrius, a sculptor of the fourth century B.C., made the statue of a Lysimache "who was priestess of Athena for sixty-four years." Possibly this was the mistress of the old woman of whom we have just spoken; very likely, too, she was the Lysimache who, according to Plutarch (*De vit. pud.* 14), replied to the demand of some muleteers that she pour a libation for them: "But I am afraid that it will become hereditary." A small round base has been found which with little doubt belonged to Demetrius's statue. The mutilated inscription upon it seems to say that the priestess lived eighty-one years, served Athena sixty-four years, saw four generations of children, and was the mother of a certain man of the deme of Phlya whose name is lost.

A remarkable series of archaic female statues was found in 1886 in a pit northwest of the Erechtheum, where they must have been thrown as refuse after the havoc wrought by the Persians. These statues vary greatly in size and style and represent a long period of artistic development. Their characteristics cannot be summed up in a few sentences. One of the group (Fig. 223) has been assigned, probably correctly, to a base which bears an inscription containing the name of Antenor, the sculptor of the first statues of the Tyrannicides in the Agora (p. 105). Some of the figures are very elaborate in their dress and coiffure (Fig. 224). The most advanced in style, as well as the most charming of the series, is one dedicated by a certain Euthydicus (Fig. 225). Very interesting are the abundant traces of colors, red, blue, green, and gray, applied not only to the borders of the garments but to the hair, eyes, and lips of the figures themselves. The influence on the style and technique of the figures produced by the artistic schools of Chios and other islands is now generally acknowledged, but they are our best representatives of the statues of Athe-

FIG. 223. — Archaic statue by Antenor (Acropolis Museum, Athens).

FIG. 224. — Archaic female figure (Acropolis Museum, Athens).

The lower part of the legs and feet of the statue have recently been found.

nian art before the Persian invasion. Originally the statues must have been set up in various parts of the precinct of Athena, to whom they were dedicated; they are now the choicest possession of the Acropolis Museum.

FIG. 225. — Archaic statue, dedicated by Euthydicus (Acropolis Museum, Athens).

### BETWEEN THE ERECHTHEUM AND THE PROPYLAEA

Pausanias continues: "There are also large brazen statues of men facing each other to fight; one they call Erechtheus, the other Eumolpus. Of course it has not escaped the notice of any Athenian who knows antiquities that the man who was killed by Erechtheus was Immaradus son of Eumolpus. Upon the base is also a statue of Theaenetus, who was the prophet of Tolmides, and one of Tolmides himself, who as commander of the Athenian fleet harassed both the land of the Peloponnesians and other people. . . . And there are ancient statues of Athena. These are not melted, but they are blackened and too fragile to endure a blow; for the flame touched them when the king, after the Athenians had entered their ships, took the city wasted of its youth. There is also a boar hunt (I do not know for certain whether it is the Caledonian boar hunt or not) and Cycnus fighting with Heracles." This is a considerable list, but of them all we know little or nothing more than Pausanias tells us. He next mentions a "Theseus about sixteen years old, lifting the stone (Fig. 226) and taking the deposit of Aegeus [his sandals and sword, as tokens of recognition which Aegeus left for his son] . . . all alike of bronze except the stone." Then with the words, "And they also set up another deed of Theseus," he introduces a digression on the Marathonian bull, closing with the statement that "the offering is by the deme of Marathon." This type is familiar on Athenian coins, and in vase paintings and sculpture.

FIG. 226. — Theseus discovering the sandals of his father Aegeus; Athenian coin.

"I cannot say definitely on what grounds they set up a

bronze statue of Cylon, notwithstanding his having plotted to create a tyranny. Probably it was because he was very beautiful and not unknown to fame, since he won an Olympic victory in the double course and had the fortune to marry the daughter of Theagenes, the tyrant of Megara." Pausanias may be correct, but a more probable solution of the difficulty lies in the suggestion that the Athenians erected the statue as an expiatory offering at the time when the city was purified from its blood-guiltiness, a short time after the perfidious murder of Cylon (p. 362).

The statues of Theseus, Cylon, and the others just mentioned must have stood between the Erechtheum and the Propylaea, toward which Pausanias is now returning. Probably they were nearer the Erechtheum, for we are now brought to two conspicuous objects which would seem to have stood about halfway between the two buildings, where the rock is hewn for the bedding of two large bases (Fig. 133). "In addition to the objects which have been mentioned there are two tithe-offerings from Athenian wars. One of these is the bronze statue of Athena from the spoils of the Medes who landed at Marathon. The statue is the work of Pheidias, and the battle of Lapiths and Centaurs on the shield and other reliefs are said to have been embossed by Mys, though, as in the rest of the works of Mys, the design was by Parrhasius son of Evenor. The head of the spear and the crest of the helmet of this Athena are visible as you sail up from Sunium. The other offering is a bronze chariot, a tithe from the spoils of the Boeotians and the Euboean Chalcidians."

Demosthenes (19, 272) calls the first of these works the "great bronze Athena," and from his remarks we gather that it was made from the spoils of the Persian Wars, and not merely of the battle of Marathon. Later it received the name of Promachus, or "Champion," to distinguish it from the other two famous statues of Athena on the Acropolis. A combination of evidence indicates that it was some twenty-five or thirty feet in height. Its site may have been the larger of the two cuttings mentioned above. This cutting is about 16 by 28 feet in size and almost exactly in line with the axis of the Propylaea, a coincidence which may or may not be significant. Mys and Parrhasius, to whom are ascribed the decoration on the shield and other parts of the statue, flourished in the latter part of the fifth century B.C.; the statue, however, seems to have been erected before 461 B.C., for a statue of Arthmius, a treacherous ambassador of the Persian king, was set up in that year "by the great bronze Athena (Demosthenes, *l.c.*)." The chasing must, therefore, have been added later.

The type of the statue is not wholly certain. Athenian coins represent it on the Acropolis between the Propylaea and the Parthenon (Fig. 227), but in varying style and of exaggerated size. A bronze statue destroyed in Constantinople in 1205 has with much reason been supposed to be the Promachus. If this identification is correct we have a description of it written by the Byzantine historian Nicetas Choniates. The statue of which he writes stood in the Forum of Constantine and was demolished in the belief that the outstretched arm had summoned the Crusaders. The goddess was represented as standing, thirty feet high. Her robe reached to her feet and was gathered in at the waist with a girdle. She displayed the aegis with

Fig. 227. — Acropolis, with Parthenon, Propylaea and its approach, Athena Promachus, and the cave of Pan; Athenian coin.

the Gorgon's head. Above her helmet nodded a horse-hair plume, and her hair was braided and fastened behind, except some locks that stole over her brow. Her left hand grasped the folds of her robe; her right was extended toward the south, whither her eyes also gazed. Her expression was sweet and yearning, and her lips were parted as if about to speak. Nicetas mentions neither spear nor shield; doubtless they had perished before his time.

The other of the rock-cuttings, about 18 feet square and still preserving several blocks of the base which stood upon it, may mark the location of the Chalcidian chariot. Herodotus saw it before he went away with the colonists for Thurii "on the left hand as you enter into the Propylaea;" but he refers to the early Propylum, and the site of the chariot evidently was changed later (p. 229). The elegiac couplets on the base, as recorded by Herodotus (5, 77) and others (Diod. 10, 24, 3; Pseudo-Simonides 132, with reversed couplets), read, in a free rendering: —

"Having subdued by their might the Boeotian nation and Chalcis,
  Athens' valorous sons, bold in the labors of war,
Quenched in dark thralldom of iron the insolent pride of their foemen;
  Now, as a tithe of the spoils, Pallas they laud with these [mares."

Fragments not of a single base but of two bases bearing this inscription have been found, one in letters of the sixth, the other in letters of the fifth, century. On the earlier base the hexameter lines are interchanged; this makes it evident that Herodotus copied the later inscription. The first probably was demolished by the Persians; the restoration may have been made in 457 B.C., after the battle of Oenophyta, or perhaps in 445 B.C., after Pericles's campaign in Euboea. Herodotus tells us that the chains of the captured Chalcidians and Euboeans were, up to his time, hung on walls blackened by fire and "opposite the megaron turned toward the west." On the hypothesis that this megaron was part of the Old Temple, the conjecture has been made that the chariot when first set up (506 B.C.) was near the Old Temple. This is possible but not very convincing, for we have no certain knowledge what or where the megaron was. The actual base may be estimated as about ten feet long.

FIG. 228. — Bust of Pericles, probably after the statue by Cresilas (Vatican Museum, Rome).

Pausanias has already told us of a statue of Pericles on the Acropolis "in another place" (p. 307); now he brings us to it. "Two other votive offerings are Pericles son of Xanthippus, and the most worth seeing of the works of Pheidias, a statue of Athena named Lemnian from its dedicators." Pausanias is now near the Propylaea, close to which these statues must have stood. The sculptor of the statue of Pericles is given by Pliny as Cresilas, and a small base bearing a mutilated inscription, which may be amended to read, "Of Pericles; Cresilas made it," probably belongs to the statue of the Acropolis. Several copies of the bust of a bearded and helmeted man of dignified and noble appearance (Fig. 228) exist and are generally thought to have been copied from this statue of Cresilas. Plutarch tells us (*Pericles* 3) that Pericles's head was "elongated and unsymmetrical, whence his likenesses are nearly all helmeted."

Pausanias's estimate of the Lemnian Athena is sustained by the appreciations of other writers. Lucian in his *Imagines* makes Lycinus ask (§ 4): "Which of the works of Pheidias have you praised most?" Polystratus replies: "What other than the Lemnian, on which Pheidias deigned to inscribe his name?" So for his ideal composite statue (*cf*. pp. 170, 254 f.) Lucian proposes that "the Lemnian and Pheidias shall furnish the contour of the whole face, the softness of the cheeks, and the well-proportioned nose." Pliny says (*Nat. hist.* 34, 54) that "Pheidias made of bronze a Minerva of such surpassing beauty that she received the name of 'Forma.'" And an epigram in the Palatine Anthology (No. 169) which apparently refers to the Lemnian declares: —

"Gaze on the beauty divine of the foam-sprung goddess of Paphos,
Then you will say: 'I approve, Phrygian, you for your choice;'
But when you next let your eyes rest on Athenian Pallas,
Then you will cry: 'What a boor, Paris, to pass this one by.'"

Himerius gives us a clew for the recognition of the type of the statue (*Or*. 21, 4). "Pheidias," he tells us, "did not always model Zeus or forge Athena in armor, but extended his art to other gods, and the Virgin's cheeks he adorned with a blush, that by this instead of a helmet her beauty might be hid." In accord with this hint a conjectural restoration of the Lemnian Athena has been made by combining a type of statue found at Dresden with a head from Bologna which had previously been taken for that of a boy, but which exactly fits the cavity in the torso. The aegis proves that the figure is that of Athena, and a relief from

Epidaurus shows us that the right hand held a helmet at which the goddess is gazing, while the left hand grasped a spear (Fig. 229). The clear-cut lines indicate that the original was of bronze. Although there is some dissent, the correctness of the identification has been generally accepted.

"The virginal face," says one critic,[1] "conceived and wrought with ineffable refinement, is as far removed from sensual charm as from the ecstasy of a Madonna. The goddess does not reveal herself as one who can be 'touched with the feeling of our infirmities'; but by the power of her pure, passionless beauty she sways our minds and hearts."

Of the multitude on the Acropolis the Lemnian Athena is the last work of art that Pausanias mentions. He closes this portion of his description with a few words about the walls, which we have already studied (Chapter III). A few other points require brief consideration.

Above archaic house-walls nearly west of the Erechtheum, in a corner of the wall of the Acropolis, are the foundations of two buildings of the early classical period (Fig. 133). One of these is a large rectangular structure, possibly a stoa; it measures about 88 by 35 feet, and is built against the wall of the Acropolis. Above the east end of this stoa is the foundation of a later building approximately 40 feet square; whether this was a shrine or a treasury we do not know. Further west, near the Propylaea, are other remains. Lowest of all is a large cistern divided into two parts. Into it flowed the water of a conduit leading from near the Brauronium. Over the remains of the cistern is the massive foundation of a building of the fifth century B.C., in the form of a stoa, about 60 by 65 feet in size. It had a front portico and a large chamber divided by a parti-

[1] Tarbell, *A History of Greek Art*, p. 189.

FIG. 229. — Lemnian Athena, restored (Strassburg Museum).

The identification of the statue as the Lemnia is disputed. The replicas from which this restoration was made are two torsos in the museum of Dresden and a head in the museum of Bologna.

tion into two rooms. Various other buildings existed within the sacred inclosure. Judging from architectural members used in the foundation of the present Propylaea, one of them must have had a circular end or apse. A considerable series of archaic pedimental sculptures found in

Fig. 230. — Archaic group from pediment of a building on the Acropolis (Acropolis Museum, Athens).

the excavations are to be assigned to early buildings on the Acropolis, but the majority of them cannot be connected with extant foundations (Fig. 230). Northeast of the Propylaea, behind the Pinacotheca, are remains of a huge mediaeval or Turkish cistern; another is found north of the Erechtheum. A series of wells was cut in the rock along the north side of the Parthenon, and others are seen in different places. During mediaeval and early modern times the Acropolis came to be thickly covered with dwellings (Fig. 231, *cf.* Fig. 200), all of which have been removed.

The bases and inscribed stelae which have been found in almost countless numbers help us to appreciate how crowded the Acropolis was in ancient times with works of art and historic records. These, as well as the splendid buildings, must form a part of the picture through which our imagination will attempt to restore the glory of the ancient citadel. We appreciate the feelings of Strabo when he says (p. 396): "But when I come upon the multitude of things in the city which are extolled in song and story by the tongues of all men, I shrink from the details, lest my description go beyond the bounds which I have set for myself."

FIG. 231.—Acropolis in 1687. From a drawing made for Count D'Ortières.

NORTHWEST SLOPE OF THE ACROPOLIS

We accompany our cicerone from the citadel. "As we descend, not to the lower city but just below the Propylaea, we come to a spring of water." This spring, the Clepsydra (*cf.* Fig. 233), earlier called Empedo, still furnishes a never-failing supply of water, clear but slightly brackish in taste. During the Middle Ages the spring-house was made a shrine of the Twelve Apostles. A long flight of steps leading down from the Acropolis through an opening in the wall is partly ancient, partly mediaeval and modern. In 1822, during the Greek revolution, the spring was fortified and connected with the citadel by the "bastion" of Odysseus Androutsos, which has now been removed. Numerous fictions played about the spring in antiquity; of these

FIG. 232.—Northwest slope of the Acropolis, with caves of Pan and Apollo.

The Cave of Apollo is the smaller of the two large niches just to the right of the center of the picture. One entrance to the Cave of Pan can be distinguished at the base of the projection of rock beneath the buttress of the wall of the Acropolis; it is small and at the same level as the Cave of Apollo.

the story told by a scholiast on Aristophanes (*Birds* 1694) furnishes a good example. "The spring got its name because it is filled when the Etesian winds blow, and ceases when they stop, like the Nile and the fountain in Delos. A bloody cup which fell into it was afterward seen in the bay of Phalerum, twenty furlongs away. They say that the spring has no bottom, and that the water is salty."

"And near by is a sanctuary of Apollo in a cave. They say that here Apollo met Creusa the daughter of Erechtheus. [Here also is a sanctuary of Pan. They say] that

Philippides was sent to Lacedaemon when the Medes landed, and on his return he said that the Lacedaemonians had postponed their departure, for it was their custom not to set out for battle before the orb of the moon was full. Philippides further said that Pan met him near Mt. Parthenion and told him that he was favorably inclined toward the Athenians and that he would come to Marathon to fight with them. On account of this message, therefore, the god has been held in honor."

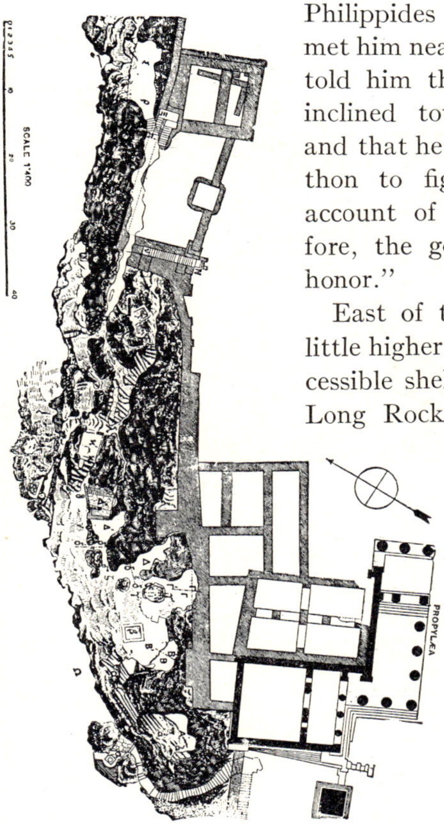

East of the Clepsydra, and a little higher up, is an almost inaccessible shelf, which must be the Long Rocks of Euripides's *Ion*. Here are situated the caves of Pan and Apollo (B and Δ, Fig. 233). The latter occupied the high and deep grotto toward the west (Fig. 232). The interior and edges of this grotto are filled with niches for votive tablets. Many of the plaques, with inscriptions celebrating "Apollo beneath the Heights," were re-

FIG. 233. — Plan of northwest slope of the Acropolis.

The Cave of Apollo is at B; the Cave of Pan, at Δ. The Clepsydra is in the projection of rock on the lower left-hand corner of the plan. The grotto at the top of the plan is wrongly identified as the Aglaurium.

covered in the excavation of the slope. Adjoining the shrine of Apollo on the west is a smaller grotto (A in Fig. 233), and on the east a high and shallow one (Γ in Fig. 233); but no evidence of use has been found in either.

The sanctuary of Pan is the low cave, running back under the rock for some distance, to the east of the cave

FIG. 234. — Entrance to the cave of Pan.

of Apollo (Δ in Fig. 233 and Fig. 234). Its deep recesses form a fit lurking-place for the shy Arcadian god (Fig. 235), as they are said to have done for the amour of Apollo with Creusa, and the clandestine meeting of Cinesias and Myrrhina in the *Lysistrata* of Aristophanes. The story of the introduction of the worship of Pan into Athens (490 B.C.) is borrowed by Pausanias from Herodotus, who makes the hero (according to our best manuscripts) not Philippides but Pheidippides. The story has been immortalized in English poetry in Browning's *Pheidippides*.

Of this picturesque and romantic spot the chorus in Euripides's *Ion* sings (vv. 492 ff.; Verrall's translation): —

"O Athens, what thy cliff
has seen!
The northward scar, Pan's
cavern seat,
With rocks before, and
grassy floor,
Where dancing tread the
Aglaurids' feet
Their triple measure on
the green
'Neath Pallas' fane,
Whene'er the god in his
retreat
Times on the reed a qua-
vering strain."

FIG. 235.— Statue of Pan, from Peiraeus (National Museum, Athens).

Before the cave of Apollo is a depression in the rock, perhaps the site of the altar at which the archons took their oath (*β* in Fig. 233); and back of this is a rugged pit, which may be the one said to have been made by Poseidon's trident for the tomb of Erechtheus (*γ* in Fig. 233). Just east of the cave of Pan some mediaeval men built a small Christian chapel; near this begins a rock-hewn stairway that leads up to the inner staircase in the wall of the Acropolis (**N** in Fig. 233). Still farther east of the chapel an enormous slice of the rock has in some prehistoric period slipped off, leaving behind it a narrow fissure through which one can worm his way to another grotto (**Σ** in Fig. 233), which has often been called the Aglaurium (pp. 156 f.). From this in the Middle Ages was built a secret staircase, of which a few of the bottom and top steps remain.

# CHAPTER IX

## The Courts and the Suburbs

### THE AREOPAGUS AND OTHER COURTS

When the Persians had occupied the city just before the battle of Salamis, they "encamped over against the Acropolis on the hill which the Athenians call the Areopagus." These words of Herodotus (8, 52) even if unconfirmed from other sources, would warrant us in identifying the Areopagus as the rugged, triangular eminence a hundred yards west of the Acropolis, to which it is linked by a ridge some thirty-five feet lower than itself (Fig. 236). The hill is upwards of 1000 feet long and 425 feet broad in its widest part; it rises 377 feet above the sea. At the east end and along the greater part of the north side it is precipitous and inaccessible, but its west end broadens out and descends in a gradual slope. Near the southeast corner has been hewn a flight of fifteen or sixteen steps, now much broken (Fig. 237), which afford the only means of ascent from this quarter.

The origin of the name Areopagus is explained by the majority of ancient writers in a supposed connection of the hill with the god Ares. Aeschylus in the *Eumenides* says (v. 689 f.) that when the Amazons pitched their tents here, "they sacrificed to Ares, whence is the name rock and Hill of Ares," or Mars' Hill, as the King James version of *Acts* has it (17, 22; *cf.* 19). Pausanias follows the more common tradition: "The Areopagus is so named because Ares

Fig. 236. — Areopagus, from the north.

In the background, at the right, is the Hill of the Muses.

was the first one judged here; and this story has also made it clear to me that he killed Halirrhothius, and for what reason he killed him. They say that Orestes also was judged here later for the murder of his mother; and there

FIG. 237.—East end of the Areopagus, from the southeast.

is an altar of Athena Areia, which he set up when he was acquitted." Many scholars, however, consider the derivation of the name from Ares as aetiological, maintaining that the name really means the Hill of Curses (ara, "curse"); the hill was the seat of a criminal court for cases of homicide, and had an association with the Furies, who are also known as the Arae.

Numerous writers agree with Pausanias in his assertion that "The white stones on which stand respectively the defendants and the prosecutors are called the stone of Insolence and the stone of Ruthlessness." Orestes is made to say in Euripides's *Iphigenia among the Taurians* (vv. 961 ff.):

"But when I came to Ares' Hill and rose for trial,
Myself upon one stand, while over opposite
The eldest of the Furies took the other place," . . .

But neither the white stones nor their site can now be found, though the surface of the rock is covered with cuttings, which give evidence that the hill was much used. Especially towards the west were numerous buildings, but of what period we do not know. We hear of a very ancient mud hut situated on the Areopagus and also of police barracks. The Amazonium was on the hill, or at all events not far away.

On the Areopagus the dignified court of the same name held its sittings, which were at night and under the open sky. Here too — though some scholars have maintained, without sufficient cause, that the event took place in the Royal Stoa (pp. 89 ff.). — Saint Paul delivered his message to the Athenians. His words, "dwelleth not in temples made with hands," lose half their force if we fail to associate with them the stately and beautiful temples within range of his vision as he stood on Mars' Hill. The spot fixed by tradition for his address is the little plateau on the north side of the hill (Fig. 238). Not far away are the ruins of a little church named after Dionysius the Areopagite, Paul's first and most distinguished Athenian convert.

FIG. 238. — Site sometimes given as that of the sermon of St. Paul.

Probably this was actually an ancient shrine, with a herm set into the rock.

"Near the Areopagus is a sanctuary of the goddesses whom the Athenians call the Semnae, and whom Hesiod in his *Theogony* calls the Erinyes. Aeschylus was the first to portray them with serpents in their hair; but neither these statues nor the other infernal divinities set up here have any such frightful aspect — I refer to the statues of Pluto, Hermes, and Earth. Sacrifices are offered here by persons who have been acquitted on the Areopagus of some charge, and by others, both citizens and strangers."

The Furies, or Erinyes, were also known euphemistically as Eumenides, the Kindly, and as Semnae, the Venerable. Their sanctuary was an inclosure surrounding and including the natural cleft at the northeast corner of the Areopagus (Figs. 239 and 46). This is the spot where the disap-

FIG. 239. — Areopagus, from the entrance to the Acropolis; at the right the chasm of the Furies.

pointed Furies vanished from sight after the acquittal of Orestes. The chasm has been much altered by time, and no longer contains the pool of water which was there in the last century; but it is a place easily associated with these gloomy divinities. The sanctuary was very ancient, and its origin was early forgotten. The statues which Pausanias mentions are known from other sources to have been three in number. The middle statue was the work of Calamis; those on either side were by Scopas.

Pausanias continues: "Within the inclosure is also a monument of Oedipus. After some pains I found out that his bones were brought from Thebes — for Homer does not let me accept the story told by Sophocles respecting Oedipus's death, since Homer says that, upon the death of Oedipus, Mecisteus came to Thebes and took part in the funeral games." Valerius Maximus informs us that the tomb of Oedipus was between the Areopagus and the Acropolis; hence we may judge that the inclosure was one of considerable extent. Sophocles in his *Oedipus at Colonus* depicts the death of the aged Theban at Colonus Hippius, northwest of the city (p. 382). As we see, however, from the words of Pausanias, the question as to whether he died in Boeotia or Attica was disputed in ancient times. The monument by the Areopagus was one much venerated, and an altar stood beside it.

The worship of the Furies was conducted by the descendants of Hesychus, the Silent, whose own shrine was "beside the Cylonium, outside the Enneapylum," on the saddle between the two hills (p. 343). Some of the conspirators with Cylon were cut down at the altars of the Furies. This may well be the reason for the establishment of Cylon's heroum at this point.

After a digression upon the Athenian courts, to which we shall return, Pausanias adds: "Near the Areopagus is shown a ship made for the procession of the Panathenaea." This ship was a leading feature of the procession and of the festival. Its sail was the embroidered peplos of Athena, and with its crew of priests and priestesses it was moved along on rollers in the festal parade. The ship is represented on a relief set in the wall of the Little Metropolis church (Panagia Gorgoëpikoös; Fig. 240), but only a bit of the design is left at the sides of a cross which has been cut over it. The course of the ship from the Dipylum Gate to the Pelargicum has already been traced (p. 115). From that point Philostratus tells us (*Vit. soph.* 2, 1, 5), "being carried on past the Pythium, it came where it is now moored;" or as often translated, "being carried on, it arrived beside the Pythium, where it is now moored."

FIG. 240. — Panathenaic ship; relief on the "Little Metropolis" church.

The form of the ship is largely obliterated by a Christian cross.

The only Pythium attested by existing evidence is the one southwest of the Olympieum (p. 168). Had the ship been moored there, Pausanias could not have seen it "near the Areopagus." Thus arises a contradiction which cannot be satisfactorily explained. An anchorage by the Areopagus may seem more natural; we have no knowledge, however, of a Pythium there. The suggestion has been made that the cave on the northwest slope of the Acropolis (p. 353) is meant; but all the evidence goes to show that this was dedicated to "Apollo beneath the Heights," and not to Pythian Apollo, unless the contrary is indicated in a dubious passage of Euripides's *Ion* (v. 285), which says: "The Pythian honors them and the Pythian lightnings." But the position of the cave suits neither translation of Philostratus. The cave is high and inaccessible, and the ship could hardly have been drawn over the cliff "past" the cave, nor could a suitable mooring have been found "beside" the cave (*cf.* Fig. 232). Furthermore, the cave on the slope of the Acropolis would scarcely be described as "near the Areopagus." Had the ship been beside the cave or below it, Pausanias must have spoken of it in connection with the cave, or with the Anaceum, or with some other building in the vicinity. The conclusion seems certain that either an unknown Pythium stood near the Areopagus, or else the Pythium by the Olympieum is meant. In the latter case either Pausanias or Philostratus must have been wrong, or the ship was not always moored in the same place, or there must be an error in the manuscripts. In leaving the subject, it should be observed that those who believe that the Pythium was the cave also create an otherwise unknown Olympieum near the Pythium. They then warp Thucydides's remark that the sanctuaries of the pre-Thesean city were situated southward of the Acropolis to include these sites northwest of the Acropolis, and locate here the priests said by Strabo to have watched for the lightnings on Parnes from a wall between the Pythium and the Olympieum (pp. 13 and 61).

In the digression already mentioned (p. 362) Pausanias introduces the most complete list that we have of the Athenian courts with the words: "But the Athenians have also other courts that are not so famous," as the Court of the Areopagus. But of these minor courts we know so little that they may be dismissed briefly.

On the Areopagus were tried cases of murder "with malice aforethought." The Parabystum, where the Eleven at one time presided, appears to have been a roofed building in the Agora. The Trigonum is known only by name. The Batrachium and the Phoenicium were so called from the colors, frog-green and red, painted on the lintels above their entrances.

The Heliaea, the "largest court of Athens, in which public affairs were tried before 1000 or 1500 dicasts," was probably in the southeast corner of the Agora near the market of the Cercopes (p. 149). The Palladium, for cases of involuntary homicide and plot to kill and cases of the murder of a slave, a resident-alien, or a foreigner, was probably south of the Ilissus. It is said to have been founded when the Athenians had unwittingly slain the Argives who were bringing the Palladium from Troy. The Delphinium, for cases of justifiable homicide, was at the sanctuary of Delphinian Apollo near the Olympieum (p. 168). The court of the Prytaneum, for the trial of animals or inanimate objects by which a human being had been killed, was on the north slope of the Acropolis (p. 158).

The Phreattys was "beside the sea," perhaps near the entrance to Zea Harbor at Peiraeus (p. 401). Here were tried persons who, having been banished by the court of Palladium for involuntary manslaughter, were charged with murder or assault. The accused in such a case was compelled to plead his cause from a boat near the shore, and was not allowed to land or to cast anchor. Besides these the names survive of other courts, as the Metocheum, the Greater, and the Middle, whose situation and functions are alike unknown. The court in which Socrates was tried was "near the prison," and therefore at the north end of the Agora (p. 129).

## THE ACADEMY

Pausanias begins his itinerary of Athens at the Dipylum on the northwest side of the city, and to this locality he brings us back at the end.

Of places beyond the walls he says: "The Athenians have also outside of the city, in the demes and along the roads, sanctuaries of gods and graves of heroes and men. Nearest is the Academy, once the estate of a private citizen, but in my time a gymnasium. As you go down to it you see an inclosure of Artemis and rude statues of Ariste and Calliste. As I believe, in agreement with the poems of Sappho [or Pamphos], these are by-names of Artemis. I am aware that another story is told, but shall pass it by. There is also a temple of no great size to which they bring every year on appointed days the statue of Eleutherian Dionysus. Such are the sanctuaries here."

A recent conjecture has located the sanctuary of Artemis Calliste a short distance to the west of the Dipylum, and near the remains of a bridge which once crossed the Eridanus below the chapel of Hagia Triada (Fig. 243). The small temple of Dionysus has not yet been found, nor the heroum of Toxaris, the heroum of Demetrius Poliorcetes, the sanctuary of Artemis Savior, and other sites known to have been near by. The continuation of excavations which have been begun in the region, however, will doubtless add much to our knowledge.

The road from the Dipylum to the Academy, according to Cicero, was six furlongs, about three-quarters of a mile in length; according to Livy, about a mile. Cicero tells us (*De fin.* 5, 1, 1) of an afternoon walk, beguiled "with various discourse," which he and some friends took along this road, to find in the Academy the solitude which they sought. A recent discovery of what is thought to be the entrance to the Academy is in harmony with the orator's estimate of the distance.

After speaking of the tombs along the way Pausanias says: "In front of the entrance to the Academy is an altar of Love with an inscription to the effect that Charmus was the first Athenian to make a dedication to Love (Eros). . . . In the Academy is an altar of Prometheus, from which they have races to the city with blazing torches. The aim of the contestants is to keep their torches alight while they run. The foremost runner, if his torch is extinguished, does not win, but the second instead; if his is not burning, the third; if the flames of all are quenched, no one wins. And there is an altar of the Muses and one of Hermes and, on the inside, one of Athena; still another belongs to Heracles. There is also an olive plant, which is said to have been the second one to appear."

The original ownership and foundation of the Academy is ascribed to Academus, or Hecademus, to whom a shrine was dedicated within its boundaries, but the first inclosing wall is said to have been built by the tyrant Hipparchus. According to Plutarch (*Cimon* 13) Cimon transformed the Academy "from a dry and arid spot into a well-watered grove with neat roads and shady walks." Such it was, a pleasant park, when the youth of Athens in Aristophanes's time are urged by Just Reason in the *Clouds* (vv. 1005 ff).

> "The Academy then shall be your resort, 'neath the olive trees hoar blithely racing
> With a comrade virtuous crowned like yourself with a chaplet of rushes;
> In the fragrance of ivy and freedom from care and leaf-shedding poplar you'll tarry,
> Rejoicing and glad in the season of spring, while the plane to the elm softly whispers."

But our most cherished association with the Academy is of Plato, who taught there, and of the school of philosophy which he founded. His successors, Speusippus, Xenocrates, and Polemo, kept up the tradition and not only taught but dwelt in the Academy. The sanctity of the Academic grove was respected until the time of Sulla, when the trees were cut down to make siege-engines (pp. 42 f.). The park must have been replanted, but Pausanias mentions only a single olive tree, perhaps the sole survivor of the

FIG. 241. — Site of the Academy, from Colonus Hippius, looking west.

sacred twelve, which were said to have been scions of the olive of Athena on the Acropolis.

The Academy contained other altars besides those named in Pausanias's list. The altar of Prometheus was sacred also to Hephaestus, and on it a relief representing both divinities was carved. It must have stood near the altar of Love, for from the altar of Prometheus rather than that of Hephaestus the torch-race is said by some to have started. The altars of Hermes and Heracles were probably close to the gymnasium. Plato himself is said to have dedicated the altar of the Muses, a reminder of his early incursions into the realm of poetry. But Athena was the chief divinity of the Academy, and near the altar was one of Zeus Morieus (from moria, the sacred olive).

If a recent conjecture, supported by reasonable evidence, that the sanctuaries of Heracles and Academus lay immediately to the west of Colonus Hippius is correct, the Academy must have extended over a considerable area in the plain beside the Cephissus River, where still are multitudes of olive trees and poplars, planes and cypresses (Fig. 241).

"Not far from the Academy" Pausanias saw "a monument of Plato. . . . In the vicinity of this place is seen a tower of Timon, who alone saw that the only way to be happy is to shun the rest of mankind." We are told by Diogenes Laertius (3, 41) that Plato was buried "in the Academy, where he spent the most of his life." Possibly his sepulcher was in the gardens which he possessed beside the Academy; these were often identified with the Academy itself. On the philosopher's tomb was engraved (*Biog. Graec.* 388): "Apollo created the two, Asclepius and Plato; Asclepius to save the body, Plato to save the soul." Lucian has told us the story of Timon, the misanthrope, and the tale was wrought into an immortal drama by

Shakespeare. Notwithstanding his hatred of mankind Timon is said to have been a friend of Plato.

### THE CEMETERIES

The road from the Dipylum to the Academy seems to have been a wide avenue. Through its middle may have run the Polyandrion, in which were set up the sepulchral stelae of those who had died in battle for the city. At either end was probably a broad plaza. The plaza near the Dipylum must have been the gathering place for those who were to take part in the Panathenaic procession. In the other plaza was the tomb of Harmodius and Aristogeiton, the Tyrannicides; here, we may suppose, Pericles delivered his famous funeral oration over the men who died in the first year of the Peloponnesian War. A long list of renowned dead is given by Pausanias, but as none of the burial places have been found, it may be omitted. From this list and other sources the relative positions of some tombs can be conjectured. Here were the graves of Thrasybulus, who freed Athens from the rule of the hated Thirty. Near by were the tombs of Pericles, Chabrias, and Phormio. "There are also monuments to all the Athenians who fell in battle on land or sea, except to those who fought at Marathon; because of their valor their graves were made on the spot." A few of the inscriptions which commemorate these national heroes are left, but only one of them can be mentioned here (Fig. 242). This is the tombstone of the men who fell in Chersonese, in Byzantium, and "in the other wars," perhaps of the campaign of Alcibiades in 409 B.C. The marble stele is about five feet high and twenty inches wide. On it the names are given by tribes, and the inscription closes with a eulogy in elegiac verse. At least one tomb bore the names of slaves who had been brave in battle. On the stone which commemorated the men who died in the ill-fated Sicilian Expedition, Pausanias says, in avowed agreement with the historian Philistus, the name of Nicias was omitted, on the ground that he was a "voluntary captive and a man unfit for war." Besides the graves that have been mentioned, among the others, was that of Cleisthenes, the reformer; farther along were the tombs of Tolmides and Cimon, of Conon and Timotheus, of Zeno and Chrysippus, of Nicias the painter, of Ephialtes, and of Lycurgus.

Future excavations may bring to light the graves of some of these distinguished men; but much better known at present

ΕΛΧΕΡΡΟΝΕΣΟΙ
ΑΘΕΝΑΙΟΝ:ΗΟΙΔΕ
ΑΠΕΘΑΝΟΝ
ΕΠΙΤΕΛΕΣ:ΣΤΡΑΤΕΛΟΣ
ΕΡΕΧΘΕΙΔΟΣ
ΠΥΘΟΔΟΡΟΣ
ΑΡΙΣΤΟΔΙΚΟΣ
ΤΕΛΕΦΟΣ
ΠΥΘΟΔΟΡΟΣ

ΑΙΓΕΙΔΟΣ
ΕΠΙΧΑΡΕΣ
ΜΝΕΣΙΦΙΛΟΣ
ΦΑΙΔΙΜΙΔΕΣ
ΛΑΧΕΣ
ΝΙΚΟΦΙΛΟΣ
ΠΑΝΔΙΟΝΙΔΟΣ
ΛΥΣΙΚΛΕΣ

ΛΕΟΝΤΙΔΟΣ
ΧΑΙΡΕΣ

ΟΙΝΕΙΔΟΣ
ΡΟΔΟΚΛΕΣ
ΕΥΡΥΒΟΤΟΣ
ΠΟΛΙΤΕΣ
ΕΡΟΚΛΕΙΔΕΣ

ΚΕΚΡΟΠΙΔΟΣ
ΑΡΙΣΤΑΡΧΟΣ
ΚΑΡΥΣΤΟΝΙΚΟΣ
ΘΕΟΜΝΕΣΤΟΣ
ΑΡΙΣΤΑΡΧΟΣ
ΕΥΚΡΑΤΕΣ
ΝΙΚΟΜΑΧΟΣ

ΗΙΠΠΟΘΟΝΤΙΔΟΣ
ΣΟΤΕΛΙΔΕΣ
ΠΟΣΕΙΔΙΠΠΟΣ
ΑΙΑΝΤΙΔΟΣ
ΔΙΦΙΛΟΣ

ΑΝΤΙΟΧΙΔΟΣ
ΚΡΑΤΟΝ
ΑΝΤΙΚΡΑΤΕΣ
ΕΥΔΟΧΣΟΣ

ΗΟΙΔΕ:ΕΝΤΟΙΣΑΛΛΟΙΣ
ΠΟΛΕΜΟΙΣ:ΑΠΕΘΑΝΟΝ

ΕΡΕΧΘΕΙΔΟΣ
ΛΥΣΑΝΙΑΣ

ΕΜΒΥΖΑΝΤΙΟΙ
ΑΘΕΝΑΙΟΝ:ΗΟΙΔ
ΑΠΕΘΑΝΟΝ
ΕΡΕΧΘΕΙΔΟΣ
ΝΙΚΟΣΤΡΑΤΟΣ
ΦΙΛΟΚΟΜΟΣ

ΑΙΓΕΙΔΟΣ
ΧΙΟΝΙΣ

ΠΑΝΔΙΟΝΙΔΟΣ
ΦΙΛΙΣΤΙΔΕΣ

ΛΕΟΝΤΙΔΟΣ
ΛΥΣΙΜΑΧΟΣ

ΑΚΑΜΑΝΤΙΔΟΣ
ΚΑΛΛΙΣΘΕΝΕΣ

ΟΙΝΕΙΔΟΣ
ΚΑΛΛΙΠΠΟΣ

ΚΕΚΡΟΠΙΔΟΣ
ΚΝΙΦΟΝ
ΔΕΜΟΤΕΛΕΣ
ΗΙΠΠΟΘΟΝΤΙΔΟΣ
Η Α Ι Σ Ο Ν
ΑΙΑΝΤΙΔΟΣ
ΝΙΚΟΔΕΜΟΣ

ΑΝΤΙΟΧΙΔΟΣ
ΦΑΝΙΑΣ

ΠΑΝΔΙΟΝΙΔΟΣ
ΣΙΜΟΝΙΔΕΣ
ΑΙΣΧΥΛΟΣ ΑΡΧΕΠΟΛΙΣ
ΣΜΙΚΡΙΟΝ
ΧΑΡΟΠΙΔΕΣ
ΝΑΧΣΙΑΔΕΣ
ΛΕΟΝΤΙΔΟΣ
ΦΙΛΟΝ
ΕΥΔΕΜΟΣ
ΑΚΑΜΑΝΤΙΔΟΣ
ΠΡΟΤΑΡΧΟΣ
ΚΕΚΡΟΠΙΔΟΣ
ΧΑΙΡΙΑΣ
ΑΣΤΥΑΝΑΧΣ
ΛΥΣΙΣΤΡΑΤΟΣ
ΗΙΠΠΟΘΟΝΤΙΔΟΣ
ΤΙΜΟΝΟΘΟΣ
ΑΝΤΙΦΑΝΕΣ
ΑΙΑΝΤΙΔΟΣ
ΚΛΕΝΟΘΟΣ
ΦΙΛΙΟΣ
ΚΑΛΛΙΚΛΕΣ
ΕΛΕΥΘΕΡΑΘΕΝ
ΣΕΜΙΧΙΔΕΣ

ΗΟΙΔΕΠΑΡΗΕΛΛΕΣΠΟΝΤΟΝΑΠΟΛΕΣΑΝΑΓΛΑΟΝΗΕΒΕΝ
ΒΑΡΝΑΜΕΝΟΙΣΦΕΤΕΡΑΝΔΕΥΚΛΕΙΣΑΜΠΑΤΡΙΔΑ
ΗΟΣΤΕΧΘΡΟΣΣΤΕΝΑΧΕΜΠΟΛΕΜΟΘΕΡΟΣΕΚΚΟΜΙΣΑΝΤΑΣ
ΑΥΤΟΙΣΔΑΘΑΝΑΤΟΝΜΝΕΜΑΡΕΤΕΣΕΘΕΣΑΝ

FIG. 242. — Inscription on a grave stele.

is the cemetery of humbler folk southwest of the Dipylum, which is often called the Dipylum Cemetery (Fig. 243). The visitor of to-day usually approaches it from the Peiraeus road on the west, but the situation can be understood better from its relation to the Sacred Gate. As one stands in the opening of the gate (Fig. 29), with the walls of the city on either side, at his right he sees the bed of the Eridanus River, and on its nearer bank the Sacred Way to Eleusis, which crosses the river by a bridge close

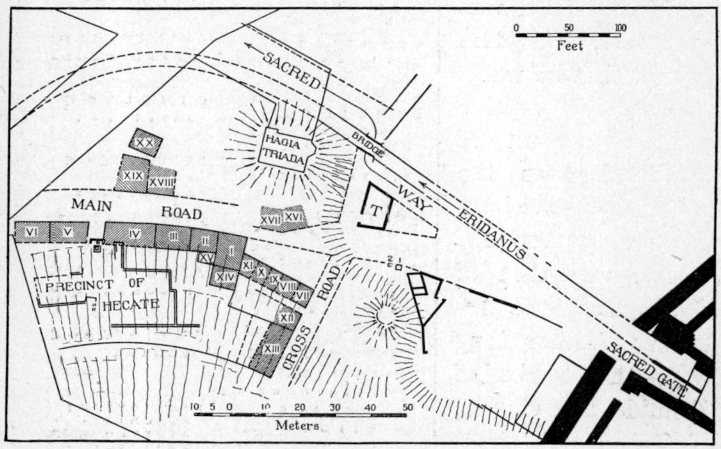


FIG. 243. — Plan of the Cemetery on the Eridanus — the Dipylum Cemetery.

to the church of Hagia Triada. To the left a branching road runs westward through the cemetery. The excavations, which are still in progress, have already thrown a flood of light upon the entire region, which is worthy of a fuller description than present space permits.

The first monuments that one sees after leaving the Sacred Gate are two shafts of marble some eighty yards to the west (1, 2 in Fig. 243). One of these marks the tomb

FIG. 244. — Part of the Cemetery on the Eridanus.

The photograph was made after the recent excavations. The plots along the road belong, respectively, to Lysanias of Thoricus, Agathon and Sosicrates of Heracleia, and Dionysius of Collytus. The area fronted by a wall of small stones, at the left of the middle, belongs to the plot of Lysanias.

of Pythagoras, consul from Selymbria in the Propontis about the middle of the fifth century B.C.; the other is the monument of Thersander and Simylus, ambassadors from the island of Corcyra about 375 B.C. On each stele is carved an epigram in memory of the honored dead. The monument of Pythagoras is perhaps the oldest formal sepulcher in the place.

The main portion of the cemetery, however, lies farther to the west (Fig. 244). Here graves are found on both sides of the road, but the majority are on the south side. Careful study of the monuments, and of the stratified deposits laid bare by the spade, has shown that the principal tombs were constructed between the beginning of the fourth century and the year 317/6 B.C. At this later date luxury and expense had become so obtrusive in the ceremonies of funerals and burial that Demetrius of Phalerum was impelled to issue an order of repression. The order was apparently obeyed, for the tombs after this time are much more modest, though inhumation in the district continued well down into Roman times, with constantly declining taste in the designs of the sepulchral monuments.

The majority of the burials of the fourth century B.C. are in family plots, each separately walled and adorned with stelae and sculpture. The earliest and at the same time most noteworthy of these is that of the family of Lysanias of Thoricus (1 in Fig. 243 and Fig. 245). In this group our interest centers in the splendid relief of the young warrior Dexileos, who is represented as a triumphant horseman riding down his foe. The bronze spear poised by the victor has been lost, but the holes by means of which it was fastened are visible in the hero's side. Beneath the relief is an inscription which tells us about all we know of the young man and his fate. It reads: "Dexileos of Thoricus, son of

FIG. 245.—Monument of the knight Dexileos, son of Lysanias of Thoricus.

The inscription on the base reads: Δεξίλεως Λυσανίου Θορίκιος· ἐγένετο ἐπὶ Τεισάνδρου ἄρχοντος, ἀπέθανε ἐπ' Εὐβουλίδου ἐν Κορίνθῳ, τῶν πέντε ἱππέων.

Lysanias. Born in the archonship of Teisander [414/3 B.C.]; died in the archonship of Eubulides [394/3 B.C.] in Corinth, of the five knights." The battle of Corinth is known to us, but not the deed of valor of the illustrious five. Dexileos was doubtless buried, with the other warriors who died at Corinth, in the Polyandrion (p. 370), and this is a cenotaph. In the same plot were interred several other members of Lysanias's family, but their monuments are less conspicuous. The parapet on which the relief stands once terminated with figures of Sirens, and the whole grave precinct with its massive wall presented an imposing aspect.

Of the other tombs on this side of the road the most noteworthy are those of Agathon and Sosicrates of Heracleia (II in Fig. 243), with the superb relief of Corallion, and that of Dionysius of Collytus (III in Fig. 243), with its high-mounted statue of a bull. Behind the stelae in the second precinct excavations have revealed the sarcophagi of several persons who were buried there, with the bones undisturbed. On the opposite side of the road the most famous relief is that of Hegeso daughter of Proxenus, perhaps the choicest of all these works (Fig. 246). Beside the cross-road toward the east (XII in Fig. 243) is the beautiful relief of Demetria and Pamphila. Here too the bones have been exhumed.

One of the most important results of the recent investigations was the finding of the original level of the ground, with the discovery that the reliefs were intended to be seen from below. As thus examined they constantly reveal new refinements of form and modeling. The men and women who were buried here were not known to fame, and, so far as we are aware, none of the monuments were made by distinguished artists. That mere stonecutters could produce works of so consummate beauty and dignified restraint is among the marvels of ancient art. The same comment is of course valid in respect to the scores of similar reliefs that fill several rooms in the National Museum of Athens.

FIG. 246. — Gravestones of the family of Coroebus of Melite.

The relief of Hegeso, daughter of Proxenus and probably the wife of Coroebus, is among the choicest examples of Greek sculpture.

Almost any one of them may be deemed worthy to rank as a masterpiece (Fig. 247).

In the rear of the cemetery on the Eridanus are the remains of a rude wall which encompassed the inclosure of a sanctuary of Artemis Hecate (Fig. 243). Hecate was associated with things of the lower world, and this fact doubtless accounts for the presence of her worship here.

The base for her statue, an altar, and other tokens, still exist in the precinct of the Hecateum.

The cemeteries outside of the other gates of the city are less interesting, though from some of them have come superb reliefs. An extensive burial ground of early date lies beyond a gate northeast of the Dipylum. Other graves are found outside of the Acharnian Gate at the north. On the east side of the city a considerable cemetery was situated along the road leading from the Diochares Gate to the Lyceum, in the vicinity of the present Constitution Square. On account of the prohibition, during the classical period (p. 62), of burials within the walls, some scores of graves lying in the deme of Coele (p. 26) must be thought to be either of very early or very late date, presumably the latter. Of single tombs in this general region may be mentioned a large rock-cut sarcophagus between the Museum Hill and the Pynx, and a larger sepulcher of two rooms, known as the tomb of Cimon (p. 65), hewn in the rock at the end of the west spur of Museum Hill.

FIG. 247. — Gravestone of Hagnostrate (National Museum, Athens).

## COLONUS HIPPIUS

Adjoining the Academy, and about a mile and a quarter northwest of the Dipylum, — ten furlongs, according to Thucydides, — is a long hill of naked rock about fifty feet high, the ancient Colonus Hippius, or Horse Knoll (Fig. 248). On its summit is now an iron fence which incloses the marble tombstones of two accomplished archaeologists,

Fig. 248. — Colonus Hippius, from the east.

Karl Ottfried Müller, who died in 1840, and Charles Lenormant, who died in 1859. On the hill is a single tree; around its base are scattered groves, and a few buildings. In his last words before he leaves the city, to visit the demes of Attica, Pausanias says: "A spot called Colonus Hippius is also shown. To this spot Oedipus is said to come (this is at variance with Homer's account, but they say it) and here is an altar of Poseidon Hippius and Athena Hippia, also an heroum of Peirithous and Theseus, and one of Oedipus and Adrastus. The grove and the temple of Poseidon were burned by Antigonus, whose army also devastated the land of the Athenians at other times."

Aside from its unhappy association with the raid of Antigonus, Colonus scarcely comes into the field of historical mention, except as the scene of an assembly held by the

Athenian oligarchs in 411 B.C. But in the vision of the lover of literature the region looms large. The dramatist Sophocles was born near the knoll, and here, in his old age, he set the scene of his last immortal tragedy, the *Oedipus at Colonus*. In the poet's time the hill was covered with vegetation, which spread all about its foot. In one of the noblest lyrics of his drama, a passage that should silence those who

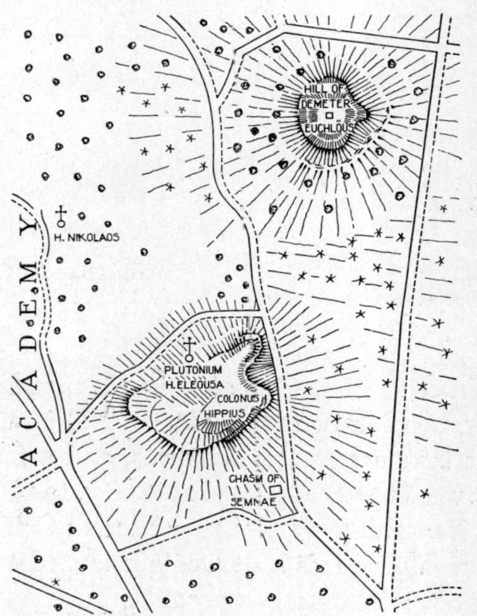


FIG. 249. — Map of Colonus Hippius and its environs.

accuse the Greeks of lack of appreciation of the charms of nature, Sophocles sings (vv. 668 ff.; Plumptre's translation):

"Of all the land far famed for goodly steeds,
Thou com'st, O stranger, to the noblest spot,
Colonus, glistening bright,
Where evermore, in thickets freshly green,

The clear-voiced nightingale
Still haunts, and pours her song,
By purpling ivy hid,
And the thick leafage sacred to the God,
With all its myriad fruits,
By mortal's foot untouched,
By sun's hot ray unscathed,
Sheltered from every blast;
There wanders Dionysus evermore,
In full wild revelry,
And waits upon the nymphs who nursed his youth.

And there, beneath the gentle dews of heaven,
The fair narcissus with its clustered bells
Blooms ever, day by day,
Of old the wreath of mightiest goddesses;
And crocus golden-eyed;
And still unslumbering flow
Cephissus' wandering streams."

FIG. 250. — Hill of Demeter Euchloüs, from the chapel of Hagia Eleousa.

Recent studies have shown, what before was inadequately appreciated, that the topography of the region is followed closely in the drama (Fig. 249). The chasm of the Furies, which has its place in the poem, is found a little to the southeast of the hill. Between the hill and the chasm was the Furies' grove and sacred precinct. On the saddle of the knoll was the altar of Poseidon and Athena, which the poet mentions also, and on the summit was the altar of Prometheus and Hephaestus. Along the western slope was the grove of Poseidon, at the upper end of which was the mystic shrine of Pluto, where the little church of St. Eleousa conceals a fabled entrance to the underworld. To the region of the Plutoneum leads the "cataract road" which Oedipus with his little retinue trod to his sudden and mysterious vanishment. A few hundred yards to the north rises the green hill of Verdant Demeter (Fig. 250), whither the faithful daughters, Antigone and Ismene, are sent by Oedipus to fetch water for purificatory rites.

# CHAPTER X

## PEIRAEUS AND THE PORTS OF ATHENS

### THE PORTS

THE fortunes of Peiraeus are so closely bound up with those of Athens that the two centers of population have always been regarded as forming one city. In ancient times Athens proper was often termed the "upper town," or Asty, in contradistinction to the joint city, the Polis. Had the Athenians after the Persian Wars been able, as Themistocles desired, to break the bonds of sentiment that held them to the vicinity of the Acropolis, Athens might have fulfilled an even more brilliant destiny than she did; Peiraeus would have been an almost ideal site for the center of a maritime empire. Failing in his far-seeing project for a new metropolis on the coast, the Athenian statesman began the fortification of the lower city and her ports, and the construction of the Long Walls, which united the two sections of the city (pp. 72 ff.).

Ancient literature preserved the tradition of a geological era when Peiraeus was an island, and ascribed the very name to association with the word "peran," "beyond" the coast. But before the earliest historical period the Cephissus had brought down the silt which thereafter connected the former island with the mainland.

The peninsula of Peiraeus (Fig. 251) is about two miles in greatest length, from northeast to southwest; its surface is uneven. The Hill of Munychia (Fig. 252) at the north-

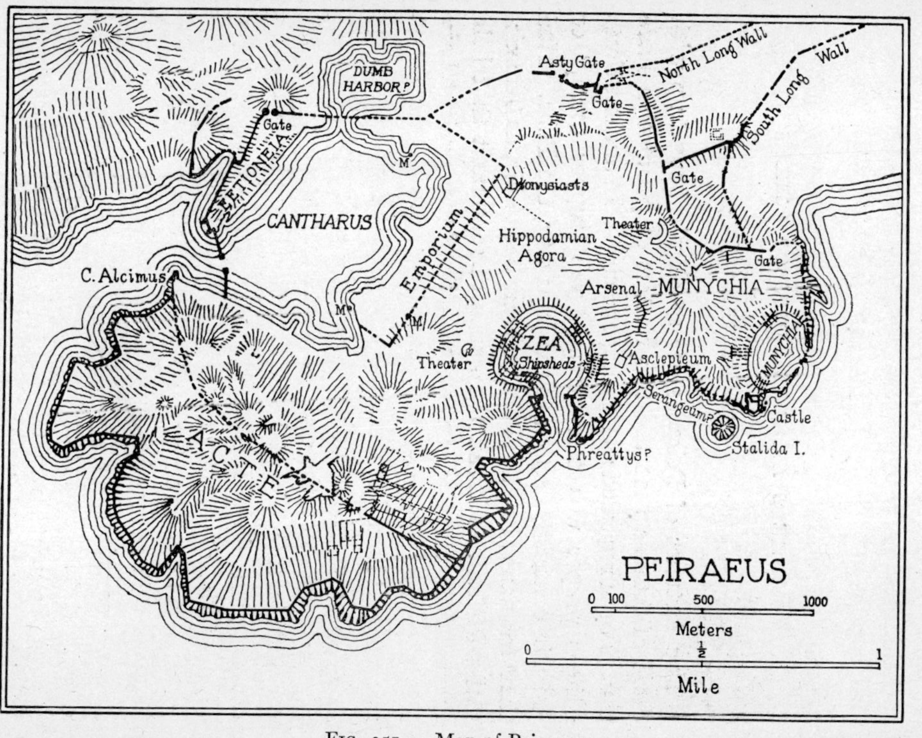


Fig. 251.—Map of Peiraeus.

east is 284 feet in height; the broad Hill of Acte at the other extremity 190 feet; and these two elevations are joined by an isthmus some 50 feet in height, which divides the city into two parts. The fortifications included also the Hill

FIG. 252.—Hill of Munychia, seen across the great harbor of Peiraeus; Hymettus in the distance.

of Eëtioneia, across the bay to the north, thus dominating the entrance to the principal port. The coast line is irregular, being indented with three large bays.

Before the Persian Wars the port of Athens was the broad Bay of Phalerum (Fig. 253), an open roadstead extending eastward from Peiraeus to the Cape of St. George, or Trispyrgi, probably the ancient Cape Colias, where now is located Old Phaleron. The Phaleric Harbor is said to have been twenty furlongs, about 2.2 miles, from the Acropolis (pp. 72 f.). At present the nearest distance to the sea is twenty-seven or twenty-eight furlongs, a little more than three miles. Hence we must suppose that the coast, which here is low and somewhat marshy, has filled in since ancient times. We hear of no quays belonging to this ancient harbor, and probably there were none; Athens had no fleet of importance before the Persian Wars.

The deme, or village, of Phalerum (p. 73), from which the bay took its name, possessed various shrines, some of

FIG. 253. — View northeast from the Hill of Munychia.

The Bay of Phalerum is seen in the foreground; bordering it are the buildings of New Phaleron. In the distance, at the left, is Athens; in the background Mts. Pentelicus and Hymettus.

which are mentioned by Pausanias. Near the harbor he saw a sanctuary of Demeter. "Here too," he continues, "is a temple of Sciradian Athena, and farther on one of Zeus. There are altars of the gods named Unknown, and of heroes, and of the sons of Theseus, and of Phalerus. This Phalerus, the Athenians say, sailed with Jason to the land of the Colchians. There is also an altar of Androgeos son of Minos. It is called the altar of Hero; but those who have the best understanding of native traditions know that it belongs to Androgeos. Twenty furlongs away is Cape Colias; on this, when the fleet of the Medes was destroyed, the waves washed up the wreckage. Here is a statue of Colian Aphrodite, and the goddesses known as the Genetyllides. The Phocians in Ionia have goddesses whom they call Gennaïdes, and these are the same as the ones of Colias." Herodotus (8, 96) speaks of the wreckage cast up on Colias and connects the event with an oracle of many years before: "Colian women shall cook their food with oars."

"The country in the neighborhood is barren, solitary, and desolate in a high degree. The stony and broken soil is traversed by the beds, generally dry, of many brooks. As far as the eye can reach, from the sea to the foot of Mt. Hymettus, ancient tombs are seen dotted over the landscape, rising in the form of mounds above the stunted bushes which cover the low ground. Melancholy at all times, the landscape is doubly gloomy in winter, when dark clouds lower on Mt. Hymettus and shut out the view across the sea to the coast of Peloponnese." [1]

After the fortification of Peiraeus, with its superior harbors, the Phaleric Harbor fell into disuse, and thenceforward the Peiraic harbors alone were developed. The three harbors of Peiraeus were Munychia, Zea, and Cantharus. A few still dissent from the current view as to the identification of these harbors, but the majority of scholars are in substantial agreement.

The Munychia Harbor is the smallest of the three and lies at the eastern foot of the hill of the same name, spurs of which almost surround it (Fig. 254). The bay is oval in shape and measures about 800 by 1000 feet. Its east and exposed side was fortified by the strong wall of the city and by terminal towers, the narrow entrance between which could be closed by a chain or rope (p. 67). About sixty

[1] Frazer, *Pausanias*, II, p. 36. But the mounds of which Frazer speaks have been found to be heaps of stones thrown up by husbandmen, not tombs.

yards off the shore, southwest of the castle which guarded the south arm of the harbor, is the bald rocky islet of Stalida,

FIG. 254. — Munychia Harbor, from the Hill of Munychia.

about sixty-five feet in height. It bears no signs of ancient occupancy.

Approximately half a mile west of Munychia is the Bay of Zea (Fig. 255), a mushroom-shaped harbor, whose head

FIG. 255. — Zea Harbor, from the Hill of Munychia.

measures approximately 1300 feet in diameter. Its throat and entrance were fortified with walls and towers like Munychia (p. 67); though at present few remains exist, and the level of the ground above the entire circuit has been raised so as to form an open plaza.

Cantharus, the "largest harbor," as Pausanias rightly calls it, lies to the north of the peninsula (Fig. 256). Its putative resemblance to the familiar drinking-cup seen in representations of Dionysus (*cf.* Fig. 104) probably suggested the name. The average width of the bay from northwest to southeast is about 2300 feet; its length from the moles at the entrance to the northerly extremities is about 3800 feet, not including "Dumb Harbor," a shallow extension to the north which is now used by freight vessels. This harbor, like the others, is almost surrounded by hills. The ancient moles have nearly disappeared, and new ones have been constructed much farther to the west, greatly enlarging its capacity. While the small harbors are at present little used and are accessible only for small craft, Cantharus is always thronged with boats, varying in size from the tiny skiffs of the "Barkáres" to ocean liners; the port is one of the busiest of the Mediterranean. The ancient quays have been overbuilt by the modern and are now completely concealed, unfortunately without an adequate study of them having previously been made.

Of the different parts of the harbor mentioned by ancient writers few can be identified. Two large stones found in the water, one near the present Custom House, the other near the entrance to Dumb Harbor, bear the words, "Boundary of the anchorage of the freight-boats;" these may indicate the limits of the mercantile quay. A projecting arm midway between these points may be the Diazeugma, or Parting. The Choma, or Dam, is mentioned

FIG. 256. — Peiraeus and the harbor of Cantharus, from the Hill of Munychia.

In the background is the island of Salamis; the darker islet before it is Psytalleia.

by Xenophon in connection with the fortification built by the Four Hundred on Eëtioneia; hence we may look for it near the mouth of Dumb Harbor. From the Choma ships of war set out, and here the senators met prior to such departures. For this reason some would locate the Choma at the south end of the peninsula near the outlet of the harbor.

The most interesting feature of the harbors was the series of shipsheds. From an inscription we understand that near the end of the fourth century B.C. these numbered 372, of which 196 were in Zea, 82 in Munychia, and 94 in Cantharus. Athens possessed at this time about four hundred galleys; but some of these were always at sea. In their shipsheds the Athenians took great pride. The first cost of them is said to have been 1000 talents, or more than $1,000,000, but at the end of the century the Thirty

FIG. 257. — Remains of shipsheds.

sold them by auction for three talents. After various vicissitudes the rebuilding of the sheds was completed by

Lycurgus (p. 39). Sulla ruined them again in 86 B.C., but afterwards they were once more rebuilt.

Abundant remains of the shipsheds have been uncovered, particularly in the harbors of Munychia and Zea (Fig. 257); these harbors were surrounded by sheds, sometimes two rows deep. The largest extant group is on the east side of Zea Harbor. Here the remains may be seen from the plaza, but the embankment has obliterated large portions. In Cantharus the sheds seem to have been confined to the coast between the present Custom House and the southern mole.

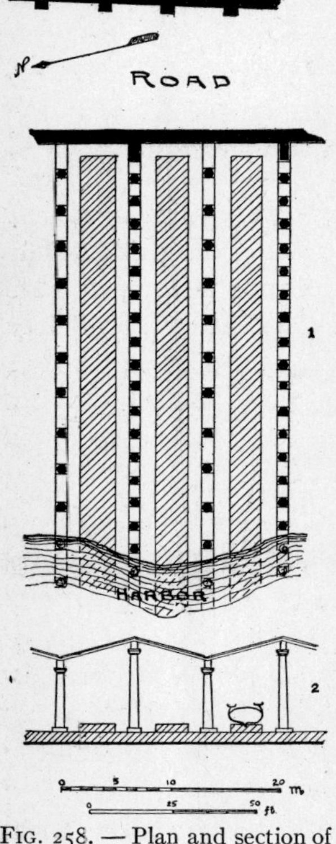

FIG. 258. — Plan and section of shipsheds.

A study of the ruins in different places has made clear the main features of the construction (Fig. 258). The sheds were of poros and were built side by side; their lower ends extend down into the water, the upper ends terminating in a heavy continuous wall about 120 feet back from the bay. In Zea this wall also supported the road which ran around the harbor. From the wall rows of columns descended the slope into the water. The alternate rows of these columns begin from antae projecting two yards from the rear wall. The rows were about twenty-one feet apart, those not starting from the antae being higher and wider spaced than the others. Saddle roofs, probably of wood, covered the sheds by pairs, the higher columns supporting the ridgepoles (Fig. 258). Through the middle of each slip ran a base three feet high and ten feet wide. This was grooved down the middle to receive the keels of the boats; the ships were warped up by pulleys to their places, where they could be cleaned and repaired.

The wooden gear of the ships, masts, rudders, oars, and the like, was kept in the ships; but for the hanging gear, such as sails and cordage, a special arsenal was provided. The Old Arsenal is known to us only by name, but a new arsenal was constructed between the years 347 and 329 B.C. This was one of the most elegant of Athenian buildings, and was planned by Philo of Eleusis. It was destroyed by Sulla, and not a trace of it has been found. Fortunately, however, we possess a long inscription containing a copy of the specifications for the building, so detailed and precise, that the Arsenal can be reconstructed with greater accuracy than some buildings of which considerable remains are left. The inscription was discovered in 1882 about 130 yards northeast of Zea Harbor. As the specifications prescribe that the Arsenal shall extend from the Propylum of the Agora (p. 397) to the rear of the shipsheds of Zea, the place where the inscription was found is probably close to the site of the building.

The Arsenal of Philo was built of poros; it was 405 Greek feet long by 55 feet wide (Figs. 259 and 260). Its walls were 30 feet high, to the bottom of the cornice. A triglyph frieze extended around the building. Light was provided by windows three feet high and two feet wide. There were thirty-six windows on each side, and three on each end; these could be closed by bronze shutters. When doors and windows were closed, the building was ventilated by slits left between the stones. The roof was made of wooden rafters, first covered with boards fastened with iron nails, and then with Corinthian tiles. In each end of the building were two doors, each 14 feet high and 9 feet wide; the doors were separated by a deep pilaster,

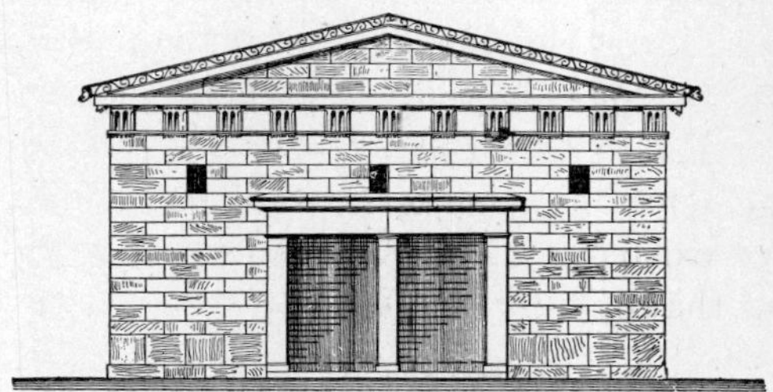

FIG. 259. — Façade of the Arsenal of Philo, restored.

or metopon, this central pilaster and those at the side being extended into the building to form a vestibule. Over the lintel of each pair of doors, on the outside, was a projecting cornice. The entire interior of the building was paved with stone, and was divided into a nave and aisles by two rows of columns, or square pillars, thirty-five on each side. The

FIG. 260. — Plan of the Arsenal of Philo, restored.

nave was intended as a public promenade. On either side, between the columns, was a stone balustrade, with a latticed gate in each intercolumniation. Through these gates access was secured to the aisles, where the hanging gear was stored. The canvas was kept in presses standing against the columns and the side walls. On upper galleries the cordage was laid on open shelves.

"Thither on the burning days of summer, one may suppose, crowds were glad to escape from the blinding glare and stifling heat of the streets, and to promenade in the cool, lofty, and dimly-lighted arcade, often stopping to gaze with idle curiosity or patriotic pride at the long array of well-ordered tackle which spoke of the naval supremacy of Athens."[1]

Of other naval buildings and docks we have almost no knowledge. Extensive shipyards for the building of galleys must have existed, perhaps on Eëtioneia, but of these we only know that one part bore the name of Telegoneia.

### THE SEAPORT CITY

Peiraeus entered upon a new epoch of her history about the middle of the fifth century B.C., when, probably at the invitation of Pericles, the Milesian architect and scientist Hippodamus arrived to lay out the city anew. Thus Peiraeus was the first European city to be built after a regular plan, with broad streets, rectangular blocks, and open squares, in accordance with the general principles which Hippodamus desired to establish for all human affairs. The somewhat crotchety Milesian later accompanied the Athenian colonists to Italy, where he laid out the new city of Thurii in 443 B.C. He is said also to have made the plan for the city of Rhodes in 408 B.C. The arrangement which he devised for Peiraeus was carried out by the expenditure of enormous sums, and his plan persisted throughout antiquity; it has in part been imitated in the modern city, as well as in other cities throughout the world.

The centers of interest in the new Peiraeus were the Emporium, along the shore of Cantharus Harbor, and the

[1] Frazer, *op. cit.*, II, p. 20.

Hippodamian Agora, at the west foot of the hill of Munychia. Into the Emporium, as says the author of the *Constitution of the Athenians*, poured the goods of Sicily, Italy, Cyprus, Egypt, Lydia, Pontus, Chersonesus, and the rest of the world, when Athens was ruler of the sea; and a passage from the comic poet Hermippus enumerates a score of stuffs which the various states of the Mediterranean furnished for Athens's use. The Emporium's northern and southern limits were doubtless the boundary stones which have been mentioned (p. 389); these belong to the Hippodamian period. Between these points stretched the principal quay, as to-day. Another inscription, found some 500 feet east of the Custom House, bears the words: "Boundary of the emporium and the street." An angle of wall discovered just south of this point seems to mark the corner of the boundary wall, which extended northwestward to the shore and northeastward to a point beyond the corner of the harbor, where it turned at a right angle and continued to the city wall near Dumb Harbor.

In this area were the "five stoae" mentioned in a passage ascribed to "Callicrates or Menecles" (Schol. Aristophanes, *Peace* 145): "Peiraeus has three harbors, all closed; one is the harbor called Cantharus, in which are the sixty docks, then the Aphrodisium, then in a circle about the harbor five stoae." An extant inscription also mentions these sites in the same order. One of the stoae must be identical with the Long Stoa. This is doubtless the one said by Thucydides to have been walled off by the Four Hundred at the time of their construction of a wall on Eëtioneia. Accordingly it must be sought at the north end of the harbor, near the present Karaïskákis Square. Another of the stoae may have been the Deigma, or Display House, a sort of bazaar or exchange, where importers gathered to show their wares. This was no doubt one of the busiest places of the city. Tradesmen of all kinds were there, bankers and money changers, and the various purchasers and small dealers. Among them was to be found the "Pretender" of Theophrastus's *Characters*, boasting to strangers "how much money he had at sea."

Apparently the stoae formed a sort of façade near the quays: behind them were the stands and stalls of hucksters. Here too were located the inns for sailors, as well as the resorts of amusement and vice in which they delighted. Possibly not without regard to the sailors was the Aphrodisium founded by Themistocles and furnished with a temple by Conon. An Aphrodisium is known from an inscription to have stood to the north of the towers on Eëtioneia, near the modern Larissa railroad station. The passage from Callicrates or Menecles, however, seems to demand another near the Custom House. "Behind the stoa on the sea" Pausanias saw statues of Zeus and the People, by Leochares, but of these we know nothing more.

The Hippodamian Agora can be located only with relation to the Arsenal of Philo, which lay between the Agora and the harbor of Zea (p. 393). The site of the Arsenal is doubtful, but we cannot go far astray in locating the Agora on the ridge west of the hill of Munychia (*cf.* Fig. 251). It must have been spacious, for troops sometimes were quartered in it. Whether or not it was surrounded by stoae and other buildings we can only guess. The existence of a propylum, or gateway, helps to confirm the supposition that it was. It was not paved, for in 320 B.C., a decree was passed "that the Agora in Peiraeus shall be repaired and leveled up as well as possible." The inscription recording this decree throws light on local conditions at the time by the regulation that "no one shall dump dirt or dung or anything else in the Agora or in the streets."

The sides of the Agora lay parallel to the principal streets of the city, of which from ancient sources we have knowledge of only one. According to Xenophon (*Hellen.* 2, 4, 11), at the time of the battle between Thrasybulus and the (probably 3000) soldiers of the Thirty Tyrants, "Those from the City came into the Hippodamian Agora, and then first were marshaled so as to fill the street which leads to the sanctuary of Munychian Artemis and the Bendideum; and they numbered not less than fifty shield in depth." From these figures and the known method of deploying Greek troops the width of this road from the side of the Agora up the slope of Munychia has been estimated at a hundred feet, or a plethron, which seems to have been a favorite measure of Hippodamus.

Some thirty yards northwest of the place where we have located the Agora, and underneath the modern theater, the remains of a private house have been found which measure about 75 by 130 feet. Adjoining it was a sanctuary of Dionysius which belonged to a society of Dionysiasts founded by a certain Dionysius of Marathon. The former of these buildings is situated on the corner of two streets, one of them fifty feet wide, which corresponds almost exactly in direction with the streets of the modern city; the difference of orientation is only four degrees. The direction of the system of streets as thus determined is consistent with the line of the walls of the Emporium and indicates with a degree of probability that the Agora and the Emporium, as might have been anticipated, had the same relative orientation. Slight evidence of a like adjustment of other streets is also found, but remains on the east end of Acte show that the streets there were orientated somewhat differently, as are those of the northern slope to-day.

Very little of the inner city of Peiraeus now remains. The site of its most famous sanctuary cannot be determined. This sanctuary was sacred to Zeus Savior and Athena Savior, and was known also as the Disoterium. As to its position we can only judge that it was on an elevation so that it could be seen by one sailing away from the city. Pausanias remarks that it was "the best worth seeing of anything in Peiraeus. Both statues are of bronze, and that of Zeus bears a scepter and a Victory, while that of Athena has a spear." Strabo asserts (9, 395) that in his day Peiraeus was reduced to "a petty colony about the harbors and the sanctuary of Zeus Savior," and that "the small stoae (stoïdia) possess marvelous pictures by distinguished artists, while the open area has statues." We have reason to believe, however, that Strabo never saw the place, and that he exaggerated its diminution in size, though he may be correct on the other points. Among the pictures which he mentions must have been Arcesilaus's painting of Leosthenes, the leader of the Greeks against the Macedonians, and his sons. A bronze statue of the father of Leocrates was also set up here, and we have a list of other objects in the precinct. From Pliny (*Nat. hist.* 34, 74) we learn that the sculptor Cephisodotus made "a marvelous Minerva in the port of the Athenians and an altar at the temple of Jupiter Servator in the same port, comparable to few." At some time during the year a great festal parade was conducted in honor of Savior Zeus and Dionysus.

As a seaport town Peiraeus was the center of many local and foreign cults which not often received recognition on Greek soil. Among the strange gods we find Isis, Serapis, Men, Baal, Ammon, Bendis, Sabazius, Attis; and how many others there were we cannot tell. In cults as in commerce Peiraeus was cosmopolitan.

Of private houses known to have been in Peiraeus our list is not long, but it contains a few of much interest. Hippodamus dwelt here in the city which he had planned; afterwards he donated his house to the state. Here too lived the younger Callias and the banker Pasion. In the house of the aged Cephalus at Peiraeus the scene of Plato's *Republic* is set; and in the same house later lived Cephalus's illustrious son, the orator Lysias.

Peiraeus possessed two theaters. Of these the older was on the western slope of Munychia Hill. Scanty ruins of it have been discovered, and the site is now largely built over. Down to Hellenistic times this must have been the only theater. Xenophon (*Hellen.* 2, 4, 32) speaks of "the theater in Peiraeus" as if but one existed, and Thucydides mentions (8, 93, 1) "the Dionysiac theater on Munychia" in the same manner. Aelian informs us (*Var. hist.* 2, 13) that "when Euripides was competing at Peiraeus, Socrates went down," which throws a sidelight upon poet and philosopher. In later times this naturally became known as the "old theater."

The younger theater is dated by an inscription at the middle of the second century B.C. The scanty ruins have been found just west of the south end of Zea Harbor. The theater is of the usual form; apparently it was never made over in Roman times, as was the theater in the City. In size it was small. The orchestra was only fifty Greek feet in diameter; the auditorium was about 220 feet wide by 120 feet deep; the scene building was about 108 feet long and 39 feet wide. The auditorium was divided by fourteen stairways into thirteen wedges; its zones were separated by the customary diazoma, or aisle (Fig. 261).

Scanty ruins remain of a few other ancient sites. Along the precipitous coast midway between Munychia and Zea Harbors, and below a series of votive niches, are a few remains of an ancient shrine of Zeus Meilichius (Gentle), associated here with Zeus Philius (Friendly) and Good Fortune. Near by are a cave in the cliff and the rock-hewn remains of what seems to be a bathhouse. This may be the one known as the "bath of Serangeum."

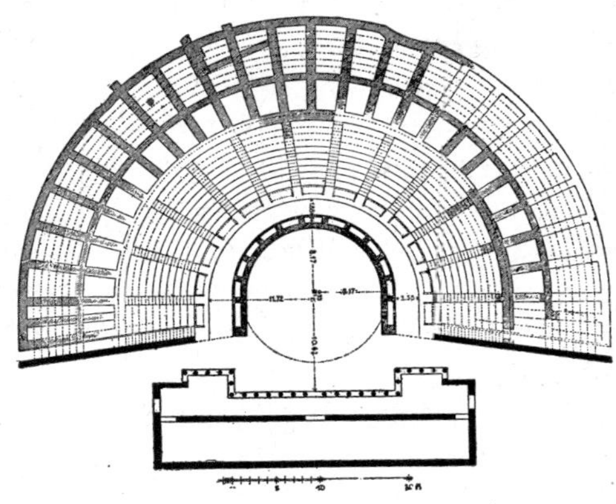

FIG. 261. — Plan of the small theater of Peiraeus.

On the ridge above this point are the ruins of the precinct of Munychian Asclepius, with an inclosure containing a temple. This unquestionably is the "Asclepieum in Peiraeus," so distinguished from the Asclepieum "in Asty" (pp. 206 ff.). Health (Hygieia) was also worshiped here, and Asclepius was revered along with other gods. Inscriptions found in the area make mention of altars on which cakes were sacrificed.

On the point of land extending hence to the mouth of Zea Harbor are numerous small pits cut in the rock; only a few of them are now seen beyond the new wall and embankment. Possibly these pits were what were anciently known as wells (phreata), and lent their name to the court called Phreattys (p. 365). If so, a cross-wall, now covered up, which cut off and helped to inclose this spit of land, would be explained.

Close by the west end of Acte are the ruins of an ancient lighthouse, and near it are the scanty remains of what has long been known as the tomb of Themistocles. Plutarch reports (*Themistocles* 32) that Diodorus the Periegete in the lost work *On Tombs* said, "that near the great harbor of Peiraeus a sort of elbow juts out from the headland by Alcimus; when you have rounded this, on the inside, where the sea is calm, there is a basis of considerable size, and the altar-like structure about it is the grave of Themistocles. And he thinks that Plato the comic poet bears witness to this in the following words: —

> "'Thy tomb whose mound is raised in this so fair a spot
> Will greet the busy throng of traders everywhere;
> The seamen, sailing in and out, it will behold,
> And look upon the emulation of the ships.'"

Thucydides says that Themistocles's monument was in the Agora of Magnesia, but that at Themistocles's bidding his bones were brought back and buried secretly in his native Attica. This meager evidence is not inconsistent with the location of the tomb at the spot in question, but recently the tomb has been thought to be on the north side of the strait west of the peninsula of Eëtioneia.

# BIBLIOGRAPHY

THE literature on the topography and monuments of ancient Athens is voluminous. English-speaking readers who wish to pursue the subject further will find Gardner's *Ancient Athens* (1902) and D'Ooge's *The Acropolis of Athens* (1908) both scholarly and interesting. Harrison and Verrall's *Mythology and Monuments of Ancient Athens* (1890) has long served as a *vade mecum* for the traveler and student, but is now in part antiquated and is out of print. Miss Harrison's *Primitive Athens as Described by Thucydides* (1906) is an illuminating discussion of a limited portion of the field. Frazer's *Pausanias's Description of Greece* (1898, reprinted 1913; translation and commentary on Pausanias's Attica in volumes I and II, with appendix in volume V) is also invaluable. The fullest and most indispensable single treatise is Judeich's *Topographie von Athen* (1905). Wachsmuth's *Die Stadt Athen im Alterthum* (1874–1890), in two volumes, but unfinished, is a masterly work to which every later student is indebted. Hitzig and Bluemner's *Pausaniae Graeciae Descriptio* (1896–1910; text and notes) is valuable. Petersen's *Athen* (1908) is a useful handbook. Other important works are Curtius's *Stadtgeschichte von Athen* (1891; including Milchhöfer's *Schriftquellen*), Jahn-Michaelis's *Arx Athenarum* (1901), and Wachsmuth's article on Athens in the first Supplement to Pauly-Wissowa's *Real-Encyclopädie* (1903).

Exhaustive bibliographies are given in these works and in Carroll's *The Attica of Pausanias* (1907). The material and discussions since the publication of the books mentioned are contained for the most part in archaeological publications; a list of the periodicals is given by Carroll, *op. cit.* pp. 221 f. Among important recent monographs are the following: Petersen's *Burgtempel der Athenaia* (1907); Köster's *Das Pelargikon*

(1909); Robert, *Pausanias als Schriftsteller* (1909); Brueckner's *Der Friedhof am Eridanos* (1909), supplemented by articles in the periodicals; Shrader's *Archaische Marmor-Skulpturen im Akropolis-Museum* (1909); Smith's *The Sculptures of the Parthenon* (1910; a sumptuous work with reproductions and text in folio); Elderkin's *Problems in Periclean Buildings* (1912); Goodyear's *Greek Refinements* (1912); Svoronos's Φῶς ἐπὶ τοῦ Παρθενῶνος (1912). Valuable contributions of Svoronos on the Academy and Colonus Hippius are published in Τὸ ἐν Ἀθήναις Ἐθνικὸν Μουσεῖον (also in German as *Der Athener Nationalmuseum*, 1910). Brief summaries of new books and articles, as well as reports of discoveries, are given promptly in the American Journal of Archaeology in the department of Archaeological News. A concise survey of the entire field of Greek architecture, sculpture, and the other arts is found in Tarbell's *A History of Greek Art* (1896), in Walters's *The Art of the Greeks* (1906), and in Fowler and Wheeler's *A Handbook of Greek Archæology* (1909).

# INDEX